LAUGHING

IN

THE

DARK

LAUGHING

IN

THE

DARK

**From Colored Girl to
Woman of Color—
A Journey
from Prison to Power**

PATRICE
GAINES

ANCHOR BOOKS

A DIVISION OF RANDOM HOUSE, INC.

NEW YORK

For Andrea, my angel

FIRST ANCHOR BOOKS EDITION, NOVEMBER 1995

Library of Congress Cataloging-in-Publication Data

Gaines, Patrice.
    Laughing in the dark : from colored girl to woman of color—a
journey from prison to power / Patrice Gaines. — 1st Anchor books
ed.
        p.   cm.
    1. Gaines, Patrice.   2. Afro-American women journalists—
Biography.   3. Afro-American women—Social conditions.   I. Title.
PN4784.G35G35   1995
070'.92—dc20
    [B]   95-8023
                                                                              CIP

ISBN 0-385-48027-X

Design by Lauren Dong

www.anchorbooks.com

Printed in the United States of America
20 19 18 17 16 15

Contents

■ ■ ■

Acknowledgments

■ ■ ■

To thank everyone who helped make this book a reality would be like trying to count the threads in a fabric. Impossible. Yet, some people must be thanked: My friend and agent Denise Stinson, who led me to another agent, Charlotte Sheedy, who also became a friend. I am grateful to you both for your faith in me and for your honesty. Yvonne Lamb, my patient friend, for gently critiquing and editing my raw writing, saving me from great embarrassment. David Groff, my editor at Crown, for a relationship that leaves me with no horror stories to tell—and for prodding me to dig deeper, in the process making my writing richer and accelerating my healing.

A major thanks goes to the institutions and people who supported me and taught me over the years as I learned how to get to this point: The D.C. Commission on the Arts and Humanities; Yaddo; The Mac-Dowell Colony; The Institute for Journalism Education, where Bob Maynard showed me a new path to follow, paved by him and others; the University of Michigan Journalism Fellows Program—especially Charles Eisendrath; also Nicholas Delbanco and Charles Baxter of the Creative Writing Program; and the Outlook section of the *Washington Post,* especially Jeff Frank, who helped me develop the article that became this book.

There are my sister-writers who have encouraged me over the years when I gave them so little validation for their faith: Bebe Moore Campbell, who also helps me with life; Marita Golden, who I admire for what she gives as much as for what she writes; Gloria Naylor, a great nurturer and healer; and Terry McMillan, who always told me to write, write, write.

To the friends I lean on: Jewelene "Gobbie" Black, who I become more like each day; Gail Dry Burton, who is like a sister to me; Fran Sauve, my Siamese twin from whom I can never be separated; and Donna Britt, whose giving spirit started this book project.

I thank God for my mother, Eleanor Gaines, whose greatest dream was to have a family, and who, in fulfilling that dream, has given me a wealth of traditions and love. To my father, William Gaines, who I love more each day and keep with me always. For my sisters and brother, who taught me there is no such thing as "half": to Shelia Williams, Carol West, Debra Spicer, and Sondra, William, and Vicki Gaines.

My daughter, Andrea, has been my inspiration before I even knew what to do with what she gives me. Now she is my cheerleader, my friend, my confidante, my love.

I will thank God eternally for bringing J.C. into my life. I thank J.C. for what he has already taught me and for the peace and stability he has given my life; and for bringing Endia, who taught me to play again.

A special thanks to my friend Benson, who continues to give me joy.

Prologue

■ ■ ■

stood with my forehead pressed as close as possible to the dark, tinted window of my jail cell. The window was long and narrow, and the foot-deep wall that framed it made it impossible to stand close. The thick glass blurred everything outside. I squinted and focused, concentrating all of my attention on the area where my mother had said the family would stand and wave.

It would be good to see my grandparents and my aunt, but it was my daughter I really wanted to see. My daughter, who would be two years old in a few months.

A couple of minutes passed, and in that small space of time I rethought my entire life and how it had come to this absurd moment, when I became a twenty-one-year-old girl in jail on a drug charge, a mother who had to wait for someone to bring my own daughter to glimpse me. I could not rub my hand across her fat, soft brown cheeks, or plait her curly hair the way I liked it. It was obvious to me my life had to change. This was my first time in jail—and I promised myself it would be my last.

Men had helped to bring me to this place: my father, whom I could not love, and my boyfriend, whom I loved too much. My father did not believe I could change. Or if he did, he kept his faith to himself, and thus, for years—even after his death—I would assume my father considered me just a little more than worthless. Looking back, I see that I have no idea what he thought, not the rigid marine who played by America's rules. Parents are like mirrors for their children; the little girl looks at her father to see herself, her female self. In my father, I saw no hint of myself, no definition, or light, no shape of who I could become.

So when I was old enough, I tried to find myself in other places and other people. When I was old enough to want a man of my own, I chose young men who toted guns, burglarized houses, robbed stores, and pulled flimflams. They were survivors, tough boys who said, "Fuck the white man and his ways." They made up their own rules and took what they wanted. When my school bus rolled past their corner, I stared out the window at them swaggering and laughing, wearing the same clothes they had worn the day before because their night was just ending. I could smell their brazenness, their raw guts that I misinterpreted as power. When you're a black child in America, your inclination is to feel powerless—and you will in fact lack power, unless someone intervenes to teach you how to possess it. I had already bought into powerlessness. Being a black girl-child meant I had about as much influence in the world as there was in my itty-bitty finger, or as much as I saw my mother hold in our family. I grabbed hold of these young men who other people called thugs, hustlers, or hoodlums. They were my power—and my freedom. What did I know about the power within me?

I did not want a man like my father, a flag-waving patriot; a marine for eternity. He was a traitor, my young self thought, serving the very system that enslaved black people. When I wore an afro and refused to stand for the national anthem, my father proudly sported the same severe haircut the military gave him when he was seventeen years old. When blacks in Washington took their anger to the streets after the assassination of Martin Luther King, my father laughed and told me, "Your people are rioting."

I thought I was revolutionary because I read H. Rap Brown,

George Jackson, the Black Muslim and the Black Panthers' newspapers. But my intelligence was misguided. In my personal sphere, I was the perfect victim for men who preyed on women with low self-esteem, women who had not yet learned to say "no." Before and after my time in the jail cell, I would be physically and verbally brutalized and disrespected in an infinite number of ways by these men. I chose them; I attracted certain men just as a magnet attracts certain metal. One day I would understand this, that if I changed, I would attract a totally different kind of man—and, more astonishing to me, a different kind of life.

Before that day came, I would hit rock bottom more than once. I bounced back each time, but I didn't know how to hold on, to keep myself from falling again. I reached some dangerously low points, like the night I was brutally beaten and raped by a man I had dated just over a month. I thought I was getting over on Gabriel, a two-bit hustler with part of his earnings invested in a big gold tooth that shone in the middle of his smile. He bought me groceries, gave me money, and paid for my daughter's day care.

Then one night he took me to a friend's house, led me to the bedroom, and ordered me to undress. *He wants me to play whore while he plays pimp,* I thought, turning coy to get in character. But once I was naked, he pulled out a black leather horse whip and shoved me on the bed. I felt the lash burn across my back. I cried out loud, shocked and in pain, rolled over, and scrambled to stand on the bed. The whip sank into my thigh. My back. Across my stomach. My chest. I fell on the bed. My flesh burned.

Then I was numb. I could not hear or feel. It was as if I existed outside of my body and I was floating somewhere on the ceiling. I looked down and saw Gab stretch my body out like an old rag doll. He climbed on top of me and had sex while I watched him from above. I was dying—and I knew it. But I felt an overwhelming grief that trembled in my bones—a sadness for my mother. Someone was going to tell her that her oldest child had been found naked, beaten to death. For my mother, I returned to my troubled life and my wounded body.

I bounced back, but I would be abused by other men in other ways.

Before Gab, before this prison cell, I had been raped before, and used heroin, hallucinogenics, uppers, downers, and nearly every drug available on the streets. Even after Gabriel's assault, I would return to jail for shoplifting and fail repeatedly at my attempt to turn my life around. I would learn that change doesn't happen overnight; that sometimes it takes years, particularly trying to remake yourself from your roots.

I would, in fact, sometimes forget my goal because I was so busy just trying to put one foot in front of the other, trying to live through one day—then another. Working in low-paying jobs as a clerk-typist and teletype operator; making it through periods of unemployment; working late nights with a catering group serving at white country clubs. Budgeting carefully, never able to save; searching for the right day-care center for my daughter, Andrea; trying to turn an ugly, cheap apartment into a cheerful home that a child would love to live in. And always, desperately searching for that man who would make me feel better. All of this made me forget sometimes that what I was really trying to do was to change my life.

But I did it—with perseverance. Before I could see the relationship between one part of my life and another, I worked on different sections of it, separately. I went to a community college to study English and took business courses to learn shorthand so I could get better secretarial jobs. I read self-help books, pop psychology that introduced me to the notion that there was untapped power within me. New friends entered my life, old ones fled. Throughout everything, I wrote. It seemed a natural progression: The child who read books to escape grew into a young woman who wrote to relieve herself of pain. Writing always consoled me, had always been my way of talking to God—and to myself.

Now, in my job as a reporter at the *Washington Post,* I run into young girls who remind me of my old self. I see them in courtrooms where they sit by loyally as their boyfriends are sentenced for selling crack, or, much too often, for murder. I see them standing in line during visiting hours at the D.C. jail, many of them toting babies on their hips. I have talked to them, told them my story even as I listened to theirs. But, like me at their age, they are largely silent victims. The media always cover their boyfriends, generally overlooking them. This oversight, I know, probably reinforces their own sense of power-lessness.

So this is my ode to those young sisters, those children with wom-anish ways, who give it up before there is really anything to give; those tender block girls who I did not have enough time to talk to because I was on deadline.

I want them to know that no matter how low they fall, they can get back up; no matter how many times they stumble, they can still walk tall. That neither racism nor sexism can stop a determined mind, or a heart beating with love for the very body that carries it. It is a lesson for all people, regardless of race or sex; for anyone who has had to overcome a challenge.

◆ ◆ ◆

My stomach hurt with excitement and fear as I waited to glimpse my daughter. I saw my grandmother first, her short, round body. Then my red-headed aunt. And finally, my daughter! She was in my grand-father's arms, laughing at him. Then my mother said something to my grandfather and he lifted my little girl onto his broad shoulders.

For years, when I conjured up this memory of them standing out-side, I saw my father holding my daughter. Then just a year ago, my mother told me that it was my grandfather who had held her—and not my father. My father had not come to see me because he had to work. I realized then that I imagined the scene the way I wished it had been, because I cannot imagine a father not going to visit his daughter in jail and because I always wanted my father to be the father I created in my head. That father, the imaginary one, would have hurried to his daughter's side, and work never would have stopped him from going there to see for himself that she was okay.

Once she was on my grandfather's shoulders, I could see my daughter's face more clearly, her big round eyes, her bushy eyebrows. She was wearing an outfit that I didn't recognize. Who bought it? I ached from the fear that already her life was slipping away from mine.

Mother pointed up to the third-floor windows, but not exactly to the one where I was standing. She blew a kiss toward the jail. Andrea watched her, then she touched her small hand to her mouth and threw a kiss too, flinging her arms wide. She laughed and I strained, as if I could really hear her giggles, trying to remember the exact silliness in that high pitch.

Mother pointed up again and Andrea looked, searching the way children do when they're not sure what they're looking for. She looked at the sky. The building. At her grandmother.

I waved, but no one saw me.

Andrea was staring at the wrong window, in the wrong direction. I imagined Mama saying, "No, baby. Over there. Your mother is over there."

Tears dripped down to my ugly green prison dress. My shoulders shook as I tried to hold back the fear, the hurt, the hopelessness, as I tried to be cool. My friend Patricia walked over to me and put her hands on my shoulders.

"My daughter can't find me," I said.

chapter one

Colored Girl

threw back my head, the way I saw white girls do on TV, and imagined my stiff braids flying across my shoulders. Vaseline, hot from the searing summer sun, melted down my bony brown legs; dust particles pricked my skin like minute splinters of glass. None of this bothered me. I scanned the street for my royal white subjects.

It was 1954 and the Supreme Court had just declared segregated schools unconstitutional, and all around me people were fighting about colored children going to school with white children. My mama had come home from the hospital with a baby girl named Shelia, and I was no longer the only child. But neither of these facts altered my life profoundly—at least not yet. I was a five-year-old colored queen, and my queendom existed on a military base in Quantico, Virginia. My subjects, my white playmates, Charlotte and Lucy, battled for my company, always presenting me with gifts and fussing about who got to spend the most time with me.

It was years before I understood how dangerous their love had been, how it swathed me in a false sense of belonging and set me up for a painful dethroning, the kind all black children in America face when they discover their country does not love them one eenie meenie bit. Neither Charlotte, Lucy, nor I knew any of this, so for part of my early life I flourished under the awe of my white friends. Charlotte and Lucy loved my caramel skin and kinky hair, the characteristics that separated me from them and from all the other kids in our neighborhood, who were white and pale, with thin, stringy hair.

Years later, when I was an adult and most of my friends were black, we talked of hating white people; I envied my black friends because their hate was so pure and uncomplicated. "I hate white people, too," I would say, before thrusting my fist into the air in a sign of Black Power. But inside, my heart beat with memories of Lucy and Charlotte, who had loved me unconditionally, in some way even more than they had loved each other. While my black friends talked about their hatred, I remembered lying in bed with my skinny legs tangled in the legs of white friends. I recalled evenings when Lucy's or Charlotte's mama called, "Dinner!" and we all ran to sit at the table together, to build houses with mashed potatoes or hide spinach in our pockets, or just giggle.

Most of my black friends would never know what it was like to be loved by anyone white. Their hate was unchallenged and definite. Mine was neither, and yet I couldn't say I loved white people. What I feel lies somewhere between love and hate; I constantly vacillate because I still carry Lucy and Charlotte with me.

Prompted by Lucy's and Charlotte's adoration, I secretly thanked God daily for my chocolate skin and cotton candy hair. Being colored, I was a rare treasure, a museum piece walking among white mortals, close enough to love or admiration for a five-year-old. But when I was an adult and a white man I was sleeping with called me "exotic" and told me he dreamed of me chasing him through the jungle with my hair wild and a gun in my hand, I thought how all my life some white people have viewed me as an alluring and bewitching alien. That wasn't anything close to love or admiration; I was being used to fulfill someone else's fantasy.

"If you wash your face, will the color come off?" Charlotte asked me one day.

"No," I giggled.

"Why are your mother and father so dark?" Lucy flung her red hair over one shoulder, a signal that she thought she had stumped me. Her tone suggested her question was an accusation, as if there were something wrong because my skin was chocolate and my parents were a deep chocolate. But I knew my parents were beautiful. They had incredible smooth, dark skin—flawless, without one blemish or mark. My mother had long, thick black hair, and my father had narrow, slanted eyes and high cheekbones.

"My mother said God baked us all in an oven and He let some of us stay in longer because he wanted different colors," I said with an air of authority. "It makes the world beautiful."

Lucy shut up, satisfied, her green eyes returning to their look of worship and awe. Anyway, both Lucy and Charlotte also knew their mothers yearned to be colored. Didn't they see them rub suntan lotion on their bodies and lie in their small backyards until their skin grew ugly and red, and finally, beautiful and dark?

Meanwhile, the girls vied for my company. We lived in a row of attached brick houses, and my family's house was in the middle. For all I knew, this was how everyone lived—in houses that all looked alike, on a reservation of land that had everything anyone needed: stores, movie theaters, a swimming pool, and a school. I would learn over the next few years just how insulated my military world was. Racial prejudice existed, but it was pushed underground and when it surfaced it was polite and gentle. No dogs and fire hoses; racist whites just ignored coloreds or, at their worst, called them "niggers."

When I came out in the mornings after breakfast each one of my friends was waiting with offerings to lure me to spend the day. Charlotte, a blond girl who tanned easily, loved to picnic under the sun in her front yard. She spread out a blanket and arranged her best doll-sized china plates for lunch. Her mother baked cookies, oftentimes my favorite chocolate chip, and she let us pour our tea from her beautiful black teapot that Charlotte's father had brought back from Japan. At Lucy's, the food was never as good, but the setup was awfully pretty. It was at Lucy's that I first used cloth napkins, which fascinated me because I had never thought of a napkin as something that could be saved and reused. We sat on the front porch and ate left-overs, sometimes warm, buttered, canned biscuits, most often cold sliced bread with jelly or butter. Lucy's mom wouldn't hear of us drinking tea, so it was either water or, if we were lucky, Kool-Aid.

I tried to spend time with both girls, alternating whom I visited first because I didn't want to hurt anyone's feelings. For some reason it never occurred to us to combine the two meals. Perhaps Lucy and Charlotte enjoyed the game as much as I did. Anyway, after this daily ritual, they cleaned up while I—the queen—ran inside to prepare for the afternoon, to pull out my jump rope, jacks, or hula hoop or one of my white doll babies.

I owned two black doll babies—Rita, a large doll who walked awkwardly if you held her hands and rocked her from side to side while dragging her forward, and Ethel, named after my grandmother, a doll with a cloth body that smelled terrible because I accidentally peed on her nightly. All of my other babies were white, which didn't matter because I was too young to realize that they couldn't really be my babies.

That summer Lucy, Charlotte, and I became blood sisters. We figured we had to perform this ritual before we started first grade because we would be too busy after that. "If we want to always be together, we got to do it," said Lucy, who told us how her brother and his friends had pricked their fingers and since then had been inseparable.

I was convinced before the last word fell from her mouth, but Charlotte, who was desperately afraid of seeing her own blood, had to be persuaded. So Lucy and I pricked our forefingers and pressed them together to show her that it wouldn't kill us. Then Charlotte did it. I took a pink ribbon from my hair and tied it around her finger like a Band-Aid.

All summer we jumped rope and ran through the lawn sprinklers dressed in our bathing suits. We shook the skinny trees that lined our street, then ran as the Japanese beetles flew out from the branches. In the evenings we caught fireflies, ripping the glowing yellow lights from their bodies and sticking them on our earlobes or on our fingers. I fancied myself as Cleopatra, who I thought was white because all I knew about Africa was what I saw in Tarzan movies. And Cleopatra's whiteness did not hinder my becoming her since at the age of six, race seemed interchangeable to me. I understood race about as much as I did death.

We laughed and played until the days folded one into another and summer, like an old pressed accordion, was silenced and put away. We went off to first grade and miraculously, Lucy and I ended up in the same class. Whenever we spotted Charlotte on the playground or standing in line waiting with her class at the water fountain we put up our forefingers that carried her blood. I loved first grade, particularly story time. When Mrs. Bloomfield, a round, middle-aged white woman, read to us, I tuned out everything in the world except her voice, which washed over me and turned me into whatever I wanted to be. I didn't just hear her; I felt the stories. I laughed and cried and sometimes turned to find, to my surprise, that none of the other children had had the same reaction.

Yet it became obvious that Mrs. Bloomfield felt differently about me. It would be years before I realized that her actions had racist overtones. She had a colored boy and a colored girl in her class, and while she tolerated the colored boy, who was slow and shy and arrived in worn hand-me-down clothes, she particularly despised me—the smart, confident colored girl who arrived impeccably dressed, walked like a queen, and was worshiped by a white girl named Lucy.

To a little girl who believed that God baked all people in an oven like cookies, Mrs. Bloomfield just seemed to have spells when she turned cranky and mean. She doled out gold stars to the white students and cleanup jobs to me. When I wanted to go to the bathroom to pee, she made me hold it until I felt I would explode. When either the colored boy or I waved a hand to answer a question, she ignored us. Halfway through the year the boy stopped trying, but I tried harder. Sometimes when Lucy pleaded, "Mrs. Bloomfield, Patrice has her hand up!" she could not ignore me. Occasionally her behavior made me believe I was bad and deserved such treatment. Adults have that power over children, the power to make children believe in their own unworthiness. It happens to black children in an infinite number of ways, particularly at school, and I wonder how many Mrs. Bloom-fields there have been and how many children they continue to damage. What Mrs. Bloomfield did was to undermine my self-esteem, and years later when I was an adult and my mother said, "I always told you you could do anything you wanted to do," I stared at her with a face blank of any such recollections. I can remember every painful signal Mrs. Bloomfield sent me, but I cannot remember one word of my mother's encouragement.

Even when I was in first grade and couldn't explain to myself why Mrs. Bloomfield acted the way she did, I hurt. She was the first person I ever met who did not like me because I was cute and polite or because I always wore pretty clothes. I had an inkling that something was terribly wrong with the way she treated me, something bigger than a child my size could understand. Children know when an action by an adult falls outside the realm of real love. When smiles are false, children absorb the tension as static in the peace in which they normally live.

Mrs. Bloomfield took the only action she must have believed she, a white woman, could use to show that she disliked having this colored girl in her class: she assigned me to cleanup duty after each playtime. While the other children flopped down on the floor in a circle at Mrs. Bloomfield's feet for story time, I hurried to put together puzzles, place game pieces in their proper boxes, and seal the cans of clay. Then I put everything away neatly on the shelves, learning early in my assignment that if I put them away hastily, Mrs. Bloomfield would pause in her reading.

"Patrice, take those boxes off the games shelf and put them back again. Neatly," she said. My classmates, upset that some imaginary cat was still stuck up a tree or a genie was stuck inside a lamp, looked at me with scorn, and I was embarrassed.

By the time I took my place at my teacher's feet for story time, the first story would be nearly over. I listened intently to the second one. On the way home on the bus, I always made Lucy tell me the first one. But she wasn't a good storyteller; she forgot details and got angry when I asked her questions.

The school year ended and I was thrilled to leave Mrs. Bloomfield.

"She's a witch," I told Lucy on the way home.

My friend looked at me as if I had cursed. "I like Mrs. Bloomfield. I want another teacher just like her," Lucy said.

I was stunned. Perplexed. I stared at Lucy but didn't say a word. Couldn't my best friend see how our teacher mistreated me? It was the first time Lucy and I had disagreed on something this important. How could I know that this was just the first time of many when a white person, even a friend, would look at something and see nothing of what I saw, particularly when race was concerned. Of course, in kindergarten, I did not know how to express my bitter disappointment in Lucy; and this inability to articulate bred a frustration and hopelessness so strong I could nearly taste it. On the bus home, I sat silent, next to Lucy, and looked out the window and my hatred for Mrs. Bloomfied grew with each tree we passed. I could feel hatred heating up inside my veins until it boiled into my head. But for now I only saw Mrs. Bloomfield as an intruder, an adult who somehow had the power to blind my best friend.

First grade passed. My mama had another baby while I was in second grade, another sister for me. Her name was Carol. My maternal grandmother, Grannie Ethel, came from Washington, D.C., to stay with us for a few weeks and help Mama, just as she had after Shelia was born. Grannie Ethel was a stumpy, round woman with arms like chicken drumsticks, fat and full near the shoulder blades. She was the only grandmother I knew, since we seldom visited my father's parents, who lived in the country, in Badin, North Carolina. Grannie Ethel and her husband, "Prince Albert" King, whom I called Grampy, lived on the top floor of a four-story walk-up apartment building that smelled of old Sunday meals and roach spray. When I visited during the summer we sat on the stoop with the other tenants and watched the Shriners' parade march right past the building.

My father loved babies, because they depended on him. By the time any of us children was old enough to have activities engraved in our memories, our father had stopped spending time with us. Grampy was my introduction to maleness. He chewed Prince Albert tobacco, smelled of Aqua Velva, and wore thin, ribbed white sleeveless undershirts with armholes that hung nearly to the waist, T-shirts my siblings and I nicknamed "Grampy shirts." Grampy is the man I remember lifting me and tossing me into the air, kissing me and calling me "Patty-boo."

Grannie Ethel worked for a while as a short-order cook in a small restaurant. Whenever we visited Washington we dropped by and she fixed us snow cones with cherry or grape syrup. Eventually, she worked as a maid for white people and brought me clothes they had thrown away, articles that seemed beautiful until I was in junior high; then the clothes turned ugly, looked like white people's second pickings—and I wouldn't wear them. Grannie's apartment was as elegant as the homes in which she worked. She had fine antique furniture, the kind I saw in pictures of white people's houses. She took me with her to the Senators' baseball games and to wrestling matches, where my normally quiet grandmother pumped her fist in the air and yelled until she was hoarse.

Second grade ended, and we were in the middle of another summer. Charlotte, Lucy, and I sat on my front porch one day, watching a moving van pull up to a house a few doors away. We were used to people moving into our neighborhood. It was a fact of life that our dads could get transferred to another base at any time. We liked to watch men unload the moving trucks, eyeing the contents for signs of children, for scooters and bikes, twin beds and boxes marked "Toys."

This time a car drove up behind the truck and a colored family stepped out.

"Wow, look at her," I said, pointing to a girl who looked to be our age. She had extremely short hair that was sticking up all over her head. Her skin was darker than that of my parents.

"She's ugly," Charlotte said, reaching back to finger the tip of her blond ponytail.

"Sure is," I agreed.

That night my mama went over to welcome the family. My parents knew them from another base where they had all lived before I was born.

"The little girl's name is Mary Ann. I want you to go over and play with her tomorrow," Mama said.

I shook my head "no" and pouted.

"Don't tell me that. I'll pop those lips of yours inside your mouth."

I smiled. My mother said the silliest things, but I knew she was serious. I went to bed wondering how I could follow my mother's instructions and visit that new girl's house without Lucy and Charlotte seeing me. The three of us had agreed we didn't want to play with her because she was too different from us and too ugly. But after breakfast the next day, Mama made me sit on her bed until she was dressed. Then she took my hand and said, "We're going to visit the Smiths."

The girl stood just inside the front screen door. She had on a cute pink shorts set with white polka dots on it, but her hair was in little teeny braids and one of them, with a barrette on it, stood straight up in the air in the center of the top of her head.

"Hi." She spoke to me without taking her thumb out of her mouth.

I didn't say a word. "Didn't you hear Mary Ann speak to you?" Mama jerked my arm. "You two go play. I'm going to help Shirley unpack."

I stood where Mama left me, but I didn't speak. I was embarrassed by this girl who did not have what white people loved: light, near-white skin, long hair, or good speech. And though I didn't fully realize it yet, I loved what white people loved.

"We useta live in Georcha," the girl said.

Mama had already told me the new girl spoke with a southern accent. "You shoulda stayed in Georgia," I said.

Mary Ann ran up the stairs to our parents and I heard her crying.

Mama yelled to me, "Patrice Jean, you want your tail whipped? You play right with Mary Ann! Take her out to meet Lucy and Charlotte!"

I started crying, so Mama came down. "Now what's wrong with you?" she asked.

I didn't know exactly what was wrong, but I knew I couldn't take that new girl out with me. "She sucks her dumb thumb," I said.

"Both of you, out on the porch!" Mama opened the door and Mary Ann and I stepped outside. Mary Ann sat on the porch, and I sat on the bottom step, peering around to see if my friends were close by. She sucked her thumb and drew on the concrete with a piece of charcoal. I got up and picked honeysuckles off the bush next to the porch. Lucy and Charlotte walked by on the sidewalk at the edge of the yard. They stopped and stared at me with squinted eyes.

"Can you come out here and play?" Charlotte said.

Mary Ann shook her head "yes."

"Not you." Lucy spat out the words.

"I have to ask my mama," I said.

"You got to play with her?" asked Lucy.

I shook my head "yes." Lucy and Charlotte shot me a look of sympathy. I ran in to talk to Mama, and when I came back and told them Mama wouldn't let me go off the porch without Mary Ann, they ran off toward the creek.

I turned to Mary Ann. "See what you did?"

◆   ◆   ◆

There were days that summer when I was forced to talk to Mary Ann because our mothers went shopping together and took us and my baby sister, Shelia, with them. (My parents didn't own a car, so whenever we went anywhere it was with other people.) My mama and I never visited the Smiths' house except before shopping trips. Although Mama didn't say it, I imagined it was because the Smiths' house wasn't as clean as ours. Sometimes the kitchen sink was full of dirty dishes and clothes were draped across the living room furniture.

On each excursion with Mary Ann and her mother, I started out as a reluctant playmate; then after an hour or so of sitting in the car with Mary Ann or walking together as we trailed behind our mothers, I was ready to talk. Mary Ann whined a lot and stared at the ground when she talked, which irritated me. But she shot marbles like a boy, snapping her finger hard and sending the glass balls spinning in place or zooming across the floor—whichever way she called it. Nothing scared her either. No bug was too large for her to pick up with her bare hands, no person too crazy-looking for her to approach.

But she always looked a mess. Sometimes her hair was all over her head and my mama combed and plaited it in the car.

"Shirley, you've got to do better," I heard Mama say often in the same preachy tone she used with me. Once in a while she even raised her voice at Shirley, which surprised me, because my mama never raised her voice at anyone, even when I thought she should, like when the store clerk ignored her, obviously because she was colored.

At those times, Shirley usually would reach into her pocketbook, light a cigarette, and sit for a moment, staring at a place that must have been empty, because it left her face a blank. I didn't like Shirley Smith, but her hair, jewelry, and makeup reminded me of Betty Boop, who I wanted to be when I grew up; that was until Mama told me Betty Boop was a cartoon character and not a real person I could be. Shirley Smith wore more makeup than my mama, bright red lipstick and rouge on her high cheekbones. She liked large, sparkling jewelry and tight clothes. Men noticed her, and I noticed that; even at eight years old, I knew their attention was very important, transforming Shirley Smith into a beautiful, special creature. That was the kind of adoration I wanted when I became a woman. I wanted to please men and make them smile, and they, in turn, would make me feel good about myself.

I figured Mrs. Smith needed attention because Mr. Smith was always working. When I saw them together, they were so different: he was stiff and stern and scared me, while she was funny and sad at the same time, but never scary.

Mary Ann liked my mama and started calling her "Aunt Eleanor," even though I told her each time, "She's not your aunt." I still didn't play with Mary Ann when I was around Lucy and Charlotte.

Third grade started and I prayed to God to keep Mary Ann out of my class. He answered me, and she wound up being the only colored child in Lucy's class.

"She stinks sometimes," said Lucy. "And her hair is so-o-o-o funny."

We were talking about Mary Ann one afternoon sitting on the edge of the bank of the creek with our feet dangling. We always went to the woods to discuss secrets or problems or anything that confused us.

"My mother said Mary Ann and her parents are niggers," Lucy announced.

"What is a nigger?" asked Charlotte.

I shrugged. "I don't know," I said.

None of us knew the definition of the word, but we knew enough to feel it wasn't a good word. Just saying it sent a vibration through us, like the ripples from the rocks we skipped across the creek.

That night, as Mama ran my bathwater, I asked her, "What is a nigger?"

She raised her eyebrows. "Where did you hear that word?"

"I heard some kids say it."

"A nigger is someone with a dirty mind," Mama said.

That made sense, thought my eight-year-old self. Mary Ann's parents were probably dirty because their house was dirty sometimes and Mary Ann didn't always bathe. When I saw Lucy and Charlotte I repeated the definition to them, adding descriptions of the Smiths' house at its worst. "Your mama was right, Lucy," I said. "Mary Ann and her parents are niggers."

That was the last time any of us actually said the word *nigger*. By winter, I had an inkling something else was wrong with Mary Ann's family, something beyond dirty minds, but I wasn't sure what. I overheard my parents whispering about Shirley drinking too much, about arguments and fights and about "that poor chile, Mary Ann."

Mama and I went to the Smiths' house one Saturday morning and knocked and called out for a long time before Shirley opened the door just a little.

"What's the matter with your face?" Mama asked.

I peeped and saw Shirley's left eye was black-and-blue and swollen shut. One side of her mouth was swollen, too. Mary Ann, her nose snotty and her hair all over her head, was hugging her mother's legs.

"You and Mary Ann go play," Mama said, and this time, without hesitating, I took Mary Ann by the hand and led her upstairs to her room. I had to pull her, and she only went after her mother said, "Go on. I'll be okay."

I knew when I saw Mrs. Smith's puffy face that her husband had beaten her. I had picked up clues from conversations between my parents about the Smiths. Although my parents sometimes argued, my father was never violent and I couldn't imagine him hitting my mother. Mr. Smith was a different kind of man, I figured, and I was even more afraid of him, because he had to be crazy to hurt someone he was supposed to love.

At that moment I felt sorry for Mary Ann because something was terribly wrong in her family and I could see that she loved her mother just as much as I loved mine. We were both kids who had no real power to change anything, living in a world run by adults who, as I had learned from Mrs. Bloomfield, could greatly disappoint you. I figured Mary Ann probably wished for a clean house, long hair, a mother who didn't drink, and a father who didn't beat her mother.

That night Mary Ann and her mother stayed at our house and Mary Ann slept in my bed. I let her play with all of my toys, even the ones I thought were too good for company to handle. I even gave her my favorite cat's-eye marble.

"Maybe you can play with me and Lucy and Charlotte one day," I said, knowing I had to discuss it with my other playmates first. But that gave Mary Ann enough hope to make her smile the longest she had smiled that day. We went to sleep holding hands. I peed in the bed that night, and I woke up that morning to discover that Mary Ann had peed, too. We laughed and changed the sheets. I didn't have to tell her to keep it a secret, and she didn't have to tell me.

Mary Ann and her mama went home, and I went outside to play with Lucy and Charlotte. I didn't see Mary Ann anymore that day, not even sitting on her porch or playing in her yard like she usually did. That night I woke up because someone was banging on the door. I heard Mama and Daddy get up.

Then Mama screaming to Daddy: "Bill! My God! My God!"

I jumped out of bed and ran downstairs. I ran past Daddy, who was on the telephone, and stopped at the door where Mama was on her knees. She was holding Mrs. Smith.

"He shot me. He shot me," Mary Ann's mama kept saying.

"Get back in here!" Daddy yelled to me, and I backed up and stood a few feet behind Mama.

"You're gonna be alright, Shirley. You'll be alright. Just be quiet," Mama said over and over.

"Where's Mary Ann, Mama?"

"Just get in here," my father said.

My baby sister woke up and started crying, and Daddy ran upstairs and came back carrying her just as an ambulance and the military police arrived. They picked up Mrs. Smith and carried her away on a stretcher. The red light flashed around the room, and I started crying.

"Go upstairs to your bed," Daddy said.

I walked up the stairs but stopped at the top and sat down, too scared to go up there alone. Later that morning Mama told me Mary Ann's father had taken her away and that the police were looking for them because Mr. Smith had shot his wife. On our porch was a large bloodstain. Lucy and Charlotte stayed near it all day, staring at it and imagining what it felt like to bleed that much. Before the day was over my father tried to wash the stain away with the hose and scrubbed at it, but it just faded a little. I think Daddy was embarrassed by that stain, because I heard him call the shooting "a shame" and he told Mama, "I hope they catch him." A week later Mama told me Mrs. Smith was out of the hospital. But she never came home and I never saw her or Mary Ann again.

"The niggers are gone," Lucy said after a moving van drove off with furniture and a box marked "Toys" that they carried out of Mary Ann's house.

"Don't say that," I insisted. A part of my heart hurt in a way it had never hurt before. There was something profoundly wrong with the way I had treated Mary Ann, something that was different than when I had an argument with Lucy or Charlotte and we called each other names and didn't speak for an hour or so. I didn't know the answers, but I knew the questions: Why had I rejected Mary Ann for Lucy and Charlotte? Why did I call Mary Ann a nigger? Was I supposed to look out for her? If I was, why?

For years afterward I was haunted by this memory of turning my back on someone my own color. When I grew old enough to realize what had happened and that the world considered me a nigger, too, I wanted to find Mary Ann and plead for forgiveness. Later when I was a young woman screaming, "Black Power!" I imagined my companions could look at me and know what I had done so shamefully to Mary Ann and see that I was really a traitor.

I was a kid, but I was a black kid. Because of my skin my life already had a complexity to it that Lucy's and Charlotte's would never have. My relationship with Mary Ann added to the pool of experience from which I would draw to answer lifelong questions about race and its meaning. It was years before I forgave myself for hating Mary Ann.

◆　◆　◆

It was well after Mary Ann left, in 1959, when someone first called me a nigger. On the news each evening, pictures flashed of young Negroes trying to get served at segregated lunch counters while crowds of angry whites taunted and jeered and even threw things at them. Those images seemed to rile some people, so that the hatred, normally asleep inside them, awakened and they acted on it, according to their beliefs. It was the middle of fourth grade when a new student, a freckle-faced white boy, joined our class. He was in my reading group, and when the group gathered at a table, the new boy, whose name was Tommy, said, "I'm not sitting next to the nigger."

I turned to see whom he was talking about and saw that he was sitting next to me. I looked at my teacher, Mrs. Hardwick, for clarification, because I didn't consider myself a nigger at all.

"We're not going to use that word in here. It's not a nice word," she said.

Tommy insisted. "My daddy said I don't have to sit next to a nigger."

Mrs. Hardwick took Tommy into the hall to talk and when they returned after a few minutes Tommy was quiet. Still, occasionally during the year, he blurted out the word *nigger*.

"One day Patrice's name will be in lights. She's going to be a star," Mrs. Hardwick told Tommy once.

Her comment filled me with such strong pride that I felt it was almost worth being called a nigger to hear a teacher talk about me that way. It was the first time I was conscious of the fact that what white people said about me would carry so much weight.

◆　◆　◆

At home, my parents bought me a piano and I started taking lessons. I joined a Brownie troop with Lucy and Charlotte and loved to sport my brown uniform, with all its badges and pins, and matching socks. At meetings we learned to cook. I discovered I could draw and paint. We went to a weekend camp on a river, where we canoed and slept in cabins. If I peed in bed, it was on a single cot where I slept alone and could hide my mishap. I was the only colored child again but I was used to it and it didn't seem to matter to any of the girls.

My father spent evenings in his lounge chair watching television. On Saturday he played golf for hours on the base golf course, where I took lessons for a short while, not because I liked the game but because I wanted to please my father. When the golf instructor required students to walk to the course for exercise, my mother withdrew me, insisting it was too long a distance for me, the only girl in the class, to travel alone in the company of boys.

Now and then, my father brought home a little animal he found on the course, once a stray dog, another time a stray duck that we kept in the bathtub until reality struck my father and he carried the duck back to its natural home. He also brought home trophies engraved with the name of the golf tournaments he had won. Mama kept up the family album, which included newspaper articles on his wins with pictures of him holding his latest trophy. He was usually the only colored person in the picture, though I recall at least twice seeing his good friend Mr. Boone standing there with a trophy, too. I never stopped to consider that this meant very few colored people played golf. Even when I was older, I seldom pondered what it must have been like for my father—out there alone, a pioneer of sorts. This was just one of his many accomplishments I never acknowledged or learned from. He was not the kind of father I wanted him to be: he was not an emotionally sensitive man, one who would notice that his oldest daughter yearned for his approval, or some sign of love. If Mama fixed my hair in a new style that made me think I was beautiful, I ran, excited, to show Daddy. But he always seemed preoccupied, not even looking in my direction, saying, "Uh-huh"— and nothing more. As I grew into an awkward, confused preteen, he added to my insecurity by not returning my good-night kisses: I kissed him on his forehead and he grumbled, "Good night," his eyes still on the television.

◆ ◆ ◆

One afternoon, the Brownie troop was riding with my scout leader in her station wagon. As we passed the golf course, my leader said to another woman, "My God, there's a nigger out there."

"He must be a caddie," the other leader said.

"No, I think he's playing golf. He . . . " She stopped abruptly, as both of them remembered that I was in the car.

Looking out the window, I saw my father. For some reason, I felt embarrassed for the women and sorry I was in the car to hear them. I sat back in my seat, silent.

Such moments came more frequently for me now, and resonated in me more deeply. My understanding of what the world thought of me was expanding. On television, I had seen angry white people shout their hatred at the colored teenagers trying to enter Central High School in Little Rock. I stared at the National Guard soldiers who did nothing. At age ten, I was truly baffled. How could anyone dislike a kid just because of her color? It seemed so absurd that I couldn't even get angry. I still had no idea yet that racism was widespread, that it even existed outside of a place I heard of called "the South," a place I figured was far away from my home in Quantico, Virginia.

◆ ◆ ◆

Near the end of fourth grade, shortly after we came home from school one day, Charlotte ran over to my house crying.

"We're moving! We're moving!" She cried so hard her body trembled. My mama ran to see what was wrong, and by the time she reached us I was wailing, too. She made us sit down and calm ourselves, but ten minutes later we were in Lucy's bedroom, where we cried until our stomachs hurt. We were inseparable over the next three weeks, until the day came when the movers emptied Charlotte's house and she and her family climbed into their car. Lucy and I waved and cried until our noses were runny. Charlotte sat in the backseat weeping on her big brother's shoulder and refused to look at us. She had given us her new address and we vowed to write forever and later, when we were older, to visit each other.

I wrote for a little over a year, even after my family had also moved. But eventually there came a day when even through letters Charlotte and I could tell we were no longer alike. We wrote less often until one day I couldn't find Charlotte's address, and then—I couldn't remember what state she lived in.

◆　◆　◆

Lucy and I spent that summer thumbing through *Seventeen* magazine, which showed us all the clothes we wished we could buy to turn our ten-year-old bodies into those of grand teenage creatures. Before summer ended, our parents, in an attempt to keep us busy and away from boredom, chaperoned neighborhood preteen dances we called "canteen" on Saturday evenings at the recreation center. We girls donned our favorite skirts and blouses and lined up on one side of the room waiting to be chosen by a boy to dance.

Up until this time Lucy and I had never needed an invitation to jump out on the dance floor. We had danced with each other, and when Charlotte had been with us the three of us would form a small circle and dance without regard to who might be watching or whether or not some boy wanted to ask one of us to step out onto the floor. This concept of dancing only with boys was new. I, for one, didn't like it at all. Another thing: I had never noticed before, but all the boys my age were white—would any one of them ask me to dance?

The pressure was definitely on. Somehow the message had been transferred to us young girls that it was an honor to be picked by a boy. That we had to stand there and wait—and hope.

When "Stagger Lee" came on, Lucy and I were content to pat our feet and move our hips a little in place on the floor. But then came "Smoke Gets in Your Eyes" and we stood still, hoping. The Platters sang, "They-ey asked me how I kneeew, my true love was truuuu-uuu-uu-uuuuue," and a redheaded, freckle-faced boy walked up to Lucy and held out his hand. I nearly fainted. The next minute, I looked up to see Lucy with her head on the boy's chest and his hands on her back. When the Platters crooned the next verse, only a fat girl with pocked skin and I were left unasked. I felt small. I wanted to feel a boy's arms around me. I wanted that same giggly feeling—only more of it—that I got when I spotted some cute guy at school looking at me. If I wasn't chosen because I was colored, that wasn't fair. The other girl was ugly and being ugly was a good reason, I concluded. And yet I still wasn't convinced that it was my color that kept a boy from asking me for a dance. That seemed too stupid to be true.

Each note of the song made my heart beat faster. Then it was over. Lucy walked back to her place next to me, smiling.

"His name is Jimmy," she whispered.

"That's nice," I said.

She gave me her quizzical look, but before we could say another word, "Mack the Knife" was playing and everybody was moving. Several of us girls found ourselves in a circle, bouncing to the music and laughing. This was so much more fun than waiting for boys, I thought.

But I was the only one who thought that. Most of the girls waited for boys even for the fast songs. Throughout the night Lucy danced on fast and slow songs not only with Jimmy, but with several other boys. By the end of the night, I had a headache that stemmed from knowing I was the only girl in the room who had not been asked at least once to dance. Even the fat girl with pimples went out on the floor twice. I considered crying, but I was too angry for that. "These white kids won't see me cry," I swore under my breath.

But it hurt. I had been rejected not just by boys, but by *white* boys, and that meant they were assuming something about me because of my color. I wasn't fat or ugly. I was cute, smart and funny and very neat, clean and well dressed, all of which should have added up to lots of dance partners. I had not factored in color.

I walked home with Lucy, who was giggling and talking about the boys she had danced with or about what so-and-so had on or some new song she heard. We were halfway home before she noticed I wasn't talking. "What's wrong with you?"

I was enraged. Mad that she had had a good time. Mad that she didn't notice that I hadn't. "No one asked me to dance," I said.

"No one?"

"You didn't notice." I stopped walking.

"I thought you didn't want to dance."

"Didn't want to!" I shoved Lucy with both my hands.

She stumbled backward, blinked, then looked at me with wide, scared eyes. Then she just turned and walked away. I watched her.

"You're no kind of friend, Lucy!" I shouted, tears streaming down my cheeks. I walked slowly home, keeping my distance behind her.

I had shocked myself with my anger, with the fact that I was willing to hurt Lucy because of it. But I was so angry at her for not noticing and even angrier because she didn't think I wanted just what she wanted: to have fun, to be thought of as worthy and beautiful enough to be chosen as a dance partner by a boy.

◆　◆　◆

The next day Lucy and I were best friends again. We rode our bikes, looked at magazines, and talked on the phone when we were apart. But by Thursday Lucy was talking about what she was going to wear to the canteen coming up Saturday.

"I'm not going," I said.

"Come on, Pat. Go," she pleaded.

"I'm not going."

By Friday we were arguing. "Suit yourself!" she shouted over the phone, and I hung up. Saturday night I sat on my porch staring up at the stars, searching for constellations and confessing to myself that I really hated Lucy.

"She's not my friend. She doesn't care about me," I said. I conjured up the memory of Mrs. Bloomfield and how Lucy had loved her. I thought about Mary Ann and the word *nigger*. Being colored was a horrible curse, a burden too large for a little girl. Why would God put anyone, but particularly children, through this? I cocked my head and thought I heard the music from the canteen. I could taste the tears pouring out of my eyes.

Before the summer ended Lucy and I were no longer best friends.

Neither of us could point to the exact day our friendship changed. We certainly didn't discuss it. But she started spending time with two of the girls she met at the canteen, and when I told her I was never going back, she dismissed me as "stupid."

Shortly after fifth grade started, my father came home with orders for us to move to Beaufort, South Carolina. Lucy and I cried together, not the gut-wrenching sobbing we had done when Charlotte left, but tears rolled down our cheeks and we pressed together the fingers we had pricked to become blood sisters.

We vowed to write each other, to keep in contact for the rest of our lives. But I think we cried, too, because a part of us knew that we had already reached the age of separation, the time when America would no longer allow us to pretend we were alike. A time to see that our country had come up with a countless number of ways to prevent us from being friends. A time to see if we were up to the challenge of hurdling the wall built to separate us.

We were so young. Only children. Not strong enough to make it over without adults to help lift us. As a grown woman I would have another best friend who was white, and we have our hurdles, too. Being older and wiser, we are able to climb over them. And I think knowing Charlotte and Lucy somehow made me want to try.

Yet to this day, I have never received a letter from Charlotte. And I have never written one to her.

chapter two

Turning Black

I n Beaufort, South Carolina, I was greeted by both "Colored Only" signs and the sight of more Negro people than I had ever seen. This was the place where I learned that people who looked like me were reviled and discriminated against. Yet this was also the spot on earth where I first felt the relief of being with my own people.

I realized I was one little girl who had always lived on the sharp edge of life—scared and nervous that one slip would sever me from my white friends. No matter how insulated my life had seemed in Quantico, I had lived as a kid on edge, trying desperately not to make mistakes, to stay on my best behavior. No drooling or stumbling, stuttering or mispronouncing a word, or doing anything that might embarrass the race or confirm what all white people—even children—thought: that colored people were dumb heathens. Living like this was like holding in your stomach all your life until the day when someone says, "Relax," and you can't because you've forgotten how; and if you let go, you still wouldn't remember how to breathe, not the natural kind of sucking in you did when you were born, when you could breathe without thinking.

My constant fear was like the background static you hear when a radio dial isn't set exactly on the station. If you want to hear the music, you try to ignore the static, and sometimes you even succeed. I wanted to hear music. To be like white children, who seemed so fiercely happy. But for me, there was always static.

In Beaufort, the static was gone, because I was no longer different, no longer the only colored one, but one among many. I could relax. I heard silence—and the beating of my own heart. I felt the soft breeze of peace a child feels blowing though her life when every face she looks at is the face of someone who cares about her, who returns her smiles and hugs her tight and believes she can do anything she wants to do.

But the "Colored Only" signs would haunt me, too. In Virginia, I was an honorary white child, a status granted to me because my marine father took an oath to defend his country to death, if necessary. In South Carolina, in 1959, white men didn't give a damn about my daddy or where he spilled his blood. They cared even less about his pickaninny children.

In Virginia, I went to a brick-and-glass building in a warm classroom with white children. In South Carolina, I wore my winter coat to my segregated school because sometimes there was no heat. On spring afternoons we sat on the lawn while white children zoomed by on shiny yellow buses, screaming, "Niggers! Niggers!" I searched their contorted faces, looking for some feature that made them different from the white friends I had left behind in Virginia.

I was ten years old. In those early weeks I did what most black children must do at some point in their lives: I began to equate being black with having a horrible, difficult life. I didn't want any part of it. I wanted to move again. In my young mind, if I left a situation, it no longer existed, because reality was only what you could see.

I had grown accustomed to seeing new schoolbooks, modern furniture, and fancy gym equipment. But at the Robert Smalls School, every book, every piece of furniture and equipment, was secondhand, passed on to Negro children after white children had thrown it away. Even as I tried to absorb these changes, some of my classmates teased me about the way I talked.

"You talk too proper," a girl said.

"You act white," another said.

I didn't understand. I cried and complained to my mother, "It's cold in that school. It smells funny. They have terrible food."

"Make friends and you'll like it. Give it time," my mother said.

Two weeks later I was in love with Negro girls with soft, thick hair like mine and boys who pulled my pigtails because they thought I was pretty. My new girlfriends and I shared our displeasure with hair that napped up. On special occasions we would run into each other in Mrs. Carter's kitchen beauty shop, where we sat patiently waiting to get our hair pressed and curled so we could look grown. I went to a birthday party at the Grand Army Hall and saw a room full of Negro children doing "the slop," our bodies twitching and our feet sliding all across the wooden floors. If the pearly white gates had opened for me at that moment, I would have entered willingly, with a smile.

But always my peace was shattered by some incident or everyday situation reminding me that the South belonged to white people. My family lived on a military base called Laurel Bay, the first place we had ever lived that didn't have its own integrated school for military dependents. On Saturdays we played with white children on the school playground, a few feet off the land belonging to the base. We peeped inside the windows at the colorful bulletin boards, but we couldn't go inside. Negro children on the base were bussed to the schools for Negroes in the town of Beaufort.

Shortly after we arrived, just in time for my sister Shelia to start first grade, Laurel Bay Elementary was integrated. The rumor was that the U.S. government purchased the school from the local government for one dollar. Older children like myself were still bussed into Beaufort, because the elementary school only went through third grade. The older white children went to a white school and the Negro children to Robert Smalls, a complex of aging buildings that housed the first through twelfth grades. The buses that picked us up were, of course, secondhand, with torn seats, scratched windows, and scuffed floors. Some mornings my bus broke down before it reached me; at other times, while I was on it, it sighed like a tired horse and just stopped. We sat where it died until another old bus arrived to retrieve us.

The bus route wound down dusty country roads and over a railroad track. At a couple of places along the way, the driver stopped and pressed long on the horn and children of all ages, most of them related, ran from different houses. I was amazed that sisters and brothers, cousins, aunts and uncles, and grandparents lived on the same plot of earth—and as I got older and discovered they owned the land, I was even more amazed, because it had never occurred to me that Negroes anywhere owned property.

Some of my classmates sat in front of wood-burning stoves on winter mornings; when they came to school they carried that warm smell with them, filling the halls of Robert Smalls with the sweet scent of freshly burnt maple.

On the first day I was led into a classroom where a young woman with dark chocolate skin welcomed me. "I am your teacher: Miss Smith," she said.

My mouth hung open, temporarily paralyzed. I had never seen a Negro teacher. Almost immediately, I was proud of her, though I could not have explained why to anyone.

"Robert Smalls was a South Carolina slave who escaped to freedom and became a navy captain, a state senator, and a congressman," my history teacher told us. I sat at attention, my head lifted by the knowledge that a school could be named after a Negro man.

The escapades of Robert Smalls aboard his steamer became etched into my mind as deeply as the story of George Washington and his cherry tree. Like the children at the white schools, we were required to watch a white woman on TV lecture for an hour each day on "South Carolina history." The only time she mentioned "nigras" was when she talked about slavery. Nigra slaves played banjos, sang, and danced. Abolitionists fought for the end of slavery, and Abraham Lincoln freed the slaves. That basically summed up the history of colored people in South Carolina, according to our TV lesson. So it was left to our teachers to augment our learning, with lessons about important Negro inventors, educators, and writers.

At Robert Smalls, teachers believed that a good whipping was as important as reading, writing, and arithmetic. Corporal punishment was an art: Teachers decorated their paddles and carved grooves into them for extra sting, fringed the ends or punched them with holes to suck in flesh. They named their belts and paddles. Legends grew around them. The man who would be my eighth-grade teacher, Mr. Fields, distinguished himself with "Joy Boy," a belt so long it left a remarkable red coil around a victim's hand.

Punishment took place in the coatroom. We would line up outside while the teacher waited inside with his belt. Before entering, we heard friends whimpering and the torture instrument slapping against flesh. As students, we used the only revenge we had: drama. The coatroom had swinging doors like the ones on saloons in Westerns we saw on television. We sauntered through those doors like bold rustlers, the wood doors flapping in the air behind us.

This was occasional, not a daily or weekly ritual, and though it sounds ugly in a world where spanking a child is considered archaic and brutal, it was quite simply a part of our lives. As adults, we all laughed about our memories of the whippings just as we did when we recalled parties, parades, and first loves. In fact, some of us agreed we were more damaged by love—by broken promises made by sincere but immature lovers who stomped on our budding self-esteem—than we were by the force used by those who had authority over us.

I was an adolescent now; avoiding embarrassment consumed a significant amount of my concentration. In the sixth grade, some fast thinking and theatrics helped me avoid grave humiliation. I was at the blackboard in my math class, explaining how I had arrived at the answer to my problem. To my surprise, the teacher pronounced my calculations wrong and told me to stand at the board until I got them right. He went on to the next four students. I needed to use the bathroom, so I waved my hand and asked for permission.

"Wait until you explain your new answer," he said.

I waited. And waited. And waited. When the time came for me to explain my new answer, I spoke fast. I ran for the bathroom but didn't make it. Pee trickled down my legs. I thought quickly—and fell to the floor, stretching out to cover the puddle.

The teacher knelt over me. "What's wrong?" he asked.

I flashed big, innocent eyes. "I don't know. I can't walk."

By now everyone had formed a circle around me. My best friends stared with compassionate faces.

"Run to the office and get help," the teacher ordered. "Don't move," he said to me.

When the principal arrived, she and the teacher picked me up. A girl pointed to the stain on the wooden floor.

"It's blood," I said, crying.

The principal and teacher carried me to the principal's car while my classmates peered out the windows. My mother and one of her girlfriends met us at the hospital. After examining me, the doctors suggested X-rays.

"Did you fall recently?" a doctor asked.

"Yes. I fell jumping over the brick wall in our backyard," I said in a voice that begged for sympathy.

A few hours later they sent me home. The diagnosis: a pulled muscle or maybe growing pains, neither of which would show up on the X-rays. My mother was instructed to keep me home a day or so, if necessary, and watch me closely for a while. I went to school a day later, limping. Two days later, in the middle of the afternoon, I couldn't remember which leg was supposedly injured, so I stopped limping. But long after this escape from embarrassment, I remained awestruck by the power of drama.

◆　◆　◆

My mother, who loved to read, filled our house with books. I would thumb through my encyclopedia, memorizing trivia. In more exotic moods, I curled up in the huge barrel-backed chair to open a page of my favorite encyclopedia, *Lands and People,* and study color photos of far-off places. I read the Bobbsey Twins books and about King Arthur and his knights. In school, I settled on English as a favorite subject and wrote adventure fantasies. My teachers also encouraged me in art, because I could draw better than most of my classmates.

In fifth grade I had joined a Brownies troop headed by my teacher, Miss Smith, and in the comfort of a group where no one would ever speak of "niggers," I made lifelong friends. Sometimes we met on the screened porch at my house and danced all over the large backyard until dark. At my house, we could hide from Jim Crow and its wretched inequities. In the real world of Beaufort and the rural towns and islands around it, postcard palmetto trees fanned out over the stench of horrid poverty, the kind of poorness that breaks spirits in half or makes men unbearably angry—like the young man I heard about who shot another man over a pack of cigarettes.

For the first time I saw such dismal poverty up close, even stepped into it when I went with a girlfriend to visit her relatives. We walked into shacks where the wind whistled across walls plastered with newspaper, shotgun houses built on stilts to protect them from the stinking, stagnant water below. At one house, an eight-year-old boy with eyes so sad it hurt to look at them told me in a dull, matter-of-fact tone that his four-year-old sister had died.

"I'm so sorry," I said.

"At least she won't be hungry anymore," he said, sounding much older than he looked.

Even as an adult, I am still haunted by another scene: a small, squat shack with a brown baby girl inside, lying on a torn, soiled sofa. There were no screens in the windows or doors and flies and gnats landed and sat on the baby's bare belly, on her forehead and cheeks, and on her legs. Her mother, busy weeding vegetables in the garden, did not have time to swat bugs.

Just up the road were the big houses and acres of farmland owned by whites, who were descendants from a generation of masters who ran plantations. The people I visited were descendants of slaves who worked that land; their descendants were still slaves, only they were called sharecroppers. They remained shackled to the land, raising crops that kept the white families rich while barely earning enough to pay themselves for tools and supplies and rent for the tiny patch of fruitless land on which they lived and on which their forefathers had also lived. As a young girl learning this history and seeing the squalid poverty it still bred, I developed a new hatred for white people, and the blame I attributed to them lay hard in my heart like a nickel-plated bullet.

◆   ◆   ◆

I was nevertheless sheltered from much of the abundance of racism that conspired to belittle the lives of my classmates. Every facility on the base, where my family lived, was integrated. There was a movie theater, where we could sit anywhere we wanted, a swimming pool, where Negroes and whites swam together, and a teen club, which I attended sometimes with a few of my Negro classmates from Robert Smalls as guests. In Beaufort, my friends stood outside cafés and ordered their food through a window and watched movies in the balcony seats, the only ones Negroes were allowed to sit in. Generally, my mother would not allow me to go into segregated facilities or to use anything that said "Colored" or "Negroes."

The first time I saw a water fountain with a hand-printed "Colored" sign hanging over it, we were at a Beaufort drugstore.

"Ple-e-e-e-ze, Mama, can I drink it?" I pleaded.

She was insistent. "No. You'll get water when we get home."

"I want to see the colored water!" I screamed, near tears. I expected an arch of red, yellow, and blue water to spout out of the fountain. My mama laughed, later, in the privacy of her home. But at the time, she grabbed my hand and yanked me away.

My father was seldom around. I had friends who spent nights at my house and never met my father. The Marine Corps sent him on cruises, and he spent months in Cuba on what my mother whispered to others was "standby," a word that scared me because it seemed to be a code that meant my father could go to war and die. The months spent apart must have taken their toll on my parents' marriage (though at times in life I would see how different they were from each other and believe that their times apart probably kept them together). With my father traveling, my mother made all of the decisions about discipline. It was a pattern that became a blueprint for our family's future, so that even when my father was out of the service and at home permanently, he never made a decision regarding the behavior of his children.

"Can we go outside?" we asked him.

"Ask your mother," he'd say, and if our mama had gone off, the lives of my sisters and I froze until she returned.

I missed my father terribly whenever he left, but after a while missing him was too painful, so I tried to ignore his absence. But I was never comfortable with it and I imagined life would be so different, perfect, like the lives of families on television, if only my father were home. In his absence, I became as much my mother's mate as a child my age could be. I was the oldest, the person she looked to to help her with the younger children, her confidante when there was no one else to talk to.

There were times when we expected Daddy to return home any day and my sisters and I were giddy with excitement. Then he'd phone to say it would be another week or so. He arrived lugging duffel bags packed with gifts, once bringing dolls from Italy and Spain. To celebrate his return, he took the family to the military club for dinner. For the weeks that he was home my mother dressed up all of us girls and we'd follow Daddy around while he ran his errands. It never occurred to me that on some of these excursions Daddy was showing off his daughters. He was a quiet, aloof man who showed little affection or emotion, and I never thought he talked about us to anyone. Then one day while we were trailing behind him, a friend of his said to me, "So you're the little girl who plays the piano." I was stunned. But it was funny, too, that Daddy talked about my piano playing, since saying I played the piano was stretching the truth. I didn't like piano lessons or practicing, but my mother believed "a cultured young girl takes piano lessons," so I banged on those black and white keys and waited to be embraced by sophistication.

Meanwhile, my body was trying to turn me into a woman, though something inside me was out of sync. My left breast grew larger than my right.

"Look at this," my mother said to her girlfriends who visited, as she lifted my blouse to display my tender, plump breast and my flat one.

She wanted an explanation from her nurse friends. I wanted sympathy and privacy, both of which were given to me in short supply now that I was an twelve-year-old woman. Even my father's friends treated me differently. They were friendly, hardworking young men who loved to laugh and party and always told me I was pretty. Now that my body had changed, a few of them liked to touch me, intimately, when no one was watching.

Once a man I called my uncle was driving me home from school.

When he stopped the car at my house, he reached across me to open the door.

"I can open it. I can open it," I said. But he ignored me and did exactly what I had come to expect: he brushed his arm across my breasts, letting his flesh linger seconds too long.

The most serious offense occurred when one of my father's friends sat down beside me at the piano in our living room. He asked me to play a song for him, and I played "Heart and Soul," my fingers bouncing on the keys. He slipped his hand under my dress, up my thigh, and inside my panties. His fingers fumbled there, tickling the edge of my vagina. I played faster. In the kitchen, my mother and father and another of their friends, unaware of what was going on just on the other side of the wall, laughed and joked. All I remember is fear and shame. This was one of my parents' best friends and a man I liked. I concentrated on playing the song, trying not to hit a wrong key, which might call attention to what was happening. When the man pulled his hands from between my legs, I removed my fingers from the piano and the music—and the laughter—stopped.

After some years, the faces and names of these men faded from my memory. What remains is the sense of their rough fingers and their hard, mean hands. I was sure something wrong had happened between me and them, but I didn't know who was to blame. This was before talk shows about "child abuse," before sex education in schools. All that I was certain of was that I was small and helpless and that I needed adults to love me, and yet I was not sure I could trust them again.

For months I brainwashed myself by repeating a message inside my head that said: *You should be ashamed for making those men do that to you. You must have done something to make them think you would like it. You can't be trusted.*

My mother says I told her a year later about the piano incident, though I don't remember telling her at all. In fact, for years I was angry at myself for saying nothing and I despised that little coward who let a man fondle her.

◆   ◆   ◆

On Valentine's Day, seven boys gave me boxes of chocolate-covered cherries; I hated cherries. Each time a boy handed me a box, I prayed for chocolate-covered nuts, fudge, or caramel. Yet my joy at receiving seven Valentine's gifts surpassed my disappointment in the type of candy I received. In Virginia, white boys had ignored me, had refused to hold my hand or squeeze me tight on a slow drag. Negro boys filled my life with sweetness, and I kept those boxes of candy in the refrigerator until the dark chocolate turned nearly white and Mama convinced me that those were not the last boxes of candy I would receive.

In seventh grade, I got my first boyfriend, a sweet, elfin boy named Will, a ninth-grader who could have gone with girls who wore stockings and had big titties. I wore ankle socks and a training bra stuffed with stockings; I was flattered to be seen with an older guy. Dating meant we wrote each other love letters; he carried my books, and at dances we slow dragged with each other—exclusively. I hugged his arm on the scary rides at the fair and sat beside him, gasping for breath, as our feet dangled together at the top of the Ferris wheel.

At dances, I was tireless, twisting and twirling nonstop for hours. No boy was too ugly or too funky for me to dance with. Though I truly appreciated a good partner, I'd dance just as quickly with someone who lacked one ounce of grace or rhythm. Basically, my rule was: if he can move, I'll dance with him.

When my good friend Jackie had a birthday party at the Grand Army Hall, I wore out the creaky wooden floors doing the slop and the Duke of Earl until my soft hair turned nappy and sweat trickled down between my breasts. We danced to "Mashed Potato Time" and acted out the "Duke of Earl." Music intoxicated me. Caught up in the beat of drums or the thump of a bass, I had no time to think about being a "nigger" or a virgin. I stepped out onto the dance floor and gave in willingly to the rhythm. That has never changed for me. I go to nightclubs and I am transformed by the joy of the dancers, revived by the fever pitch of their pleasure. Especially on Friday nights, when I swear people dance to keep from dying.

◆   ◆   ◆

Most Saturdays in Beaufort my family, which now included three sisters—Shelia, Carol, and Debra—went into town. I was sure all of the Negro people in the world were there, though my mother insisted it was just people from nearby communities and islands, places with magical names like Frogmore, Lady's Island, and Saint Helena. Men carried 50- and 100-pound bags of rice on their shoulders and hefted them onto the backs of their pickup trucks, where children sat, playing with Bo-lo bats while they waited. Women walking straight as sugarcane balanced full bags of groceries or baskets of fresh laundry on their heads. When some of the Saturday people spoke, beautiful, melodic sounds floated from between their lips. I knew it was a language, but it sounded like a type of music with words. Mama said they were "geechees," people who lived on the islands, and they spoke a language called Gullah that blended African words with English. All I knew was that their voices, especially in chorus as they walked down the streets, tickled my ears and pleased me inside my chest.

My classmates whispered about "voodoo," generally in the same sentences with the name "Dr. Buzzard," the Negro man known as the grand witch doctor or high priest of voodoo. He kept a cat in a bottle, turned water to blood and back to water again, and made rain or lightning, whichever he wanted. He could make a man who hated you suck your toes and coo his love. At least, that's what people said.

There was an unspoken agreement between the Negro and white communities: Negroes celebrated Memorial Day, and whites celebrated the Fourth of July. It was one of those traditions that cropped up in towns across the country, quietly bred by racism to keep people separated in a peaceful way. Memorial Day festivities began with a parade of marching bands and small floats and cars decorated with crepe paper and handwritten signs. Negroes lined the streets selling food from card tables and wooden crates.

"Deviled crabs!"

"Crab gumbo!"

"Fried chicken and potato salad!"

Choosing what to eat was as much fun as eating. At the end of the day, everyone went to the fair.

I was in my first and only parade in Beaufort, riding on the hood of a car until the engine toasted the back of my dress. I represented the Honor Society, waving to people with my hands in elbow-length navy blue gloves, dreaming I was some southern beauty queen.

◆ ◆ ◆

By the time we left Beaufort in late 1962 I was thirteen, my sister Sondra had been born, and my mother was pregnant again. We now had five girls in our family. My father was transferred to Albany, Georgia, but my mother and we girls headed North to Washington, D.C., to live with my maternal grandparents. After months of watching the evening news flash pictures of civil rights demonstrators being beaten and arrested in Albany, my parents had decided that that city was too dangerous and chaotic for their children. Daddy and Mama bought a house in the Washington suburbs of Maryland, in a new middle-class community for Negroes called Glenarden Woods. While it was being built, Mama and we girls lived with my grandparents. Daddy would stay in Albany for two more years, until he finished his twenty-year career in the Marine Corps. After he retired, he'd join us and we'd live in one house forever, something I couldn't imagine, though I wanted it badly.

For years I had envied people who had friends they had known all of their lives. I was in the eighth grade, and it seemed to me I had spent my life saying good-bye to people, making new friends and leaving old ones. I had learned to do whatever was necessary to make myself lovable and popular, to win new friends in a snap.

The day before we moved, Will rode with me on the school bus. We wrapped our arms around each other, and as the bus slowed down at my house some of the older girls whispered to me, "Kiss him. You should kiss him good-bye." My face must have looked like one big question mark. "It's okay. Do it," they answered. I kissed him flat on the lips and hopped off the bus with tears streaming down my cheeks. I was too sad to reflect on my achievement, to appreciate that I had just done something I had never done before.

Will and I wrote each other long letters, pledging our love for eternity. Our correspondence lasted a year. The next time I heard anything about him it was from friends who said he was living in New York and had a drug problem. In later years he returned to the South, burned out from drugs and alcohol, a shell of the energetic boy I knew. This was ironic to me because by this time I had had my own bout with drugs and I also had a phone book full of names of abusive ex-lovers with troubled lives. *Could the pattern have started in seventh grade?* I asked myself.

"You always wanted to take care of people who were like stray dogs," a girlfriend said to me when I returned to Beaufort as an adult. "If they were sick, you wanted to make them well."

◆　　◆　　◆

Leaving Beaufort was unbearably painful. In addition to missing friends, I was going to miss the junior high prom. At my going-away party, I opened a present, pushing back the tissue paper to find a sparkling crown, the kind of tiara I had expected to wear to the prom. I cried like a baby, breathless, clutching my stomach. Some of my girlfriends sobbed, too. We cried until our noses ran and we were sick with headaches. Mr. Fields sent a boy to the bathroom for rolls of toilet paper for us to use to dry our tears.

I had come to Beaufort as a little girl who had no idea what it meant to be a Negro. I was leaving a child who loved the story of Robert Smalls, the smell of Negro people in the morning, and the musical speech of black women who balanced baskets on their heads. In the South, white people would not let me forget I was black. Forcing me to stare in that mirror cast long shadows on my life but also helped me see treasures I had never seen before.

In Beaufort, I learned that there were many different expressions of black life, more than I would ever see on television. There were black teachers, property owners, poor sharecroppers, farmers. I also learned to hate white people. No one told me to hate them; no one had to. When people toss you seconds, treat you as if you are less than human, call you names, forbid you to sit in the front row of the movie theater or at the lunch counter of a diner, you don't have to muster up hate; it comes like a flood—and you spend your life building a dam to hold it back. Hate was the new static in my life. It would be there, in the background, forever.

The dam I built was called "the White People." This is the group whose faceless members are the caretakers of segregation, the proud descendants of slave owners, the conquerors who disrespect all cultures except their own. Though I would always have white friends, I learned to separate them from the White People. Somehow, I reason, my white friends have escaped receiving the gene or the arrogance or God-knows-what that creates conquerors. This thought keeps me sane and prevents me from hating *all* white people. But I know that some of my black friends, who have known atrocities much greater than what I've experienced, or perhaps feel them more deeply, do not separate white people into "good" and "bad." They lump them all together and hate each one equally.

◆ ◆ ◆

Of course, change crept into Beaufort over the years as it did in other small towns in the South, leaving nothing untouched. Today some of my classmates hold jobs that blacks weren't allowed to have when we were growing up; one is a teacher at Laurel Bay Elementary, another is director of Emergency Medical Services for the county, and my best friend, Jackie, is a banker, the first black person hired at the Bank of Beaufort in 1969.

Robert Smalls, like many formerly all-black schools, was torn down, and the Beaufort County Multi-government Complex was built in its place. A new ultracontemporary Robert Smalls Middle School for black and white children was built a few miles away on a road renamed Robert Smalls Parkway.

What has not changed is the permanent impressions I carry in my soul. It was in Beaufort that the world told me that being black meant I was not good enough to sit in a classroom next to white children. It told me I did not deserve heat in my school or new buses, or to learn that people my color had ever done anything significant. Also in Beaufort, I learned from black teachers and my own peers that we deserved much more than the world was ready to give us.

The world, as run by white people, could not be trusted to tell me the truth, I concluded. So if I couldn't believe what the world said about me, I couldn't trust what it said about other people, about people who were considered handicapped, or people who were gay, about juvenile delinquents or people on welfare, about the capabilities of women or the definition of a man. If the world lied, I decided, it was up to me to search for the truth.

chapter three

Womanish

itting with my grandmother at her second-story bedroom window in the evening, I saw black women in sparkling dresses and men in dark suits going to dances at the Knights of Columbus Hall across the street. Black people in Washington, D.C., were always going places, and I loved watching them. My grandmother must have been fascinated, too, because she sat on a short iron stool peering out her window for hours each day, first at the people going to regular jobs and later in the evening at the drag queens and prostitutes working the streets. In the afternoons I joined her, after running to the store to fetch us a bag of Mary Janes, Squirrel Nuts, and some penny cookies, which we ate as we sat. This was our cinema, and my grandmother, whom I never knew to attend a movie, was contented with the picture show outside her house.

By this time she had retired from working in white people's houses and cooking greasy food at a neighborhood diner. Now all she did was go to church on Sundays, shop occasionally, and sit at her window. Her morning watch started after Grampy left for his job as a maintenance worker on the airstrip at National Airport.

Mama said Grannie had been an excellent dancer and used to go to dances whenever one of the big bands was in town. Once she won five dollars in groceries in a dance contest at a Count Basie show, Mama said. I couldn't imagine. The Grannie I knew loved to laugh and jone on people and was known for her sharp tongue, but she was prudish about getting involved in the world she would watch from her window.

"If God wanted me to fly, He woulda given me wings," she said, explaining why she only traveled by bus and, if pressed, by train.

She didn't attend parties and seldom had company. If Grampy had different interests, he hid them. They lived in a brick row house on a corner with a bus stop out front and next to the corner store where I bought our penny candy and cookies, in the heart of a black community called Shaw. We were surrounded by the culture of our people. The campus of Howard University was a few blocks away. Up the street was the Washington headquarters of the Southern Christian Leadership Conference, a black-owned bank, the Washington Afro-American newspaper, and a string of other black-owned businesses. Not far away was Howard Theater, where over the years I would see the most famous black singers and comedians, including Otis Redding, Redd Foxx, and the Temptations. One day I saw Marvin Gaye standing outside and I was too amazed to say a word. On my way to the drugstore, usually running errands for my mother and grandmother, I passed the Scurlock Photo Studio, stopping to stare at the black-and-white photos of black people who looked different from any I had ever seen: couples dressed in expensive, fancy clothes; women with silky hair and thin noses, their faces tilted upward; men with clear, piercing eyes that fixed on the camera in a way that told that they owned something, their faces free from lines of fear or worry.

In 1963, every black person knew change was coming. Even I, at the age of fourteen, could feel it in the air. Federal troops had escorted Negroes into the halls of the University of Mississippi, which I thought was one of the most important institutions owned by white people. If blacks were going to classes there, then anything was possible. Besides, John F. Kennedy was president, and my grandparents said he was a good white man, one we could count on to help lead us into equality.

Some evenings my mother and I walked up U Street to eat in one of the black-owned restaurants. We passed record stores that advertised "African music" and "revolutionary sounds," and I wondered what kind of songs those were. We passed small clubs and when a door opened I stopped to get a glimpse. I seldom saw anything, but balloons of music, jazz and sometimes calypso, floated past me. Occasionally Mama and I went to one of the big movie theaters and afterward we ate at Ben's Chili Bowl, where you might see politicians and street hustlers sitting side by side at the counter.

◆ ◆ ◆

Across the street from my grandparents' house was my junior high school, Garnet-Patterson, a blond brick building with a wall built around the asphalt school yard. After Robert Smalls's sprawling campus, Garnet-Patterson looked like a jail. At lunchtime I sat on the hard asphalt and watched girls jump double dutch, trying to capture the rhythm of their feet in my head. I was too afraid of not being accepted to admit I didn't know anything about double dutch. I was too afraid of failure to ask anybody to teach me, so I feigned disinterest.

I thought it would be easy to make new friends, especially since all of the kids were black. This time, instead of having to cope with race or with being teased about being proper, I had to deal with being called "country."

Until I got to Washington, I thought my black jacket my grandmother bought me the previous Christmas was leather.

"That's pleather," a girl explained to me one day in a loud voice that brought snickers from classmates.

"P-l-e-a-t-h-e-r. That's plastic and leather."

"Country girl!" a boy yelled to me in the hallway. I wondered if I smelled like burnt maple wood.

I was severely wounded. At this point in life, there was nothing I wanted more than the approval and respect of my peers, so I vowed to change. To become more likable, more hip. Some things were out of my hands, such as the white nylon socks hugging my ankles, which my mother insisted I wear. She wouldn't let me wear makeup either.

But I improved my wardrobe by paying more attention to what my classmates wore and asking them where they shopped. I was beginning to get some compliments when my grandmother told me she was getting me a green suede coat with a white rabbit fur collar for Christmas.

"Is it re-e-eal?" I asked.

"Of course," she said. "It's a real *coat*." She emphasized that last word as if it was followed by a giant period—and she dared me to comment.

But I heard her tell my mother she got it on sale for thirty-nine dollars and I knew I was in trouble. When she brought it home, it was imitation suede, just as I had suspected. She saw my disappointment and her body seemed to swell in preparation for me. I had never refused a gift from my grandmother and had been taught to always be grateful for what people do for you. Yet I knew I would be too ashamed to wear an imitation suede coat in front of friends who owned real suede and real leather coats.

"Grannie, this isn't real," I snapped, though I meant to say it differently, softer. I was about to add some words when she cut me off.

"Why don't you just buy your own coat?" she said.

The next day the green brushed-cotton coat with the collar that looked like cotton balls disappeared. Though I was too young to get a job, I accepted the challenge of buying what I wanted in the future. It would be two years before I could buy a suede coat, but when I did it was a navy blue, real suede coat. I'd brush my hand across it and watch the blue change shades. My classmates admired it, which only reinforced my new belief that when you're young, being nice is enough to earn friends, but when you're older and in the city, you have to dress well and be cool to earn respect—and friends. Clothes were more important than books, I concluded, so I watched my fashion idols at school and read fashion magazines, vowing to stay on the cutting edge of trends.

Shortly before my family moved to Maryland, my period started and my mother proclaimed me a woman. "You know what that means?" she said, sitting on the edge of my bed. Her voice heaved the question in the air, and it hung there on its own, waiting for some answer that I didn't have.

"You have to be careful now," Mama said, looking at me with raised eyebrows.

In the summer of 1963, we moved from Shaw, where I could open a window and hear buses braking at the stop in front of the house and people talking as they passed at any time of the night. Our new neighborhood was quiet except for the sounds of children playing during the day. It was the first time we had ever lived in a community where everyone was black, though that wasn't what struck me initially, since I had been surrounded by blacks in South Carolina and at my grandmother's house. What struck me first was that our family had never lived in a new house. We had always lived in nice brick houses in well-kept neighborhoods—in fact, our last house in South Carolina was more modern than our new home—but we had never been the first family to live in a house. Our new home had freshly cut hardwood floors, thin, new grass, and a large backyard with skinny young trees. I spent those early weeks helping my very pregnant mother unpack our belongings and shop.

After Beaufort, I was more aware of my race. This was due in part to my experience in South Carolina, but also because it was the early sixties and everyone was talking about race and the civil rights movement. My mother, her friends, my grandparents, even people on the streets were discussing the latest protests they had read about or seen on the news. I sat and watched the evening news, intrigued by the sight of girls no older than I was being carted off to jail because they tried to do something as simple as drink out of a water fountain labeled "White." I knew the faces of the black leaders because I followed the stories about them in *Jet, Ebony,* and *Sepia* magazines, all of which my parents and grandparents subscribed to. We had been in our new house just a few days when we heard on the news that Medgar Evers, head of the NAACP in Mississippi, had been killed. I knew Medgar Evers because I had seen pictures of him and his children and wife. I had read about him and heard people talk about him, so I cried as if a relative had died. I cried because Medgar Evers believed in a stinking world that didn't care anything about him. And I was awe-struck that my family could be moving into a beautiful new house at the same time that a man was gunned down in front of his house in Mississippi. I expected to see the face of the killer on the evening news, to hear Walter Cronkite announce the verdict after the mur-derer was sentenced to death. But nothing happened, and this hurt me, deeply. I indicted all white people for Medgar's death. I took his killing personally, as if the racist who shot Medgar had wounded me, too. I demanded an answer from God: how could Medgar Evers die and the world go on as if nothing had happened?

But I learned that nothing could stop the protests and demonstra-tions. Not water hoses, dogs, bullets, or bombs. My grandparents were talking about a big civil rights march being held in Washington, which they were going to participate in with members of their churches. They said black and white people were coming from all over the country and that all of the civil rights leaders would be there. I begged my mother to let me go, but she and my grandparents thought I was too young to attend.

"There could be trouble," my grandfather said.

"Why you going then?" I asked.

"Trouble's my middle name," said Grampy, shadowboxing the air, doing what he called his Cassius Clay imitation.

When I heard the word *trouble,* I thought of the images of march-ers being beaten by white police officers wielding billy clubs. I figured my grandparents would not get close enough to be beaten, but me, I would probably be with the young marchers and we would get hurt. Right then, I realized I didn't have the guts those children in Arkan-sas, North Carolina, and Mississippi had. I didn't want trouble or pain, so I stayed home.

Yet the mere fact that the march took place just blocks away subtly changed me just as it changed those who heard Dr. King speak that day. When the March on Washington became a historic event, I thought of how ordinary it had seemed to me, as if it were only the advent of a bolder color in the texture of our lives. It was just ordinary people marching; my grandmother stayed up all night frying chicken for people who were coming; people could make history by packing

fried chicken in a shoe box, putting on comfortable shoes, and carrying a homemade sign. History was made by regular people, not just
the wealthy, not just those who were white. It was people's unity that
made them powerful, the fact that for one day they could put aside
their differences and focus on one problem they all wanted to change.
This was a form of power I had never considered.

I was watching the news a couple of weeks later and saw that a
Birmingham church had been bombed, killing four girls. Three of
them were fourteen years old, like me. I imagined what it was like for
them, sitting in Sunday school one moment and blown to death the
next. For weeks the questions exploded inside my head: What was the
Sunday school lesson they heard? What were they wearing? Who
planted the bomb? How could anyone hate that much? I couldn't
read enough in the newspaper or see enough on television about the
killings. I saw photos: the damaged stained-glass windows, the grieving parents, and a girl's shoe in the church rubble. I woke up every
morning for several weeks feeling as if a coffin were lying on my chest.
I had felt this way for about a day after Medgar Evers died, but the
excitement of moving into a new neighborhood had overpowered my
anxiety. This time the feeling lasted longer. And it would happen several times again: when John F. Kennedy was killed, when Martin Luther King was assassinated, when police gunned down the young
Black Panther Fred Hampton, and when George Jackson was killed.

Shortly after school started for me in Maryland, my brother, William, was born and we celebrated the family's first boy. Meanwhile, I
was trying to make new friends again. This time the kids in my neighborhood snubbed me. Though I didn't know it, it was a ritual to ignore
newcomers, to test their endurance and, perhaps, see if they deserved
friends. I think I would have failed had it not been for Jennifer.

One afternoon my mama yelled, "Pat, you have company!" I
thought she was joking, because I didn't know anybody, but after her
second urging I ran to the front door. Standing in the foyer was a
black girl with skin the color of light brown sugar and freckles all over
her face.

"I'm Jennifer Jackson. They call me Ginny." She stretched out her
bony hand.

We went to the basement to talk, mostly about school and clothes. Years later, I would think of our meeting that day and proclaim her an angel. She stepped out of the crowd and reached for me, and the spell that caused others to snub me was broken.

I soon found out, though, that a lot of people thought Ginny was stuck-up and sneaky and avoided her. Actually, she was just quiet and fragile, while I, having been dumped into new environments all my life, was used to leaping into the middle of the unknown. What I would find out years later was that I was just as fragile as Ginny, only my facade was so tough that for a while I even fooled myself.

We became best friends despite our differences, coming dangerously close to falling into the weird practice of dressing exactly alike. We showed up at the school bus stop once in matching oversize bows that we had made and pinned to the backs of our heads. We cut and curled ourselves into similar hairdos. Most strangers thought we were sisters; some guessed we were twins. If some new boy I didn't like asked for my name and number, I gave him Ginny's, and she did the same.

My first love was still music, but boys had entered my life and nothing would ever be the same. Songs took on new meanings; words became as important as rhythms. I took music with me everywhere I went, keeping my transistor radio plugged in my ear, even sleeping with it. I went to basement parties and danced until my clothes were soaked with sweat, then helped friends sneak in bottles of liquor to spike the punch. On warm nights some of us girls rode with older boys in their souped-up Fords and Chevys as they drag-raced down dark, snaking roads.

At the bus stop Ginny and I studied the older girls in flaming red lipstick and stockings; in the evenings we imitated them, the way they walked and swayed their hips, the way they talked in all-knowing tones. We thought we were grown because we were in high school— but our mothers thought differently, and so we hid our stockings in our pocketbooks each morning until we got around the corner, where we put them on standing behind neighbors' bushes or sitting in someone's car, slipping off our white socks and hooking our nylons onto our garter belts. In the afternoon, we hopped off the bus, unhooked our stockings, rolled them up, and stuffed them back into our pocket-books before heading home.

I was getting bored with school, but I fell back into the habit of reading when the bookmobile started visiting Glenarden and I could search its narrow bookshelves for life stories of black people. I developed an appetite for biographies and autobiographies, a hunger to know how other people lived their lives—specifically, how they overcame obstacles and challenges. Somehow it comforted me to read these stories, even though I never discussed them with anyone.

But books couldn't keep me away from the streets. My hormones, or something deep within me, said that what I was learning inside the walls of school was useless because what I needed to survive was really knowledge of what was going on outside. Ginny and I studied boys, the way they walked—whether they pimped, swayed, strolled, sauntered. We looked at their shoes and their eyes, their haircuts, and the way they carried their chins, straight or tilted up or down. We studied their dress, the colors they wore, whether or not they created their own style by wearing everything just a little different than expected, like a part in their hair when no one else wore parts or a jacket zipped to the neck when everyone else wore theirs wide open. We decided that the type of boy we liked was the one who walked, talked, and lived like he owned the world. Unfortunately, most of these boys did not attend school; they stood on the corner as our school bus rolled past.

We couldn't explain our attraction to them. More likely, one of us said to the other, "He is so-o-o cool. He don't take no shit off no-body."

Already for me, there were only two kinds of men: men like my father, remote, subdued, obedient, and men who held out and fought, seizing power whatever way they could. My father was like those eye-rolling Uncle Toms I saw in old movies. "Yessur, massa," would have flown out of his mouth if he had been a slave. I could not respect such a man. The guys Ginny and I liked were defiant, even arrogant. But a black man needed to be arrogant; you couldn't earn respect being a yes-man. My life had shown me that black people had very little control over their lives: we were told where to go to school while someone else determined the quality of that school, whether we got used books or new books, a used bus or a new bus. I knew that if we were to have any power, we would have to fashion it out of our own existence; the young men I was attracted to were the kind of men to do that. They defined what power was for them and they exuded that power in their walk and in the way they thumbed their noses at traditional notions, like working for white people or going to school. They were free and I was powerful when I was near them.

Once I had decided what type of man I liked, it seemed easy, at age fifteen, to take the next step, to find someone to love. I found Bennett, whom we called "Ben," a guy two years older who had already been expelled from several schools and was attending mine when I met him. When he walked near me my knees buckled and I got giddy inside. I loved his thin mustache, near-ebony skin, the sculpted shape of his head, the fingernails he so proudly kept manicured.

Ginny liked light-skinned boys, and she fell in love with Michael, a boy with gray eyes whose family had a reputation for marrying only people with skin as nearly white as theirs. Ginny and Michael both knew his family would never accept her. She had freckles, but still her skin was not white enough. In a spirit of rebellion, she and Michael clung to each other.

Maybe I was rebelling, too. My parents would never approve of Ben. He dropped out of school for good, shortly after I met him, and he hung out in front of the 7-Eleven store that had been built behind our house, just where my mother could see him rolling dice in crap games. My father was still away, so my mother was the lone authority in our house. She would not allow Ben to visit me, unaware that her resistance was the glue that held our love together long before we developed any other bond.

To my parents, I'm sure, Ben represented all they had worked to avoid. My father had run away from home to join the Marine Corps not only to make his life better, but so that he later could lift his own wife and children from the almost certain poverty of the red clay country of North Carolina where he was raised. My mother, who dropped out of college to give birth to me, imagined her daughter would marry someone who had at least a high school degree. My parents were from the generation that lived in the heat of segregation and heard old people whisper about slavery. Their lives were dedicated to uplifting the race by uplifting their own family, and they did not believe Ben could raise one branch of our family tree.

But I didn't consider any of this; any hint of elitism turned my stomach. Mother felt disdain for Ben until she found out I was no longer a virgin; then she hated him.

Shortly after we met, Ben and I had started necking and having long heavy-petting sessions. Generally, they ended with his whispering in my ear, "Let me make love to you. If you loved me, you'd let me have it."

I said, "No." But after each session my words got softer and I grew weaker.

One night, walking home from a dance, we stopped on a path in the woods and kissed each other until we were wet from sweat and excitement. He slipped his fingers inside my panties and my vagina. Instead of the fear I had felt with my father's friend at the piano, I experienced sizzling pleasure. I groped inside Ben's pants and felt his dick hard under my hand and I got more excited. Right then I made up my mind: soon I would go all the way.

Ginny had already slept with Michael. I was surprised and hurt because she kept such an important event a secret between us until Michael told Ben, who of course told me, and I pressured Ginny to tell me if it was true. It was the beginning of a change in our relationship, a slight moving apart. I thought girlfriends, particularly best friends, told each other the most important things, all that was left over after we told what we could to everybody else. If we kept secrets from each other, that meant girlfriends were no different from boyfriends; so carrying this disappointment with me, I moved closer to Ben.

Ginny remained my best female friend, though, and her admission that she was no longer a virgin was the encouragement I needed to give up my own virginity. We drew up a plan where I would hook school to meet Ben. Michael had a car, so he and Ginny picked me up at the bus stop and dropped me at Ben's house.

Although he lived less than a mile from my house, Ben's neighborhood looked like a small rural town, with old frame houses, a general store that was also a post office, and some dirt roads that sprouted off paved ones. This was the original town of Glenarden, divided from my family's subdivision by a single-lane highway. The people in my neighborhood referred to the side on which Ben lived as "across the tracks," which was the same as "the other side of the tracks," a place where people lived who could not bolster your family tree.

Ben lived with his mother, grandmother, two sisters, and brother in a small one-story wooden house along a dirt road. I knocked at the door, my legs trembling from fear. He swung open the door and put a large hand on my thin shoulder, pulling me to him. He kissed me on the lips, his mouth locked tight over mine, and the two books I carried under my arm slid to the floor.

It was so quiet inside that I heard my conscience whispering, *Your mama is going to be disappointed in you,* and I considered leaving. But Ben led me to the sofa and his hands moved fast. Over my tiny breasts. To my neck. Down my back. To my bra. Fumbling. Down to my panties. In seconds, I was lying there half-naked, with my skirt up and my legs sprawled open. Ben stripped to his boxer shorts. I closed my eyes. I felt his penis probing my vagina. I clutched the back of his undershirt. He thrust his hips. A piercing pain shot from between my legs. I moaned. He shoved. I squirmed. He slowed down. I was wet inside. He pulled out.

"Are you okay?" he said. "That was good."

I smiled faintly, but between my legs I burned and throbbed. We ate peanut-butter-and-jelly sandwiches and watched television and I tried to ignore my aching body parts. Holding him, being held, watching television with the taste of peanut butter on my mouth, I felt as though I had opened up myself and swallowed another person, so that now I had two halves inside me. Half of a young man's life and half of my own. The afternoon passed quickly, until it was time for me to go to my bus stop so I could walk home and greet my mother.

I couldn't tell her about what had happened, so after having sex I clung to Ben, the only person who shared my awful, wonderful secret. It was an unhealthy neediness, leaving me vulnerable to the whims of someone else, a person so young he didn't even know what he wanted out of me—or life.

I understood later that day how dependent on Ben this one act made me. He called, his voice filled with anger.

"Why did you tell me this was your first time?"

"What do you mean?" I said softly into the phone. "It *was* my first time." He had said nothing about his suspicions to me earlier.

"Then where did you learn to move like that?"

"Move like what?" For some reason, I sensed he had discussed this with another guy and together they had come up with this question for me.

"The way you wiggled and rolled your hips. You rocked—"

I cut him off. "If I did, I don't remember. I don't know. Maybe women do it naturally." My lips quivered from the pressure of holding back tears.

I hung up on him, lay on my bed, and wept with my face buried in my pillow so none of my siblings or my mother would hear. I had given Ben my most valuable possession—myself. There was nothing left to give. If he rejected me, he would be saying that who I was was not good enough.

This was a problem I was to have most of my life. Sex confused me. I could be a perfectly sane person in a relationship—until I had sex with a man. Then I thought I was in love, or even worse, I suddenly was weaker, so that when a guy did something I normally considered wrong and totally unacceptable, I would pretend it was cool, feign acceptability, pledging my loyalty nevertheless and forgetting my own well-being and my good common sense.

Ben apologized the next day and I pretended he had never phoned to question my honesty. A month later, my period didn't come on, but since I was prone to irregular periods, I wasn't too worried. Then a few more weeks passed and my mother, who kept up with my menstruation as if it were her own, began hounding me with questions: "Isn't it time for your period? Have you had sex with that boy? Pat, if you're pregnant you'd better tell me so I can do something."

I caved in after nearly two months. "Do you think you might be pregnant?" Mama asked.

I nodded "yes."

Mama stood in front of me with tears dripping down her cheeks. I cried because I had hurt her.

For the next week Mama and her girlfriends gave me every home remedy they knew for aborting a baby. I confronted nothing as horrible as a coat hanger, but I drank all kinds of concoctions, usually hot drinks mixed with black or red pepper or dry powders mixed with turpentine. Mother's nurse friends gave her all kinds of pills for me. While I gagged, a crew of women sat at our dining room table clucking their tongues and watching closely to make sure I didn't waste a drop or a pill. One day they hovered at the bathroom door while I sat on a bucket of searing hot water mixed with some herbs and dried mustard. I walked out of that room with a red rim around my butt that I expected to wear for life. I sat on the toilet, praying and making all sorts of promises to God—or I sat on the edge of the tub, waiting for the blood I normally dreaded.

My period came unannounced during one of my well-deserved naps. I'll never know if I was really pregnant, and sometimes I regret I ever told my mother. I don't think she told my absent father; his silent condemnation would have been more painful than any home remedy.

Mama forbade me to see Ben again, or to have sex again before I married. I would of course disobey her, and I deeply resented her gestapo intrusions in my life. I thought of how lucky Ginny was to have a mother who regularly sneaked into Ginny's room to tuck packages of rubbers in her dresser drawer.

While I was living through my crisis, Ginny and Michael eloped, which upset both their families. A week or so later her parents had the marriage annulled, and I believe his parents ordered him not to see her again. Ginny mourned the loss, but somehow, unlike me, she let go. Before high school graduation, Michael was a distant memory.

I was convinced that my mother didn't know anything about love, but if I could show her how much Ben and I loved each other, she'd back off. As for Ben, part of his determination to see me may have at first been based on sheer defiance. He wanted to prove to my mother he had more power over her daughter than she did. Even at the time it seemed to me like a classically male—but very exciting—power to wield.

I couldn't give up sex; by the third try I was enjoying it too much to deny myself the pleasure. I hooked school more often to be with Ben. One of those mornings I went with him to the house of a guy we both knew. In a back bedroom we made love with our clothes on. We had just finished and I was stretched out across the bed with my dress up over my hips when I felt someone watching. A guy I knew stood in the doorway. I jumped up and pulled my dress down. Ben got up off the bed, zipped up his pants, and, without a word, walked out.

His friend Derrick walked over to me. "It's me and you."

"What do you mean?" I asked.

"You got to put out or get out," he snapped.

Ben was gone.

Then Jimmy, the friend whose house we were in, walked in and stood behind Derrick. I was scared of Jimmy because he had a wild and unpredictable temper. But he left the room and I relaxed some. By now, I had figured they were thinking of pulling a train on me. I was nearly incapacitated with fear and the thought that Ben could be in on it, or that these guys I thought of as friends could so easily betray me. But they appeared confused, as if they weren't sure they really wanted to follow through, so I decided to call Derrick's bluff.

"Derrick, I'll tell your father if you put a finger on me," I said. Derrick was profoundly afraid of his father.

"I'll call your mother now and tell her you're here," he responded. He picked up a phone in the room and dialed my number. I grabbed the phone and we were struggling when Jimmy ran in to say his mother was coming.

"Damn, I thought she was at work," Derrick said.

"You need to get out of here," Jimmy said to me.

I was relieved, but before I could make it outside the house his mother was inside. I flopped on a chair in the living room, next to Ben.

"What's going on here?" she asked as soon as she walked in.

Jimmy had told her he was staying home with a toothache, and now he held his hand to his jaw.

"Your friends gotta go," she said, eyeing me suspiciously.

"Hi, Mrs. Watson. I was just leaving," I said, rushing past her and out the door.

Ben followed. As soon as we were safely away, I began to yell and curse. "You set me up! You were gonna let Jimmy and Derrick and anybody else who came in there pull a fucking train on me!" I walked and screamed, tears streaming down my cheeks.

Ben caught up with me, grabbed me, and pulled me to him. "You know me better than that," he said. "I love you."

As I look back, it's hard for me to believe that I gave in so easily, that right there on the spot I forgave him for what was nearly unforgivable. But why should he have given more to me when I demanded so little? How could he respect someone who didn't respect herself? And yet I feel compassion for that long-gone self, for the poor hurt child who was so desperate for a man's touch, the woman-child who craved those three tender words. Already my wounds must have been much deeper than I understood.

I forgave Ben. No more questions. No more doubt. I was too afraid of the truth.

◆ ◆ ◆

My father came home to live with us, but he was a stranger to me. By the time he returned from the marines and moved in, I had found my own man to fill the wound in me that longed for affection and love from a male person. All children who miss their fathers find a replacement. Some lavish their affection and adoration on uncles and grandfathers, or on the good friends of their mothers. If this affection is returned in a healthy way, it nourishes the child's self-worth and neutralizes the effect of the absent father. But this doesn't work all the time—and not for all children.

Fathers are just as important to girls as to boys. As an adult, I have seen young black boys who miss their fathers turn angry at the world, their rage festering into violence against women, whites, and even their own black brothers and sisters. As a reporter, I have seen young men turn a drug dealer into a father, a drug crew into a family. At the same time, I have seen girls who miss their fathers try loving their way into a man's heart. These young women are usually considered promiscuous, but I recognize them for what they are: lonely and fatherless.

Some fathers, like mine, are absent even when they are physically present. By the time my father came home to live with us, his time unbroken by assignments abroad, I was a stranger to him. He didn't like the way I walked or talked, the way I had grown into womanish ways while he was away. He didn't know it was all a fake, that I was really a little girl in a big girl's body, that what I wanted and needed most was a father to call me "princess" or to treat me like a queen. My deepest self knew that before I went out into the world and found a man to love I needed to be loved by the first man in my life. I needed a rich and basic love by which to judge the love of all other men.

Maybe I made it difficult for my father, too, because he could probably tell I didn't like him. He still barked orders in Marine Corps lingo, expecting us to rise before the sun to start our chores. "Get up and swab the deck!" he'd say, meaning "scrub the basement floor." When his children answered him, it was always with a "Yes, sir" or "No, sir." Stiff, formal words that wedged between us, pushing us further apart.

He went to work immediately, finding a job cleaning government office buildings at night. Within a year, he was working as a grave digger at Arlington National Cemetery. In a way his coming home was worse than his being away. When he was home, I could see and feel what he didn't do. No kisses. No hugs. No "I love you." My mother, who is very affectionate, taught us to always say good night to each other, to kiss good-bye, to never go to sleep angry. This had been in-grained in me already before Daddy came home, so I kissed and hugged him and hoped he would do the same.

I wanted to hear my father say, "I love you." And he never did, not to me, not once in his life.

I was angry with him about this, not down-and-out dirty anger, but a subtle, nagging anger, like the hatred I felt for whites. And this anger kept me from looking at my own faults. When I was old enough to suspect that my protruding front teeth could not be my only flaw, I was still too overwhelmed by the wrongs I saw in my father to take a look at myself.

My father's reluctance to accept the responsibility of being an authority in our house infuriated me. One night, I asked him if I could go to a party and, as usual, he said, "Wait until your mother comes home."

"But she already said I could go," I argued.

"Well, wait until she comes home."

I gave him the address of the party—two blocks away—and the names and phone number of my friend's parents, who promised to be present throughout the night. Daddy knew the family and yet he would not give me permission to go.

When my mother got home, the party was nearly over and I was enraged. Mother tried to calm me.

"He's not my father, anyway," I blurted.

"What do you mean?" She looked shocked.

"It takes more to be a father than just clothing and feeding somebody," I said. If I wasn't sure about anything else, I knew I was right on that one.

My mother looked at me hard and walked away.

Because Mama made all the decisions about child rearing, Daddy could blame her for our misbehavior, for my loss of virginity and my drop in grades. It also set up Mama as the punisher and the unpopular parent. She appeared powerful, but it was actually Daddy who was the controller.

She was totally dependent upon him for money. When he was in the Marine Corps and away, she received a check, but now that he was home, he decided how much he wanted to give her—and when. In the grocery store, the cashier rang up the total and my mother turned to my father with her palm stretched out. Seeing this, I vowed to always have my own money, to never be dependent on a man.

Both my parents came from poor families, but my mother was the only child and she was raised by a single mother for years. My father was from a larger family, with six sisters and a brother, raised in the country. He feared poverty more than Mother did. He had dropped out of high school to join the Marine Corps, perhaps to relieve his parents of one of the mouths they had to feed. It also afforded him the chance to learn a skill (though, with its postintegration tracking of black soldiers, what the government taught him was how to cook) and an opportunity to travel, no small accomplishment for a teenager from Badin, North Carolina. But I wouldn't understand most of what motivated my father until much later in life. I was an adult with a grown child of my own before I acknowledged that my family would never have lived as well as it had if it were not for my father's allegiance to his country.

◆ ◆ ◆

Ben was a reminder to my parents that I was determined to define my own destiny. They still forbade me to see him, so I sneaked, meeting him at parties, at the neighborhood teen dances, or at some house where I was baby-sitting. I even sneaked him into the house several times, having sex in the basement while my father slept upstairs and my mother was away.

My mother and I argued almost daily about Ben. She hung up on him when he called. One day, she met him for a talk on the corner near our house, and as I looked out the window Mama lifted her umbrella and whacked Ben across his head before he cut out running.

"He said you would come to him whenever he wanted you!" she screamed as she came in the house, panting.

I was punished often, made to stay inside and forbidden to use the telephone, usually for staying out past my midnight curfew. A few times I sneaked out the window of my bedroom, dropping my clothes out first, then climbing out myself. But there was no way to sneak in, so I faced more weeks of punishment.

By now I admired the Black Panthers and believed all blacks should carry weapons, and thus I despised my neighborhood. People who lived in split-level houses couldn't possibly know anything about life. Of course, I was too young to face the truth, that I didn't have a clue what was going on inside those houses, that life was much more than what I saw. I associated the genteelness of my neighborhood with the urge to be white, which is a terrible distortion of the truth and one that some blacks, particularly children, suffer from. We buy into the notion we hate most, that anything nice is white, that wealth is white while poverty is black.

I tried quitting Ben, but I was addicted to him and to the high I got watching him count money he won gambling or listening to him and his buddies talk about the latest flimflam they ran on some dumb, no-nhip joker. Ben had eased his way from shooting crap on the street to gambling with old heads in big-stake all-night card games. Meanwhile, he tired of low-paying "jobs" like flimflams and petty theft, so he moved up to robbing stores and gas stations and sticking up people on the street. I listened to Ben and his friends, the way they would spit out stories of their latest triumphs. They breathed heavy with excitement as they talked, laughing as they described the fear on someone's face. I longed to know what it felt like to have that much power, to face a situation where you were totally in control because you held the gun and people did whatever you said. I knew I couldn't do what Ben and his friends did; the closest I could get was to listen, imagine.

I admired Ben, too, because he took care of his family, a burden he accepted as his responsibility, though he was just a child himself. As the oldest, Ben proclaimed himself the protector of and main provider of his mother, grandmother, and siblings. His mother and grandmother had drinking problems, which meant he sometimes took care of them physically, too, cooking meals and undressing them for bed.

Since I myself was a child in search of a man who was affectionate and fatherly, this was endearing. I was too young to question if any of this responsibility affected Ben negatively, or to wonder if he was missing something that he needed, too, some security, peace, or strong, basic parental love that I could never provide.

Mama had just put the last curl in my hair one evening when I stood up to walk over to a mirror and a pain hit me, like hot knives ripping the pit of my stomach. I doubled over, unable to stand. Five minutes later, I was too weak to walk and crying loudly from the pain. Mama and a friend rushed me to the hospital.

The diagnosis was syphilis. I was hospitalized for a week, in intensive care part of that time, fed intravenously and kept high on morphine. I didn't know anything about venereal diseases, but I wasn't about to believe the doctor who said I caught it from Ben and that Ben knew he had it and should have told me. Ben tried to visit me, but my grandmother instructed the hospital to keep him out. Most of the time I was semiconscious, half-hearing the doctor, who proclaimed me lucky to have escaped death. Then, in a voice laced with sympathy, he warned that the disease might have left me sterile. I thought it was a scare tactic, that he had conspired with my parents and grandmother to keep me from Ben. Not for a minute did I even consider that I might never have children.

Ben was waiting for me when I got off the bus after my first day back at school. In a weak, weepy voice, he told me how much he had missed me. His doctor, Ben said, told him that *I* had given him syphilis. "We'll probably never know which one of us gave it to the other," he said. "But it really doesn't matter." I forgot what the doctor had said. I wanted to believe Ben. And I did.

◆　　◆　　◆

In the summer I was going into eleventh grade, my family was notified that I was one of a hundred black students being bussed to integrate a white school. I was devastated, even though I didn't love school the way I used to. Fairmont Heights, the black school I attended, was small, with about twelve hundred students; you could get to know nearly all the students in your grade level, the people who would graduate with you. At DuVal, the white school I would now attend, there were about twenty-seven hundred students and more than six hundred in eleventh grade alone. Only a few blacks already attended the school.

When our bus rolled up to DuVal High School on that first day, everybody on board stopped talking. We stared, dumbfounded, at a sign that said: "Student Parking Lot" and behind it rows and rows of souped-up Novas, Chevys, and sports cars. At Fairmont Heights, students parked on the street, which wasn't a real problem because very few students had cars. This student lot was larger than the teachers' lot at our old school.

All of us students—black and white—were afraid of each other, our fear stemming from the myths and stereotypes we harbored. Also, black students walked in feeling unwanted, forced upon people whom we didn't really want to be with, anyway. We came with attitude plus the added burden of trying to represent every black person in the world. We believed we needed to be perfect, to avoid those slipups that might cause a blond head to shake in disapproval or blue eyes to lock in knowing glances that said, "See, I told you; they are so dumb." This burden translated differently in each black child's life, causing some of my black classmates to become hoodlums, while others, like me, didn't raise a hand to answer a question if we had the least bit of doubt we might be right.

There were no angry crowds chanting racist epitaphs or police dogs snapping at our heels like I had seen on television, when other children integrated schools. We had some fistfights and the police were called to patrol the hallways, but still, no more than twenty-five students ever took part in those. Yet we black students suffered greatly. It is hard to explain what it feels like when you are a black teenager taken from a school run by black adults, where there is a library full of *Ebony* and *Jet* magazines and books about black people—and you're put in another school, where for weeks you may not see an adult who looks like you, hear familiar language or music, or see one reflection of your culture. There were no black teachers or black counselors, no black varsity cheerleaders or majorettes, and in what we considered a cruelty of fate, most of the custodial crew was white. I felt empty. Lonely. Insignificant. Invisible.

Eventually, I made friends with some of my white classmates, but we seldom socialized outside of school. Yet I was still prey to their values and styles. At times, it seemed life would be easier if I just gave in, became whitelike. When white girls started ironing their hair to make it straight, some of them convinced me to try it. So I, the baby Black Panther, crouched next to the ironing board with the iron in one hand and my shoulder-length hair stretched as far across the board as it would go, while my little sisters stared at me, their mouths dropped open. What they were seeing was assimilation at its worst, their frustrated sister trying desperately to fit in, attempting a different approach to what had been ailing her since she had walked into DuVal: she wanted to be accepted.

◆　◆　◆

My fifth sister, Vicki, was born. Mama followed her usual ritual: after the first labor pains, she washed and ironed enough clothes for us to wear for a week, wrote notes, and gave us orders to follow during the time she would be gone. She made sure there was enough food in the freezer for my grandmother to cook meals for us while she was away. Then, after two hours of Daddy begging her to let him take her to the hospital, Mama left, reappearing several days later with a new baby. All of this gave her children the impression that giving birth was a minor inconvenience accompanied by some quick, sharp pains. When each of us girls found out the truth, through our own experiences, our admiration for Mother was sealed and we considered her no less than awesome.

While Mother was in the hospital this time, I hooked school with some friends and went to the Howard Theater in Washington to sit in the dark, cool theater and dream of fame. Back in Maryland, we passed my house, headed for the bus stop so I could pretend I was coming from school. I ducked down on the floor of the car as we passed, but my family's house stood on a hill and my grandmother, the woman who watched the world from her window, was at our picture window looking out—and she saw me.

When I got home, my sisters were running around like chickens and screaming, "Go put on some pants! Grannie saw you today! Daddy's going to whip you!"

My father, the man who deferred all matters regarding discipline to his wife, had never whipped me. But one of my sisters warned, "He went out to get a switch, but he came back with a tree." My little sisters were already teary-eyed, which scared the heck out of me.

"Pa-a-at!" My father called from the basement. "Come on down here."

I walked down slowly, trying to look brave, but trembling inside. I passed my grandmother, who clucked her tongue but looked at me with sympathetic eyes, as if I were taking my last steps. My father stood in front of me with a thick branch in his hand.

"Come on. You know what you done." He didn't say another word. He grabbed my arm and whacked me on my butt. I thought he was finished, but he sat down and pulled me across his lap. He wore out my behind.

When I stopped crying, I heard all of my sisters crying a sympathetic chorus for me. This was the first and last time my father beat me. I can only guess that with my mother removed from the picture, my father had been forced to look at what was happening to his oldest child, at what her life was turning into. I think it scared him to face the possibility that I might fail. In his anger, all he knew to do was to beat me.

◆ ◆ ◆

But no beating would break me of the life I had embraced. By my last year of high school, I skipped classes, hooked school, came in hours after curfew, and disobeyed my parents regularly, mostly to see Ben. I didn't use drugs and seldom drank, though one night I got rip-roaring drunk and crashed a party my parents were having, walking in with my fishnet stockings around my ankles, my bulging eyes red, and dry puke on the black velvet collar of my chesterfield coat. I am told that my mother slapped me. And that I smiled.

◆ ◆ ◆

My parents threatened to send me away to a school for juvenile delinquents, but time drummed on. We all argued and hurt in that house until finally I was nearing graduation. No one spoke to me about college or what I wanted to do for a living. My parents must have figured they had done all they could for me.

There would be sixty-three black students and six hundred whites in my graduating class of 1967, which was considered the first fully integrated class at DuVal. Twenty years later at a class reunion five blacks—including Ginny and me—and three hundred whites would show up to reminisce in a banquet hall decorated in the school's orange and black colors. For the first time for most of us, we blacks and whites danced together. We were old enough to have been changed by time and history, old enough to see more similarities than differences in each other.

My white classmates told me they hadn't realized the problems we black students were having back when we integrated DuVal; they were so overwhelmed with being teenagers, worrying about acne and girlfriends and boyfriends, cars, and hair.

Ginny and I had never discussed those school days, opting instead to forget them. But that night, she said, "It wasn't that the white students mistreated us; it's just that they didn't treat us at all."

In a way, their failure to notice our suffering made us invisible and hurt us more than hatred would have.

◆　◆　◆

On graduation day in 1967, someone called my name—"Patrice Gaines!"—and I sauntered across the long stage to be handed my high school diploma. My family cheered, their joy sounding frighteningly close to the hysteria that comes from witnessing something hard to believe. I knew my grandmother was somewhere up in those bleachers saying, "Praise God!"

I was vowing to myself to never set foot in another school. Since first grade, education had caused me more grief than pleasure. It taught me to despise authority—teachers who hated you because you were black, counselors who didn't care whether or not you came to school because they didn't believe you would ever consider college, anyway.

I celebrated my graduation with my family, Ginny, and a few friends at a barbecue in my backyard. But by nightfall I was wrapped in Ben's arms. I didn't know what was next; I didn't care. As long as I could stay near Ben, I believed my life would turn out right.

chapter four

Giving Birth

was a skinny teenage girl who had just stopped wetting her bed at night, but already, by the summer of my eighteenth year, I believed life was meaningless without a man. While Jennifer packed her clothes to go off to college, I stayed behind to be with Ben. My parents, who had only dreamed I would graduate from high school, waited for me to turn myself into a useful adult with a job.

But no one would hire me. I scored high on tests and impressed job interviewers, yet once a company found out I had missed nearly a third of the school days my senior year, the interview ended. I looked around for a school close to home and found the Cinderella School in Washington, where I enrolled in fashion merchandising, a career I chose after reading the school's brochure. I figured becoming a buyer would come natural for me, considering that I worshiped clothes and loved to shop. A school counselor secured me a part-time job she said would help my career, so for the next year I sold table linen in a downtown department store.

My parents and I still quarreled about Ben, and during one particularly fiery argument, shortly after my eighteenth birthday, Mother demanded I quit him, or move. Fifteen minutes later, I headed for the apartment Ben shared with his uncle. Twenty-four hours passed before I called my mother. She was crazy from worrying.

"Where are you?" she asked, her voice cracking.

"Don't worry about that. I called to let you know I'm fine."

There was silence. Then, "When are you coming home?"

"I'm not." I heard Mother crying.

"Do you need anything?"

Deep inside, I wanted to go home, to sleep in my own bed and eat my mother's cooking. But I also wanted to punish Mother for trying to keep Ben and me apart.

"No, I'm fine. I'll call you tomorrow."

I went home a few days later.

After another argument, I went to live with my girlfriend Donna and her roommate. Donna worked at the store in the records and electronics section, which was on the same floor as my department, and we had gotten to know each other during fifteen-minute breaks. She was married and a couple of years older, and while her husband was in Vietnam she had a girlfriend living with her. Mama thought Donna was mature and hoped my new friend might have a calming effect on me.

At Donna's we did whatever we wanted to do. We played Aretha over and over again, singing at the top of our lungs, "You make me feel like a natural woman," trying to match the sensuality and sincerity in Aretha's voice. I stood in front of the refrigerator, holding the door open for minutes while we considered what to eat, hearing my mama's voice saying, "Close that door! You're letting out the cold air!"

At Donna's we trimmed each other's mod-style haircuts to precision, not knowing that in less than a year we would all be wearing Afros. At night we watched *The Carol Burnett Show* and laughed really loud, just because we could, or watched *Ironside* and tried to imagine Raymond Burr as someone other than Perry Mason. We ate junk food, shopped often, and went to nightclubs and concerts, cool as we wanted to be in our miniskirts and tent dresses with matching tights.

It was late 1967, a wonderful, exciting time to be free of parents.

The world swirled around us, changing fast, though never fast enough. Thurgood Marshall was appointed to the Supreme Court, but we dismissed him as a token. We didn't want tokens; we wanted rebellion. I remained a bullshit revolutionary, talking the talk but never really taking any action. I listened to Stokely Carmichael and H. Rap Brown on street corners and at churches. I cheered and applauded, thrust my fist in the air to show my solidarity, then went home to watch television.

My mother, worried I wasn't eating right, sometimes caught three buses and rode for two hours to get to Donna's apartment in Washington to bring us groceries. After the summer, tired of living out of a suitcase and sleeping on the sofa in an apartment too small for three people, I returned home. I made a mental note, though, that at Donna's I didn't call Ben as often as when I was at home. But I couldn't see the connection yet, the association between Ben and being lonely, between keeping busy and not feeling lonely. I was too young to understand that I was using Ben to fill some void I was carrying with me—and that if I could plug up my leaking heart some other way, I wouldn't want Ben.

For now, he controlled my life. He suggested stealing from the department store, and I did not object. My only concern was about getting caught, since at the time I didn't think stealing from a store was wrong. When the Ten Commandments said: "Thou shalt not steal," it referred to stealing from individuals and not institutions that stole from the masses, I reasoned. I was stealing from the capitalist pigs, performing a revolutionary deed, taking from a huge department store that was hardly distinguishable from any government building in the city, a representative of the white racists who owed me. But deep inside I harbored doubts, suspicions that it was wrong and that stealing is stealing, no matter the situation.

But those doubts were not strong enough to stop me. Our scam went like this: We waited until the older, trustworthy clerks went to lunch, leaving me alone in the department. If one of them stayed, I just lured her away from the cash register. Then Ben or a friend of his walked through the department, and as they passed the register, they hit it quick. Bam! The drawer flew open. They snatched greenbacks and fled. The other clerk and I stood, flabbergasted. When security arrived, I gave them a description that slightly contradicted the other clerk's memory.

At other times, we used a more laid-back approach. One of our friends would come to me to buy something, I'd slip an extra hundred dollars or so in her change, and we would meet later to split up the money. In the end, Ben and I always spent our share on clothes and concerts, since there was nothing else we wanted. We never paid at restaurants because Ben always had a scheme to get the food free, or we simply sneaked out and ran like hell when it was time to pay.

I also swapped merchandise with other clerks. They took the French lace tablecloths in my department and gave them to their mothers and grandmothers as gifts. In return, I picked out merchandise from their departments—stereo equipment, records, and clothes for my sisters and brother.

My mother welcomed the clothes, since it meant less money she had to beg for from my father. But years later, when I was the parent of a teenager, I rethought my mother's actions and decided they sent me the wrong message, that her acceptance said it was okay to steal, that there could be such a thing as stealing for a just cause. I fancied myself a fairy godmother bearing gifts, combating the pain and misery I thought my father caused my siblings with his selfishness. In actuality, his actions were not premeditated, as I imagined. My father was a cheap man who never lost the taste of poverty, kept fresh by memories: long, hard winter months when his mother struggled to keep the family together while his father was in an asylum suffering from tuberculosis. As a grown man hundreds of miles from Badin, North Carolina, my father still lived as if he were poor, refusing to pay to have repairs done on our house, so that broken things remained broken, since he was too busy working to fix them himself. He never owned more than one suit at a time and wore the same few undershirts, shirts, and pants over and over until his children insisted he wear some of the shirts they purposefully bought him for Father's Day. If there is such a thing as a poverty mentality, my father had it—and he couldn't shake it.

◆   ◆   ◆

I woke up one morning, lifted the screen of my bedroom window, and stuck my head out to breathe in fresh air. My father had just spread fertilizer across the front yard. One whiff, and I rushed to the bathroom to puke. Standing over the toilet, I remembered my period was late.

That night, while Ben and I were walking to a friend's house, I blurted out my suspicions.

"I think I'm pregnant," I said.

He stopped walking. "Are you sure?"

I braced myself for denial or rejection, but Ben's face turned soft and he said, "I hope you are."

We sat that night and laughed and talked about what our baby would look like and what we wanted our baby to have. But when I was alone some days, being eighteen and pregnant scared me. I had a sense there was so much I hadn't done yet and that having a child at such an early age drastically limited the possibilities in my life. This was the message I had heard repeatedly from my parents.

Actually, the thought of having a human being of my own appealed to me, particularly since, being young, I believed you could own a person. A child would love me regardless of whether or not I thought I was worthy—and my soul craved that kind of love. All my life I had been judged—by the color of my skin, by my intelligence, by my clothes, by the boy I dated.

Ben and I set a tentative date to elope. Then, a week before the big date, he received a draft notice from the army, and we had to consider the real possibility of separation. We knew there was a war going on; we watched Vietnam on the evening news: the daily death count. The bodies arriving in boxes at the airports. And in the magazines the color photos of blood. Young men bleeding on helicopters. Wounded in trenches. Lying on stretchers with bandages and mangled limbs dangling.

The draft had rumbled on like a drumroll in our lives, louder and louder. Each time one of my classmates was drafted, the word passed down the grapevine. Yet because neither Ben nor I knew anyone who had died in Vietnam, the war was still distant to us, an event in some country we couldn't find on a map.

This was before I understood what a horrible occurrence war is.

Before I knew that one of my elementary classmates from Beaufort had died in Vietnam while I was pregnant; and years before there was a Vietnam Memorial, where I traced his name with my finger and cried over my sixth-grade picture of him, a dark-skinned little boy with a flattop haircut.

For Ben and me, the draft was an intrusion we resented, but we couldn't imagine he'd really go to Vietnam. I spent the night before he left for the army crying in his arms until I fell asleep, and yet I woke up still believing he would con his way out of going. But he dressed that morning and left, while I stayed behind at his family's house, where I could watch him walk away as if he were just running to the store and would be back in a minute.

My mother, who had guessed that we might elope, begged us to wait awhile, convincing us that it would mean more if we married after our love had been tested by this separation. Ben and I figured this was a chance for us to prove to Mama that our love was strong enough to survive our being apart. Plus knowing we were going to be parents made Ben and me hope even more for a peaceful relationship with Mama in the future. So we agreed to wait. Mama confessed to me years later that she had prayed for months that Ben would be drafted—and with him gone, she hoped to persuade me to leave him forever.

What Mama hadn't counted on was my being pregnant. She had always been my official period keeper, and since she had found out just weeks earlier that she was pregnant, periods and the lack of them was a subject at the forefront of her mind. She snooped around for used sanitary napkins, sniffed the air for the scent of blood. She hounded me. "Isn't it time for you to come on? When are you due? Are you pregnant?"

Finally, I told her my suspicions. She went with me to the doctor, and when he confirmed that I was pregnant, Mother sat and cried hard, just as she usually did when she believed my life was spiraling downward. I was ashamed of myself for disappointing her, and I was scared, too, because I had no idea how I would take care of a baby—physically or financially. Mama said later that the baby was my escape from her and Daddy, that I would get married or pregnant or whatever to create my own life, one separate from theirs.

Mama and Grannie wanted me to have an abortion and they had even gotten Ben to agree to pay for it, but it was my choice and I said, "No." Mama waited for the right time to tell Daddy I was pregnant, while I walked around the house with my stomach hidden under tent dresses. Daddy chose to treat my pregnancy like the Immaculate Conception, a baby conceived only by me. He could not admit to himself that his grandchild belonged to Ben, too, or that Ben had actually put his penis inside me, my father's virgin daughter. Ben was still forbidden to come to our house, and my father never spoke his name.

"I don't want to have anything to do with it," were the first words Daddy spoke to Mama about my pregnancy. A moment later, she said, he added, "She's not the first girl to get pregnant. At least she finished school." For years I didn't know he had said this, so that what I remembered most was that he still did not allow Ben to visit. I was aware of my father paying more attention to me than he normally did, but even this made me sad, because I interpreted it to mean I had to get pregnant to be treated kindly by him; and then I wondered if it was me he was treating well or if it was his not-yet-born grandchild.

He made sure the refrigerator was stocked with whatever I craved: sweet potatoes for the sweet potato pudding my mother whipped up for me every other day, strawberry sodas, and Argo starch, which Mama and I ate while watching television. This was my father's way of saying, "I love you." Unfortunately, I was too young to recognize it and I ate all of the food enjoying only its taste and not the pleasure of knowing it was a gift.

Grannie refused to let me go to church with her anymore. "I love you, but I don't want you to be embarrassed in front of the church," she said. I translated this into what I knew was the truth: Grannie didn't want her church to know her granddaughter was guilty of the horrible sin of being pregnant and unwed.

In April, a month after Ben left, Martin Luther King was killed, and I gave up for years any flicker of hope that blacks and whites could live together peacefully, or that America would allow blacks equal rights. On the radio, Nina Simone's haunting voice sang, "What will we do now that the king of peace is dead?" and my heart pounded madly because I wanted to scream in frustration. If they could kill a man who preached nonviolence, who turned a cheek and never struck back, what would they do to me or all those like me, who were not sure we had King's patience or faith, to kneel when we felt like fighting.

While I sat with friends in my suburban neighborhood, telling each other about our anger, our brothers and sisters in the city lit the skies with their rage. We screamed at the TV images of the riots: "Burn the muthafucka down!" "Shoot those crackers!" But at no time would it be clearer than it was that day that our lives were different from the lives of some inner-city blacks. While we cried and shouted from our comfortable split-level homes, miles away black smoke billowed in the skies, and even the stores where we shopped on H Street in Northeast burned to the ground. Angry young men threw Molotov cocktails and ran through the streets carrying televisions, boxes of shoes, coats, and records. In the heat of rage, where reasoning and logic no longer exist, black men pulled white men from their cars and shot them or kicked and beat them, trying to make any white man pay for the death of a man who did not believe in vengeance.

Even in the suburbs, though, we were angry and hurt and the two emotions were equally strong, so that we were rational and mournful one minute and insane and full of rage the next. I rubbed my stomach, thought about my baby, and wondered if some of my friends were right when they said, "I would never bring a child into this world." Some of the boys in our neighborhood, unable to channel their anger into conversations and shouts at a television, went into Washington to join the rioters. I went home.

"Your people are rioting," my father said when I walked in the door.

We were still on the opposite sides of the political fence, and we had always jabbed at each other about racism, the Vietnam War, and what I considered police brutality, which he usually saw as necessary force. He was unrelenting in his patriotism, and he loved to taunt me with it.

"They're your people, too," I snapped.

"My people don't burn up their own neighborhoods." He said this matter-of-factly, as if he were stating the absolute truth.

"Your people don't do anything," I said.

"If they didn't do anything, you wouldn't be here," he said.

"Here?! You mean here in this neighborhood?! Where is this?! This is nowhere! Look at where those white kids I went to school with live! You think they'd settle for this?! This is nowhere!"

I was shouting and he just looked at me. "You're sick," I said, turning to head for my bedroom.

My father's voice was still calm, and the evenness of it mocked my anger. "I'm sick? I'm working every day," he said. "Your people are out there burning and stealing."

"I feel sorry for you," I said, running to the bedroom before the tears in my eyes ran down my cheeks.

"Feel sorry for yourself." He returned to his newspaper.

◆   ◆   ◆

My mother had adjusted to the truth of my pregnancy. She was always this way: she yelled and threatened and wept, but in the end she forgave and accepted. Now we enjoyed waiting for our babies together. We ate our peculiar snacks together, laughed at each other's cravings, and when our tummies were so fat we couldn't stand on the scale and read our own weight, we read the numbers for each other. We shopped together, picking out identical outfits for our babies.

I quit school, since Mama and I had already concluded that Cinderella wasn't worth the money we were paying and I was spending more time working at the department store than I was sitting in class. So I started working full-time at the store. I was so small that I still didn't look pregnant, particularly dressed in the fashions of the day, high "empire"-waist dresses and tent dresses in bold stripes. At work, it seemed more guys flirted with me than ever before, but it could be that I just noticed now that Ben was away.

I was particularly attracted to Phillip Miller, one of the college students who was working at the store for the summer. I explained to him in great depth that my heart belonged to Ben, the only boy I had ever had sex with and the man I intended to marry. But I was drawn to Phillip, a toffee-colored, willowy guy with a pug nose, a very thick mustache over his babyish lips and unforgettable eyes that seemed to turn from soft green to gray and back, according to his mood. There was a sexual tension between us, which I had never experienced with anyone other than Ben. It confused me because I didn't know enough about sex or life or being a woman to interpret it. Was it normal? Why did I feel it for Phillip? What distinguished love from lust? Or, for that matter, from loneliness? At my tender age, I had based all of my decisions on my feelings. Anyway, I'm not sure there's a way to teach children like me to stop and think before they act. I was driven by a desire to fill a huge hollowness in me—and to do anything to stop the pain that grew from it. So all I knew was that this feeling with Phillip was something I had thought I only felt with Ben—and I wondered if it meant that I didn't love Ben, or that I was falling in love with someone else.

I fully expected that once I told Phillip about my pregnancy, he would go off to date other girls while we remained friends. In the evenings he gave me driving lessons in a park along the Potomac River. One evening I asked him to park so we could talk. I rambled on for fifteen minutes about life being full of surprises, how you could meet someone you could have loved if only you had met him sooner; then, in the middle of a thought, I said, "Phillip, I'm pregnant."

He was silent for a few moments; then he asked, quietly, "Are you getting married?"

"I don't think so," I said.

"Do you love him?"

"Not in that way." The truth was I was confused and I was making up my answers on the spot.

Phillip and I continued to spend part of every day together. We were comfortable with each other, laughing easily and talking for hours about Martin Luther King and Malcolm X, about nonviolence versus armed rebellion, about how the mythical world of equality looked and whether we would live to see it. Though Ben and I had discussed the same topics, our conversations were always made up of superficial comments like "Malcolm knew what he was talking about," or, "We're gonna kick whitey's ass one day!" With Phillip, I discussed the evolution of jazz while listening to Charles Lloyd's *Forest Flower*. With Phillip, there was the lure of intellect, a chance to use some of the knowledge that came from the books I devoured.

This was a first for me, the recognition of the importance of friendship between a man and a woman, the appreciation of good conversations and respect for each other's knowledge. But this is in retrospect, because even though I knew my relationship with Phillip was different, I couldn't identify at the time exactly what made it so.

Ben and Phillip were worlds apart from each other, not in the way they dressed or walked, not in some concrete way I could point to. It was in some way that had to do with how they saw themselves, what they thought was important in life, and how they made me feel. Phillip made me feel good about myself. Somewhere between birth and this young adulthood I was now stuck in, I had begun to believe I wasn't worthy of a boy who went to college, who had never been in trouble, who came from a middle-class family. I wasn't nice enough, smart enough, or pretty enough.

My mother liked Phillip, too, and I was surprised to find that this mattered to me. When my mother looked at Phillip as if she was pleased, I felt proud to be with him. I had forgotten how good it felt to have the approval of your parents.

At best I could only conclude that Phillip was different because he had attended college and, unlike Ben, had not had to be a man-child responsible for augmenting the family income and taking care of relatives with drinking problems. My mother's theory was simpler: "Phillip is the first gentleman you ever met," she said.

Phillip was an only child from an upper-middle-class family and had spent part of his life on a college campus in upstate New York while his father was an administrator at the school. Now Phillip's family lived in Virginia, just outside of Washington, while he attended Hampton Institute.

During that summer of my pregnancy, he indulged my cravings, running to the store to get me sour pickles and to the one bakery downtown that carried the pound cake I loved. He laughed as my face got plumper and he massaged my swollen ankles. He put his hand on my stomach each time the baby moved and he oohed and ahhed at the bulges made by the small limbs just on the other side of my skin. Before the summer ended, we both accepted that our feelings went beyond friendship, and on one of our evening drives we proclaimed our love for each other.

Ben sent me an engagement ring, which I returned with the kind of letter he told me servicemen joked about, while their hearts fluttered, lightly threatening to fly out of their chests to flee the pain. I felt sympathy for Ben, for his whole life—for his upbringing, for the trouble he had gotten into in high school, for his getting drafted. But I did not take responsibility for my part in what had happened between us, and I could not see that my sorrow was condescending. Ben never answered my letter and, for months, disappeared from my life.

◆　◆　◆

On August 26, 1968, Phillip and I stood in front of the justice of peace in Arlington, Virginia, and promised to be faithful 'til death do us part. I was six months' pregnant, with swollen ankles and a belly that made me look like I was wearing a basketball under my short white empire-waist wedding dress. My mother was our only witness, and she cried through the entire ceremony because she believed I still loved Ben—and that Phillip knew it but was determined to change me. Phil's parents, who were not at the brief service, were disappointed because in their dreams their son completed college and then married a girl who was also a college graduate. They certainly didn't think he would marry a pregnant girl, and in their wildest nightmare he wouldn't marry a girl carrying someone else's baby.

◆　◆　◆

Phil and I moved in with his parents, into a comfortable brick split-level home with a garage and a large picture window on the back overlooking a pond filled with goldfish. Phil's parents decorated a nursery for the baby with beautiful white Italian provincial furniture.

One of the things that Phil and I had in common was our indifference toward our parents, what we saw as their lack of identity with blackness. My parents and their suburban neighborhood frustrated me because I thought it was all so whitelike; Phillip's parents, the Millers, exasperated us even more. In retrospect, it probably was their money and success we rallied against. In our eyes, the gulf between activists like the Black Panthers and our parents, who appeared to have forgotten where they came from, was wide enough to drown in. In a way, Phil and I were no different than thousands of young adults in the sixties who thumbed their noses at the lives their parents lived. In our case, we wanted evidence that our parents were doing something to bring about change for those blacks who were nowhere near the doors of opportunity that were opening. We didn't want our parents to sit back and be comfortable, because in our minds the time for relaxation had not yet come; it was still time to fight.

Phil started wearing an Afro, and his mother insisted he enter the house through the garage so neighbors wouldn't see him. He didn't like that rule, but he obeyed. He knew how far to push his parents, and he warned me they would never accept me if they knew he was not the father of my baby. I was against lying this time, but he insisted. So he told his parents that we had dated several times each summer when he came home and that I had occasionally come down to visit him in school. On one of those trips, I got pregnant.

They reluctantly accepted his story, maybe because the alternative was too great: they would have to reject a baby who just might be their first grandchild. It was also easier for them to believe my lie, that I had tricked their son because he was my meal ticket to a better life.

They tolerated me, the lower-class girl whose father worked in a cemetery and whose parents had a slew of children. They criticized everything I did. Both of them corrected my English. Mrs. Miller showed me her nylon negligees and soft silk pajamas and suggested I buy the same.

"Why don't you get your nails manicured?" she asked. "You need to take care of yourself."

At breakfast, they watched with disconcerted faces as I ate my bacon with my hand. "Why don't you try using your fork?" Mrs. Miller said.

I followed their lead, keeping one hand in my lap and off the table whenever I ate, never picking up chicken with my hands because they didn't. Eventually, my friends stopped visiting, complaining to me that the Millers made them feel unwelcome.

Phil and I were married and yet we were just at the beginning of a relationship, the time when every day presents you with a small thread of truth about your partner and day after day passes until you find you have enough truths to weave a strong relationship that can bear the weight of challenges. We were discovering what position the other slept in at night, hearing the timbre of our first arguments, and finding out how long the words from them reverberated in our lives.

Two months after we got married, Phillip got drafted. His parents hired a lawyer to keep him out of the military, but the best the lawyer could do was get a promise that Phillip wouldn't be sent to Vietnam. This wasn't unusual for an only son, but it was a blessing nevertheless, since the war monster needed all the young men it could get and it was gobbling up young black men at an accelerated rate.

With their son gone, the Millers questioned me more intensely about the history of our relationship. I recited the answers Phillip had had me memorize, until a couple of weeks before I was due to have the baby, when I moved back to my parents' house in search of peace.

Mama and I passed the days eating starch and sweet potato pudding and shopping for our babies. We were finally more alike than different, two women waiting for children to enter the world. Phillip was stationed in North Carolina, and on weekends he came home to visit.

Early on November 10, my due date, Mama started having labor pains. She wasn't due for another week. I felt cheated, yearning to be first and afraid she wouldn't be with me when I went into labor. Mama was her usual calm self. She ironed clothes and gave out instructions about cooking and curfews. Before she left for the hospital, I packed up to go back to the Millers. Daddy was going to be running back and forth to the hospital, and we all agreed I should be where someone could drive me to the hospital if necessary. My grandmother came over to stay with my sisters and brother.

A few hours later, just as I sat down for dinner at the Millers', my grandmother called.

"I hate to tell you this, Pat. The baby was born dead," she said.

"What baby?" I couldn't imagine she was talking about my mother.

"Your mother's baby."

"My mother's baby died?" I had five healthy sisters and one brother. My mother didn't even have hard labor pains like other women; babies slid out of her womb, perfect and strong.

"It was another girl," my grandmother said.

"How is Mama?"

"Upset, but fine."

"How did the baby die?"

"It came out wrong."

"What do you mean?"

"It was . . . what do you call it? Breech? Yeah, breech. The feet came out first, before the head. It was born dead. It was God's will."

I hung up. When my grandmother started talking that "God's will" stuff, my mind blanked out. Why would God will such a thing? How could a baby be born dead? If the baby was born, it was alive. It couldn't be born and be dead at the same time—could it? Could *my* baby be born dead? Mama and I had rubbed our palms across each other's navels and felt our babies move. I had seen my sister's kicks ripple my mother's belly.

I couldn't eat dinner.

The next day I went with my father to visit Mama. Daddy was so uncomfortable, it was difficult watching him. He fidgeted with his hat and couldn't sit still in her room, so he paced the hallway outside her door while I visited. Mama looked old and young at the same time, a speechless, bewildered child who had just seen something too ugly to explain. She was still in the maternity ward, watching other people feed their babies and hold them for the first time.

I wanted to hide my stomach so I would not remind her of her loss. She hugged me. We cried together, and in that frozen moment I knew we understood each other better than we ever had before. It was impossible to return to who we had been before Mama lost the baby, to that mother and daughter who misunderstood, to a daughter capable of deliberately worrying her mother, and a mother who did not trust her daughter to be an adult. We were both mothers, even if I hadn't delivered my baby yet, and together we had shared something no one else on this earth had shared with either of us.

My sisters told me later how they waited for Daddy to come home to tell them whether they had a new sister or brother. Everyone had just sat at the dinner table when he walked in. My sisters said, "He sat down and before we said the grace, he said, 'Your mama won't be coming home with a baby. The baby is dead.' " For years, they remembered he said it in a tone that sounded like he was saying, "So okay, let's get on with it. Pass the butter beans." It was two sentences at the beginning of a meal.

At the hospital, my mother asked the nurse to let her hold her dead baby. Against the advice of her male military doctors, Mama held her cold baby and fixed in her memory forever a picture of how beautiful her daughter looked. It was important to Mama to touch her baby's flesh, to see the nose and eyes and mouth of the baby that was hers but would never go home with her. Then she wrapped her daughter in a receiving blanket and gave her back to the nurse.

I tried to comfort Mama when she came home. We talked about what we had lost. We would not tote our babies on our hips while we shopped together. People would not question them one day about who was the aunt and who was the niece.

"I'll give you my baby clothes, but I can't look through them yet. Maybe I'll keep a couple of things," Mama said to me.

I couldn't imagine my baby having two sets of everything. It was too sad to consider, so I just nodded.

On the night of November 18, I was lying in the bed at my parents' house and I started having burning pains in my side. I called out to Mama and she came in to sit with me and keep track of how often the pains hit. A couple of hours later a girlfriend rushed me to the hospital while my father sat in the backseat. At the hospital, though, I was disappointed when the nurse proclaimed, "She hasn't dilated enough. Take her home."

I went home and an hour later was asleep. By nine o'clock the next morning, we were back in the emergency room, and this time I was admitted. They put me in a room and I slept for hours, exhausted from a night of unbroken rest. Around 3:00 P.M., someone woke me up.

"It's time to have your baby," a nurse said.

I thought she was kidding until a sharp pain shot from my left side to my right, nearly cutting off my breath. Another nurse walked in with a paper for me to sign so they could give me a spinal anesthetic. I remembered my mother saying, "Whatever you do, don't let them give you a spinal. It's risky. If you move while they're doing it you could be paralyzed, and it's painful."

I shook my head no.

"What do you mean, 'no'?" the nurse asked.

"I won't sign. I'm not having a spinal."

I was in the bathroom, gripping the sink in the middle of a pain, when the nurse walked in again.

"You have to sign," she said.

I heard my mother's voice in my head, much louder than the nurse's: *They'll try to talk you into it, but don't let them.*

"Who says?" I asked the nurse.

"The doctor."

"I won't," I said, figuring I trusted my mother more than some strange white man I had never seen before. "I'm not getting a spinal."

The nurse shot me a hateful look and stomped out of the bathroom.

I was lying on the cot when she and the doctor walked into my room, one on each side of me, insisting that I get the spinal anesthetic. I just stared at the ceiling.

"We want to make it as comfortable for you as possible," he said.

I heard my mother: *They just want to make it easy on themselves.*

This was in the years before men were in touch with their feelings, before Lamaze was popular or fathers were allowed in the delivery room. All of my doctors were military men used to barking orders and having people roll over and obey. As far as they were concerned, the only thing a women needed to know before giving birth was to hold her legs open wide and push. *Pregnancy, labor,* and *delivery* were medical terms, secret rituals these men were not about to share with a silly young black girl who they were sure would not understand a word, anyway.

I didn't get the spinal injection, and in retrospect I think the doctor and nurse decided then to make my delivery a hellish experience. I had asked for an overhead mirror to be put in the delivery room so I could watch the delivery. A nurse said she would get one. But the mirror wasn't there, and when I asked about it, the doctor snapped, "It's being used for something more important."

I was at the mercy of these strangers, all of them white and from the military and most of them males. They frightened me with their callousness. In addition to feeling mistreated, I was haunted by the memory of my mother's ordeal and her stillborn baby. I gripped the bed as a hard pain hit. A nurse folded straps across my wrists and tied my hands down.

"No!" I screamed. "Please, I won't fight. Please untie me. I won't hurt anybody. Please."

Mother hadn't told me that my hands would be tied, and I thought the doctors and nurses had singled me out for punishment for refusing the spinal. Being strapped down was worse than being in labor. Years later, when the memory of the labor pains had faded, I remembered vividly the agony of being tied.

One kind nurse stepped forward to hold my hand, and that calmed me. With her hand in mine, I concentrated on listening to my baby's heartbeat. Then there was one last grueling push. The doctor tugged with forceps. Finally, a tremendous release.

"It's a girl," a nurse said.

It was 4:35 P.M., November 19, 1968. At age nineteen, when most of my friends were at college, packing to come home for Thanksgiving to tell stories about their fall semesters, I had brought a person into the world. I imagined God had told a spirit there was a troubled soul on earth who needed her love and wisdom—and that spirit, being brave, studied me for just a short time before replying, "Yes," to the challenge. Then, at exactly 4:35 P.M., she looked at God. He said, "Now!" and my daughter fell willingly into my life.

"It's a girl," I whispered to myself. And while it had never mattered to me whether it was a girl or boy, it suddenly felt as if a girl was what I had always wanted.

"Eight pounds and three ounces," a nurse said.

I looked at my daughter, who was slimy and gray, with her mouth open wide, crying, and a peace like I had never known washed over me and warmed me to the bone.

Phillip and I had picked the name Andrea out of a college yearbook one night. We decided that if the baby was a boy it would be named after him, but a girl would be "Andrea." I liked the way the name came out of my mouth, the first syllable round and full of breath, the next short and slightly harder, but flowing into the last, which released the name to the air again. Her middle name was Kristal, which conjured up for me a feeling of clarity and pureness.

"Ouch!" I yelled, as the doctor stitched up a tear near my vagina.

I will always remember his last words to me: "If you had listened to me, you wouldn't have all this pain."

Over the next few hours Phillip and his parents arrived. They pressed their foreheads against the glass to the nursery and talked about how beautiful Andrea was.

"She's gonna have good hair. She's gonna have good hair like her daddy." Phillip's mother repeated this often in the coming months, laughing as if she were joking. But she was serious. She wanted the baby to have "good hair," which meant curly or straight hair, not kinky hair like most black people had.

The next morning, when the nurses brought the babies in for their feedings, I admired everyone else's child and waited for my own, but they didn't bring her. I started to cry, convinced she was dead.

"What's wrong, Mrs. Miller?" a nurse asked as she passed a baby from her arms to the arms of another mother.

"Where is my baby?" I said between my whimpering.

"We don't bring them for a while when they're newborns. You'll get her the next feeding," she said.

I didn't believe her. I cried harder. She left, shaking her head. A few minutes later she returned with my baby. I held Andrea against my chest and squeezed her so tight she cried. Then I held her in the cradle of my arm and saw that her eyes were crossed. I started crying again.

"What on earth is wrong now?" the nurse asked.

"My baby's cross-eyed," I sobbed.

The nurse laughed. "Honey, newborns can't control their eyes. Your baby is fine."

◆ ◆ ◆

They buried my mama's baby while I lay in my hospital bed recuperating from childbirth.

"I named her Angela for 'Angel,' " Mama told me on the phone. "I want her buried in the dress she was going to wear home."

My sisters told me a marine carried the tiny pink casket under his arm while a group of marines followed. I left the hospital the day after the funeral. My first stop: my parents' house. My mother sat on the living room couch and tears rolled down her cheek as she held Andrea and kissed her. Before I left, Mama put some of Angela's clothes in a bag for my baby.

◆ ◆ ◆

I didn't know anything about a baby. What's wrong when the baby cries? Is she hungry? Is she sick? Has she had enough to eat? Why is her stool yellow? Why is she spitting up?

All I knew was that I wanted this child's life to be different from mine, to be minus the fears of being alone. Of being wrong. Of being inadequate.

Phillip adored the baby. He talked to her in baby talk, fed her a bottle in the middle of the night, and lay down beside her when she took her naps. Mrs. Miller shopped for the baby nearly every day.

◆ ◆ ◆

I got high with Phillip for the first time when Andrea was a few months old. We drank a bottle of cough syrup and I walked around a mall in slow motion, my eyes stretched wide, trying to look normal. After that, we shared a bottle of cough syrup occasionally on weekends. Generally, he and I got along well, but Phillip was spoiled and he liked to get his way; he insisted on always being right. The first time

I disagreed with him and raised my voice to tell him so, he slapped me so hard I was dizzy. Afterward we went downstairs for dinner with his parents. I smiled and kept my left hand in my lap while I ate and spoke perfect English.

Whenever I looked at Andrea, I saw Ben—in her bushy eyebrows, high forehead, and long, narrow nose. Mother told me he had called to find out if the baby had been born and she had warned him to stay away from me.

Phillip and I were still learning about each other when he received orders to go to Korea. I assumed I'd go with him, but my mother and my in-laws said Korea was too dirty a place to raise a child. The truth was probably that they didn't want their grandchild living across an ocean from them. My father, who as a marine had moved his family around the country, said, as if there was nothing more natural, "Go with your husband." It didn't cross my mind that maybe my father was thinking about those times when he had been separated from his family, or that he was considering the damage done to a family when the father is missing. I never thought about his motives for the recommendation because I never took his advice seriously. I didn't trust my father or his word. So I stayed home and said good-bye to my husband.

But I wasn't the kind of girl who could be alone. As far as I was concerned, when Phillip left for Korea, he took our love with him and our relationship was doomed. I didn't understand that love stays with you—always—it doesn't enter and exit as people come and go.

With Phillip gone, the Millers stepped up their battering. Each time we sat down to dinner they found some way to bring up my visits to their son when he was in college. When Mrs. Miller and I were alone she rephrased old questions and politely asked again, "When did you get pregnant?"

I fled to my parents' after one particularly difficult session of questioning. The more I thought about the questions, the angrier I became. And then when I went to a friend's house one evening and smoked a joint, my rage ballooned. My life was fucked up because I was living a lie, I thought. My mind would not let go of this notion: a lie, a lie, a lie.

The only way to set it right, to start again, was to tell the truth. I called Mrs. Miller. "Andrea is not your real grandchild," I said in the detached tone of a person high on drugs. "Isn't that what you want to hear? You're absolutely right. She is not your flesh and blood. Your son is not her father. He knew it all the time."

Mrs. Miller was too hurt and shocked to answer. She loved her son enough to ask me those questions about getting pregnant, but now, faced with the truth, she realized she loved her grandchild enough to forget.

She called me at my mother's house the next day. "Pat, I don't care if Phil isn't Andrea's father," she said. "I love that little baby and I'll always love her. She's my grandchild."

I hung up the phone.

chapter five

Riding the Horse

I was walking down a hill near my parents' house, pushing the stroller with my five-month-old baby in it, when I saw coming toward us a man who looked like Ben. But Ben was supposed to be in Vietnam, and anyway, this man was taller, older, and clean-shaven. He walked closer. I squinted. The man widened his mouth into a familiar smirk.

Ben stood in front of me. Mesmerized. Staring at his baby.

"She's pretty," he said, without moving his eyes from Andrea.

I couldn't say a word. I was deeply uncomfortable. This was the first time I had seen Ben since I had written that letter announcing my departure from his life.

"Can I hold her?" he asked.

"I don't think so."

He moved to the side and I walked away, feeling his eyes on my back like floodlights glaring on my guilt.

"I thought you were in Vietnam," I said.

"Got wounded. They sent me home."

"You have to go back?" I asked, half-hoping he had to go back to somewhere, anywhere other than here.

"No," he said.

◆ ◆ ◆

Phillip called from Korea, angry that I had told his parents the truth about Andrea, but also pleading with me to wait for him to come home on emergency leave before I made any drastic decisions. His words tore at my heart, but I was convinced I was righting a wrong, telling a truth I should have told long before now.

Each afternoon when I took Andrea out in her stroller Ben would meet us to walk with us. "Wanna go see Sly and the Family Stone in concert? My treat," I asked one day, the words slipping from my mouth, unplanned.

Ben accepted, and after the concert we went to a cheap tourist home to spend the night. The next day, our relationship picked up where it had ended more than a year before, as if nothing had ever happened to separate us. In my heart, I believed I had been given a rare chance to set things right.

I bounced so easily from Phillip to Ben, and then back to Ben again, that years later I wondered if it wasn't another example of how in my youth I could not love someone who was absent. When a man left me, I strayed, probably like many girls whom people call promiscuous, but who are actually lonely. We have to have a man to feel complete, and it has nothing to do with sex. It is more like an illness or addiction, because we hurt to the point of near-insanity when we are by ourselves. The antidote is simply to learn that we are already whole, already have all we need inside us. But that is easier said than done.

By the time Phillip came home I was in love with Ben again, driven, I convinced myself, by a determination for my daughter to be with her real father. There was no way to explain this to Phillip, and so we spent a night crying together and talking in circles until our heads were spinning and we were exhausted. By the time the sun rose, he reluctantly agreed to a separation.

◆　◆　◆

When my head ached from the jumbled, confused thoughts I had about my own life, I escaped by reading, filling myself with someone else's ideas or life. Now I turned my attention to young black revolutionaries like H. Rap Brown, Stokely Carmichael, and Eldridge Cleaver. I read the poets who spoke of blackness as a royal gift rather than a curse, and who kept my head and my fist raised in pride: Nikki Giovanni, Sonia Sanchez, Haki Madhubuti, and Amiri Baraka. And I bought dozens of cheaply printed poetry publications from the proliferation of black poets whose work appeared and then disappeared just as quickly a few years later when publishing companies said black was no longer in. Each week I bought the newspapers of the Communist Party, the Black Muslims, and the Black Panthers. In addition to the writings of black authors, I read the works of young whites hellbent on changing the country, groups like the Weather Underground and the Yippies, people like Abbie Hoffman and Jerry Rubin.

It is impossible to describe the feelings that came over me when I looked at pictures of Black Panthers, young black women with huge Afros, young black men dressed in black leather jackets and black berets, toting automatic rifles. The men were hot, fierce brothers, exuding power and sensuality with their leather and guns. But that feeling alone would trivialize what I truly felt. It was even more than pride. Much more. Something came alive in me, and my heart beat faster and stronger. They were audacious. They taunted white America, "Stuff your racism down your throat and gag on it, muthafucka." They seized control of their own lives and assumed responsibility for their communities. Their work made me feel powerful, too. "All power to the people!" they chanted, so that I believed anything was possible. This was a magical time when young black men with guns were not menaces to me but "brothers"; they knew I was their "sister" and they would never stand in an alley and point the barrel of a gun at my head.

I wore my hair in a huge Afro, discovering it would billow in the day if I braided it at night and then took it out and teased it in the morning. I wore heavy earrings made of African beads, jeans, and suede vests with fringes. My mother and grandmother, always looking for proof of my insanity, found it in my new hair. They were women raised to believe that pretty hair was straight hair: in the North Carolina projects where my mother grew up, if your hair was kinky you were dirty or deranged, too crazy to care about your appearance. "Why would you want to walk around with nappy hair?" my mother asked, while my father looked at me as if I were the enemy, what he was trained to fight against.

I thought of my hair as a halo announcing my pride in all that black people were and had ever been. I would never change it, I declared; I couldn't see ahead to when I would be a woman with my hair dyed red and straight and yet be blacker than I was when I had an Afro. In 1969, I thought my Afro separated me from the Negroes and the coloreds and pulled my head higher, so that I walked straighter, a pure and visible version of the African princess I thought I was until the age of five, with Lucy and Charlotte, my hair braided and beribboned.

A coworker at Western Union, a black man several years older than I was, brought me political essays as well as literature and I read James Baldwin for the first time, Claude Brown, and Ralph Ellison. Nothing I had ever read in high school even hinted that I could receive such contentment from reading, that there even existed people who had expressed exactly what I was feeling and believing. In the pages of these books I could see clean through to the truth, while in my own life I was lost in a muddle. You could read words and hold them in your head until they became a part of you. I began writing, mostly bad poems about my despair. And I hoped, as I wrote, that my words would lead me to my truth.

Ben and I listened to music we would have shrugged at a few years earlier, going to hear people like African vocalist Miriam Makeba and her then husband, trumpeter Hugh Masekela; we went to concerts by Nina Simone, Wes Montgomery, and Ramsey Lewis. In high school, I had rebelled against jazz because it was the music of my parents, always blaring in our house, competing with my albums: Mary Wells,

Martha Reeves and the Vandellas, and the Temptations. My parents played Miles Davis and Sarah Vaughn. Now, under the influence of Black Power, I listened more intently to jazz because I knew it was music invented by black Americans.

But one period of black pride, when I was already grown, was not enough to erase years of damage to my self-esteem. It felt good to be black, yet it still felt bad to be me.

One evening Ben and I dropped by an apartment to visit a friend who had been in Vietnam with him. Ben and the guy went upstairs, and I sat in the living room watching television. A half hour later, I walked upstairs to look for them. I knocked on the bedroom door, which was shut. Then, not waiting for a response, I pushed open the door. Ben was in a chair, with a belt pulled tight around his forearm, sticking a syringe in the bend of his arm. His friend, also holding a syringe, jumped when he saw me.

"It's all right," Ben said to him, then he pulled the syringe out and looked at me with glassy eyes.

"What are you doing?" Of course, I had an idea, but the question came more from shock than curiosity. I had never seen anyone shoot drugs, and I had no idea Ben used any drug other than marijuana.

"I'm shooting smack."

"Smack?"

"Her-ron" was the way Ben said it. His voice was slurred and his eyes blinked, as he fought to keep them open.

"How does it make you feel?"

The other guy laughed.

"Real good," Ben said. "You wanna try?"

I don't know what makes a person stick a syringe of heroin or crack or any other drug in his body, but I didn't give it much thought at all before saying, "Yeah." Maybe I had made the decision slowly, over the years, long before being asked; maybe I was ready for heroin before I even knew it existed.

Among my earliest memories as a child are recollections of the severe pain I felt when I was about four or five years old and realized people killed each other. It made me extremely nervous, and I kept a weak stomach. At night I woke up with nightmares, dreaming that bombs were being dropped on our house. The slightest hint of meanness from one person to another hurt me deeply. I was so depressed about how people treated each other that I wasn't sure I wanted to live in this world, though I would not consider suicide until much later in life.

To be capable of shooting heroin requires that you do not love yourself at all, do not look upon yourself as a miracle, or a perfect creation of God. At that moment when Ben offered me drugs, I loved him more than I did myself. I was too addicted to him to do anything other than what he suggested. I followed men. What they did, I did. What they told me to do, I did. I wanted their approval, an ounce of care I could pass off as love. It made me higher than any heroin I ever shot into my veins.

When I looked at Ben, high on heroin that day, he was more peaceful and calm than I had ever seen him. Everyone in America was, it seemed, on some sort of drug, whether they were black or white, rich or poor, all of us looking for ways to relax, reasons to laugh, to feel during a time of war something that could pass for peace. If someone else had asked me if I wanted heroin, I would have hesitated. But I trusted Ben with my life.

His friend handed him another packet of heroin. Ben rinsed out the syringe he had used. He poured the powder in a spoon and with an eyedropper added a few drops of water. He held a match under the spoon until the heroin dissolved into the water. He dropped a cotton ball on the spoon to soak up the heroin and, supposedly, leave behind impurities. Then he used a syringe to suck up the solution from the cotton.

"Are you sure?" he asked me.

"Yeah," I said, sitting down.

He looked pleased. "You want it in this arm?"

I held out my right arm with my palm facing upward. He wrapped the strap around my upper arm, and I watched the blue veins pop up. He stuck the needle in one of my veins, and the dope disappeared into me. He pulled the plunger and my blood flowed into the syringe.

"Are you okay? This will give you a rush," he said.

He pushed and pulled the plunger of the syringe a couple of times

so the dope mixed with my blood and flowed in and out. In and out.
Each time, I got higher. Before he pulled out the needle, I was extremely high and the sweet, bitter taste of heroin was in my throat.

The music playing in the room began to play inside me, warm waves from a saxophone rippling my blood. I had never felt so good. My head and eyes were heavy, and I heard Ben laughing.

"You're nodding," he said.

It was true, my head bobbed. There was no time. Hours or minutes passed. At some point we went into another bedroom and made love, nothing passionate or frenzied, but rather a slow dance of ecstasy. Heroin slowed down everything to a pace that felt natural to me.

I loved heroin. It silenced the confusion in my head and I was in sync with the world. Every weekend—Friday, Saturday, and Sunday—I held out my arm and Ben shot me up. Occasionally, I got high on a weeknight, but generally I didn't touch it when I had to work. Always I went out to get high, so Andrea wasn't with me.

With such self-imposed rules and restrictions, I do not believe I had a heroin habit. At least not a physical addiction. My body never craved the drug; my mind did. My addiction was psychological, not to be confused, though, with some attempt at being "hip." I needed to feel good, to ban the fear and anxiety that had been my jail guard for years now, the constant feeling that I was not good enough. And now, not good enough to be a mother. I wanted to live where there was no hypocrisy, no racism, no one hurting someone else. I wanted a perfect world—and I didn't know how to get it. Meanwhile, I had to live with me, this person I believed was bad, stupid, and unlikable. What I had in common with friends who were physically addicted to drugs was an engulfing self-hatred. When you hate yourself, you don't hear people say, "Gosh, you're smart," or, "You're a talented artist." Or if you hear them, you don't believe them.

I don't know why I never became a hopeless addict. Ben struggled with heroin longer than I did, developing a serious habit at one time, kicking it, struggling with a drinking problem, successfully fighting off that, too. What first saved me were memories of a better time, when as a child I believed I was good and smart—beliefs my teachers, friends, and family had reinforced. Because I didn't always have faith, though, in the present or the future, I used heroin. But because I had my memories, I only used it occasionally. I had this; my family's steadfast love—and Andrea, who made me want to try, even though I was afraid.

As a reporter years later, I would interview men and women who had contracted AIDS from sharing dirty needles, and I saw no difference between me and them except time: I shot heroin before AIDS. Once I interviewed a man over lunch and as he sat across from me, it seemed so clear to me that if I turned the table around just a notch, he would be the reporter and I would be the addict with AIDS. As I became less ashamed of my past, I could encourage people I interviewed to believe in themselves and their future. I could tell the woman I interviewed in a drug rehabilitation program, where she was trying to break a heroin habit, that I knew, personally, how difficult it is to stop doing something that makes you feel so good and to try to find that natural something in life that makes you feel even better. I could tell the young man who did not want to admit to me that he had been to jail that I had been in jail before, also, for possession of heroin and for shoplifting. In every case, the person I was interviewing let down his or her guard and talked straightforwardly and honestly. But first, each looked at me in disbelief, which only reinforced for me the distance I had traveled.

◆   ◆   ◆

In the fall of 1969 Ben was transferred to Fort Bragg, in North Carolina. Shortly afterward, his family moved to Charlotte, North Carolina, and Andrea and I went with them. We moved into a brick rambler in a quiet neighborhood with yards that looked loved and shade trees two decades old. Ben reported for duty at Fort Bragg, Andrea and I stayed behind with his mother and grandmother and Ben's niece and nephew who lived with them.

I expected to find a job as a teletype operator and let Ben's grandmother, Mrs. Anderson, baby-sit Andrea while I was at work. But it was soon obvious that that was impossible. I was fond of Mrs. Anderson and Ben's mother, Mrs. Smith, both enormously resourceful

women whose wit kept me laughing. I knew they had drinking problems, but I didn't know what that meant as far as living with them
each day. I soon found out. They bought liquor every morning and
spent the day drinking. When they ran out of liquor, they begged me
to go to the store; when I didn't, they called a cab and paid the driver
to go get it for them.

When they were drunk, they disregarded everything else. I cooked,
cleaned the house, and cared for Andrea as well as Ben's nephew, who
was two, and his niece, who was six. Occasionally the women stopped
drinking for a day or two and we caught up on all the housekeeping
and I slept late. But mostly I was Cinderella before the ball, scrubbing
and cleaning and washing the clothes, cooking the meals, and bathing
the children. By the time I moved out, my love for Ben's mother and
grandmother resembled hate, and I severed my ties with them, disillu-
sioned about the family I had chosen to be my daughter's flesh and
blood. Years later, after Ben's grandmother became sick and died and
when his mother overcame her drinking problem, I had left my
daughter no ties to these women, no way to mend what had been
broken.

After Ben went to Fort Bragg, I stopped shooting heroin. A couple
of weeks later I found a job as the second black teletype operator to be
hired by E. I. Du Pont. The first, a young woman named Roberta,
became my friend immediately, the two of us united by our color and
by the racist attitudes that kept most of our white coworkers away
from us.

Ben left Fort Bragg for what was supposed to be a weekend visit; he
stayed away six months. He was never suited for the army, or for any
organization that required discipline or that he follow orders, particularly when most of the orders came from white men. He made up his
mind he wasn't returning—and he didn't. He was declared AWOL,
but no one came after him, so he traveled back and forth from Maryland to North Carolina, hustling and working jobs that paid him cash,
so his name wouldn't show up on Social Security records. But he was
always looking over his shoulder, sleeping light. After being AWOL
six months, he turned himself in, tired of the fugitive life. The army
locked him in the stockade. On weekends, I donned my black wet-

look maxicoat, combed Andrea's curly Afro, and went to Fort Bragg, riding the Greyhound for four hard hours, stopping in a string of small towns where the bus station was a bench inside a grocery store or a post office.

My coworker Roberta and I moved into an apartment together in a new complex of plain square brick buildings with more parking lots than grass. Because I was now farther away from my baby-sitter and didn't have a car, Mama and I decided Andrea should return to Maryland, where Mama would care for her until I got settled. Twice a month I rode a Greyhound bus north now, eighteen hours round-trip, leaving on Friday afternoons and returning late Sunday, spending what was left of the weekend with my daughter. To help me survive the trip, I gobbled downers so I could sleep during the ride.

Phillip visited me in Charlotte after he returned from Korea. It was the last sigh of a relationship, the farewell of two cheerless friends who avoided any discussion of the past or the future, because I couldn't bear the memories of when we were happy and he couldn't tolerate the possibility that I might be happy without him. In the parking lot at Du Pont we lingered in a soft, remorseful good-bye kiss. And then he was gone. He told me his parents were having our divorce papers drawn up; a few weeks later they were in my mailbox, with this caveat: "No children were born of this union." I signed my name on the line that said: "I acknowledge this to be the truth."

Phillip was absolved of all responsibility, which seemed only fair to me, and I saw neither him nor his parents again for years. When my grandmother suffered a stroke about seven years later, I got the urge to look up Phillip, prompted perhaps by memories of living with him at Grannie's. I took a girlfriend with me and we found Phillip, who was an insurance adjuster, living in sprawling rambler in a rural neighborhood in Maryland. By this time he had married a second time, had a son, and was separated from his wife. I was unprepared for what happened: The man I had entombed in my memory as an intellect spoke in rambling, circular sentences that didn't make sense. But once we were outside, I was ready to dismiss my interpretation of his behavior until my girlfriend asked, "Was he high, or has he always been that crazy?"

Phillip had smashed a long-held-sacred memory in which I immortalized him as the safe, sane man I had married. The visit was so disturbing that to this day, when I see him on the subway or walking downtown I always take a sharp turn and disappear, fleeing my past.

The army discharged Ben, basically to get rid of him, and he moved back to Maryland, because he considered Charlotte redneck country, too slow for his liking. I stayed behind. I was reveling in my first taste of freedom. Besides, Ben promised to visit often and, of course, our separation had already changed our relationship. I had new friends who introduced me to hallucinogenic drugs like LSD, purple haze, and mescaline.

I enjoyed the gentle pace of life in Charlotte. Strangers, even white people, nodded and bid you, "Good morning," as you passed. Of course, there were minor discomforts. I didn't see as many black people as I was accustomed to seeing in Washington, and it took me a while to get used to having so many white people around me in public. But then there was "West Charlotte," the type of section of town that exists in most cities, a community where you can hang out and never see one white person. Nightlife was extremely different than in Washington. Charlotte clubs closed about 1:00 A.M., which was traumatic for a young woman who could dance all night. I was introduced to juke joints, private houses where liquor was still sold long after the legitimate clubs closed—small, cozy, dimly lit places where people danced until daylight to the forty-fives on the jukebox. When I wasn't dancing, I was at the bar eating a pickled pig's foot or a pickled egg.

I was twenty-one, living in my own apartment, away from my father's eyes. I could have whomever I wanted in my house. When Ben came to visit, we partied hard. Defiantly. He brought the heroin and I tried to plan something special for us to do, a party or a concert, to prove that Charlotte wasn't the hick town he thought it was. He and a friend, James, came one weekend in June 1970 and I bought tickets for us to attend a Steppenwolf concert. We shot up and smoked a joint before heading to the show.

"Here, put this in your pocketbook," James said to me as we walked out of the apartment. He handed me our pack of works—the syringes, the spoon we used to cook the heroin, and a couple small packets and capsules of heroin.

I hated nodding in public, but it was nearly impossible not to after shooting up, so we all sat in the audience at the concert with our heads bobbing up and down and jerking. Ben and James went to the bathroom and I stayed in my seat. Steppenwolf played their last number, "Born to Be Wild," and I realized the guys had been gone for quite some time. I stood up as people began leaving and saw Ben and James over by the bathroom surrounded by a few white guys with long hair and ragged jeans. Then I saw some policemen, and I knew the guys had gotten busted.

I would find out later that undercover agents had watched the three of us most of the night. Moments later, the police came after me. I started running but couldn't find the exit.

"How do you get out of here?" I asked some young drugged-out white boy. We stood out. We were a minority in the overwhelmingly white crowd, we looked as high as we were, and Ben and James wore their Northern cockiness in their exaggerated swaggers.

"Take the door," he said, laughing.

I looked over my shoulder to see several police officers running my way. I jumped over seats and skipped down steps two at a time. They got closer. I threw down my purse. A second later, a firm hand squeezed my shoulder and I stopped. Another officer in uniform grabbed my arms, and one of the guys in jeans picked up my pocketbook.

"Lose something?" he asked.

I was too high to be scared. I wanted to spit in his face. They handcuffed me and put me in the back of a police car. I watched them search the trunk of Ben's car.

At the police station, they took each of us—separately—into a room to be questioned. They had arrested the guys after James sold an undercover agent a joint of marijuana for five dollars.

"Goddamn," I said, when the police told me. I was thinking about the arrogance of Ben and James. While I would have wondered, *Why would someone pay five dollars for a joint?* they had assumed, I was sure, that the guy was dumb because he was white and from the South. On the other hand, they considered themselves too hip to err, certainly too cool to be busted. Soaring on heroin and with that kind of attitude, they were easy game for the undercover agent.

Their misjudgment would cost us all. Ben was the luckiest because he didn't have any drugs on him, his only crime being that he was with James when James sold the joint. Ben was released from jail the day after our arrest. James would serve eighteen months in a North Carolina prison. My fate would fall somewhere between those two.

In the interrogation room, I sat in an old wooden desk chair while two white officers in uniform and one of the long-haired undercover guys stood around me. It was really a small office with dull light green walls and several desks. The overhead fluorescent light was bright and the three of them stood in front of me, though occasionally one or the other would pace and walk around behind me, making me nervous and irritated.

"I've seen you around Oaklawn," said the stringy-haired undercover cop, who looked to be in his early twenties.

"You haven't seen me," I said indignantly.

Oaklawn was a main street in West Charlotte, running past housing projects at one end and large brick homes at another. Just past the brick homes, Oaklawn ran into Beatties Ford Road, the main business street in the black community. At that intersection, where there was a Chick-N-Rib carryout on one corner and a pool hall across the street, people congregated to buy and sell drugs. But I had never bought drugs off the street; my friends delivered my drugs to me. I was pissed at this white boy for thinking all blacks bought their drugs on the corner.

For the next hour, the men threatened me and offered deals, trying to entice me into giving them information about the drug ring they said was run by Ben and James. There was no dilemma for me because I didn't know anything to tell. They did get my attention when they said they could prove that Ben and James came to North Carolina regularly to bring me heroin to sell in Charlotte. But they were bluffing.

"Tell us your source—who the big man is—and we'll let you go," the undercover cop said.

They thought I was so important I wanted to laugh. But I disliked cops immensely. Most people my age that I knew hated them, too. They were pigs. When I looked at them I saw the National Guard members who stood at the doors of white schools blocking the entrance to black children; I saw cracker cops in Alabama, who ordered their dogs to attack black civil rights demonstrators; I saw J. Edgar Hoover and the vicious cracker madmen who had killed Fred Hampton and God only knew how many other Black Panthers. In my neighborhood, the county police were legendary for the number of black people, particularly young men, they killed each year in incidents reported as "self-defense." I had no respect for "pigs" or any authority, having learned to dislike the system that held power over me and did such things as force me to go to segregated schools with inferior supplies, then to better-equipped buildings with white teachers that didn't want to teach me. Authority was white cops, white teachers, crazy white bosses, and the only black people on the list: my mother and father. I had no respect for such authority because none of them recognized the truth when they heard it.

As I sat in the police station, what angered me more than anything was the idea that these "pigs" thought they could buy me with threats and promises and, furthermore, thought they knew my price.

"I ain't telling you nothing," I said indignantly, as if I knew something to tell. "Even on the streets, we have a code of ethics and loyalty."

That was my ode to the revolution, my kick in the teeth to the "pigs." Let them think they can't break us, that all of us people on the street stick together. I thought I was being revolutionary when I was in fact counterrevolutionary, fighting over what I thought was a principle when I had gotten caught with heroin in my pocket and, worse, in my veins.

"We can see to it you never get out of here," the undercover cop said, nearly spitting on me. "I'm sure I've seen you buying or selling on Oaklawn."

That was a threat, I was sure. But I was too high and too young to be scared. I sneered at their whiteness and their arrogance.

"Give me my time," I demanded in my cockiest tone.

They set my bond at $100,000. "To give you time to think," one of them explained. They figured a bond that high would definitely mean some time in jail, because it would be a while before it was reduced, and they assumed, rightfully so, that my family didn't have that much money.

I called Roberta and asked her to call my parents. Then two white female guards watched as I stripped and put on the long hospital green cotton dress they gave me. I followed the women down a long corridor and through thick steel doors.

My high was wearing thin. I was tired. It was nearly three in the morning and deathly quiet. The guards stopped in front of a dark cell.

"This is it," one of them said.

I stepped inside.

Then the heavy doors slammed shut. And I was in the dark.

chapter six

Locked Up

Three black women stared at me in the dark. The oldest, a woman with wild gray hair, tore my arrest papers from my hand.

"Whatcha in for?" a younger woman with braids asked.

The older woman read my papers: " 'Possession of a controlled substance . . . heroin. Possession with intent to distribute. Possession of a needle and syringe.' "

"You high now?" the third woman asked. She was a thin, pretty girl with golden bronze skin and a curly black Afro.

"Yeah, she's high. Look at her eyes," the gray-haired one said, handing me my papers.

I was speechless, tired, and suddenly scared. Everything I knew about jail I had learned from watching bad television movies, old black-and-white films where women fought each other with crude weapons made from forks and the matrons who guarded them were lusting lesbians. Only the heroin flowing in my veins kept my body from rocking and my cool veneer from vanishing.

"That's your bed over there, over mine. I'm Tanya," said a woman about my age. She stood in front of me with her hair in five thick braids, the two front ones curled up like a ram's horns. She stuck out her hand. I shook it and walked over to the bed.

"Tell us how you got picked up," said the older woman. "My name's Odessa."

"I'm Patricia," said the one with the curly Afro.

Tanya patted the thin mattress of her bed and invited me to sit. The other two women sat on the bed across from us. For the first time, I noticed other women in bunk beds around us. There were eight of us altogether. Everybody else was asleep while we talked for nearly an hour. I told them about my arrest, and they told me why they were in jail.

"I was drunk in the streets," said Odessa.

"A-gain," added Patricia, laughing, then explaining, "I sold cocaine to an undercover agent."

"I cut a woman," quipped Tanya.

I wondered if the woman had died, but I was too afraid to ask. They interrogated me more thoroughly than the three police officers had, but in some strange, inexplicable way the longer our conversation trailed on, the more fun it became. I had not expected them to be witty, and their laughter relaxed me. The more I listened, the more threads of similarity I found in our stories. We were tied to each other by poor judgment, by bad decisions in love, which was what put most of us in jail. Tanya had cut another woman in an argument over a man; Patricia had been busted with her boyfriend, who had her strung out on coke and stealing for him. Like me, the women there for drug charges had gotten them following behind some man. Ben had introduced me to drugs, and I had carried them for him. It was the same for most of the women in my cell: they got busted carrying drugs for boyfriends—because nobody was married—or they had habits because a man had encouraged them to use his drug of choice.

"I need to go to sleep," I told them after nearly an hour of talking. My high was wearing thin.

"In the morning, we'll give you some pins so you can pin up your dress," said Patricia. "Then you'll have on a minidress like us. Just 'cause we in jail don't mean we gotta wear these long mammy dresses."

This was my first introduction to what women could do for each other, separated from the outside world and from men. Normally, we nurtured our children or the men in our lives, our parents and grandparents, or anyone within reach who would accept our nurturing, not turning our healing talents on our own selves or our women friends. But stuck here together—without children or men or parents—we were forced to nurture each other. I sat between the legs of women who combed and parted and greased my hair. In our time together they would take their worn hands, marred from needles or from protecting their faces from some man's fists, and braid my hair into intricate patterns, as if I were their child. We cried when we talked about the children we could not see, the missed graduations, first words, and small hugs; we laughed—oh, how we laughed—uproariously, our wanting howls bouncing off the cold walls and escaping through the steel bars into the dark of the night, while the rest of the city slept.

We didn't have televisions or radios, so we passed the days playing cards. I had never played cards before, but the girls taught me several games and I was thankful. One day I drew a picture of a man and we propped him up against the wall so he could watch us. He became "every man," recipient of the painful memories and rage of all of the women. Therefore, he was abused repeatedly.

"You ain't good for nothin' but staring," Odessa said to him.

"Watch this, honey. I'm gonna beat their asses," I said to the paper man, while in a rare brazen mood.

After losing one afternoon, Tanya yelled, "Whatcha looking at, muthafucka?" and stabbed the paper man with a pencil until he had holes in his face and chest. I balled him up and threw him across the room.

"You're a sick bitch," I said.

Tanya laughed hysterically.

"That was the only man we had," Odessa said, pouting as if she were upset.

"Shit, eight women shared him," said Patricia.

"Make yourself another one," Tanya told me.

By this time we were all laughing again.

"Hell, it's men that got me here," I said. "I ain't fooling with another one."

Tanya winked at me. "I ain't fooling with your ass either," I said to her, and we all laughed.

Everyone had a love-hate relationship with Tanya. She didn't know how to accept nurturing and didn't trust people, so she was always doing something she thought would keep her a step ahead of the next person. Her petty lies tried our patience, and sometimes we forgot that what she was really craving was love. Most often, though, in this place where we could focus on each other, we remembered to be patient and gentle, to recognize the loneliness we saw in other women. This was an exceptional time for me, though I didn't truly understand its significance until later. I knew that though I was imprisoned, I was enjoying myself in a way I hadn't in years. Of course, I wanted to get out immediately, yet I felt a respect for women—including myself—creeping up on me. Then before it could take hold, I was gone, turned loose again into a world that revolved around men.

At night, I tossed and turned, worrying about what my parents would say when they found out about my arrest. What did they tell my little sisters? What did Roberta tell the people on the job?

But my shame and embarrassment resonated from my ego and not from a sense of having done wrong. I was embarrassed only because I didn't want everybody to know I had been arrested; I wasn't ashamed because I used drugs or thought I had done anything wrong. I was humiliated because I had confirmed the suspicions of people like my white coworkers, who thought being black and using drugs were synonymous. I was ashamed because I believed my father, like my coworkers, never had faith in me and that I had confirmed his bleak expectations for my life.

On my first night, after I went to bed, I felt a hand on my back.

"Move over." It was Tanya.

"What the hell are you doing?"

"If you're gonna live here, you gotta play by the rules. I'm the head of this house. The daddy. So move over."

I inched over because I was too afraid to refuse. She flashed me a crazy wide grin. Her face had been pretty once, before she lost a front tooth and pain etched a map across her taut skin, showing every time her life dipped and went in circles. On one cheek was a scar, like an old cut, and a dark oval, like a burn, on her forehead, over her right eyebrow. Her ginger skin was dull. When she smiled, her lips always stiffened, as if they were doing the most unnatural thing they could do.

"Tanya . . ." I barely got her name out before she grabbed me by the back of my neck and thrust me against the wall. Her lips bore down on mine. I screamed and pushed her back by the shoulders. It was all reflex action, because if I had stopped to think, I would have been too afraid to fight back.

She stopped. "Girl, if you push me off I'll kill ya," she said. Her eyes were cold. She laughed, a terrible, hollow sound, and I retreated inside myself.

"Tanya." Patricia spat out the name in the dark. "Tanya, why don't you leave her alone."

Tanya turned to look back in Patricia's direction and teetered on the edge of the bed. *Push her off,* I told myself. But I didn't have the guts. She twisted around to stare at me. With her lips shut tight and her eyes fixed, she climbed down from my bed. Silent.

I sat up with my back against the wall and wrapped myself in my blanket.

"You okay, Pat?" Patricia whispered.

Words stuck in my throat. I grunted, then managed to utter, "Okay."

I lay down with the cover still wrapped tightly around me like a cocoon, my back pressed against the wall. Time passed and I cursed myself for being a coward, for not knowing how to fight or even having the guts to try. My ears strained for the comforting sound of Tanya's snores. Eventually, I dozed off, but not before I realized the awful truth about myself, that if it had not been for Patricia, I would have been a victim—again—because I wasn't as tough and streetwise as I pretended. Inside me there breathed a little girl in a swing who wanted nothing more than to soar high—up, up, up into the blue sky—as her pigtails flapped in the wind.

◆   ◆   ◆

"Your breakfast is here." Patricia woke me up, holding a metal plate with scrambled eggs, bacon, and toast on it. "There's coffee over there," she said, pointing to a matching cup on the picnic table in the middle of the room.

Two steel picnic tables were bolted to the floor. Everybody at the table watched me. There were women I had not seen the night before. All of them were black. I nodded to acknowledge them.

"Good morning," I said. "Thanks, but I don't want it," I told Patricia.

"You'd better eat."

"I'll eat lunch. I feel sick."

"It's those drugs you took. If you know what I know, you'll eat breakfast and skip lunch," Odessa said, and several women laughed.

I got up, searching the wall for a clock; there wasn't one.

"What time is it?" I asked.

"Five-thirty," Patricia said.

"How do you know?"

"Don't exactly. But breakfast comes between five and six," she said.

I had hoped she would point to a clock. One of the first details I noticed about jail was that I didn't see any clocks, an extremely difficult adjustment for a girl in a hurry. My life was based on racing, on living only for the day, on spending all the money I had, shooting all the dope I could get, on not trying to figure out the effect one moment had on another or how moments became days and then years, and how all of this established patterns that were extremely difficult to change because you had not realized the importance of the moments. I did not think about the future, what I wanted to be or do. Time was important to me, only because I wanted to know the hour so I could rush ahead, though I wasn't really going anywhere.

The absence of clocks was just one of an infinite number of conditions in jail aimed at reducing our sense of self-worth, which was ironic, because those of us who were incarcerated had walked into jail already thinking so little of ourselves. I was reduced to a number and a last name, to an existence that did not allow privacy, unable to express my singularity by the way I dressed or wore my hair. Yet I saw in some of the women just how easily they had accepted that this small space and these limited freedoms would be the perimeters of their lives. Would their lives be any freer outside?

◆ ◆ ◆

I jumped off the bed, curled my toes around the thongs of my shower shoes, and took my plate from Patricia. "Thanks," I said.

The thick aluminum tray was divided into three sections and reminded me of a plate from which animals ate. The food was cold, the toast was dry, and there was no butter or jelly. The only silverware we would ever get was a spoon.

"Good morning." Tanya was sitting at the table, her plate nearly empty.

I sat down across from her. The other women introduced themselves. In the light I could see that Odessa, who looked to be in her sixties, was probably the oldest. I picked at my food but decided it was too cold. Normally, I didn't drink coffee, but at least it was warm, so I sipped. "Where's the cream and sugar?" I asked.

Tanya laughed. "This is jail, girl. This ain't no café."

"No cream or sugar?" I needed confirmation.

"Nope," said Patricia.

"You want your coffee?" Tanya asked, clearly excited at the prospect of having another cup.

"No," I said.

She reached for it. I put my hand on her arm to stop her. For a moment our eyes locked on each other. "You want my coffee, Patricia?" I asked, not taking my hand off Tanya's arm or my eyes off her.

"Sure." Patricia laughed.

Tanya moved her arm, but her eyes remained on me. "Bitch," she snapped.

I gasped at my nerve, remembering my fear of Tanya just hours earlier. But that morning, tired and disgusted about being in jail, I didn't care if she tried to beat my ass. I needed to feel power over something—or someone.

On my second day, a guard called out my last name and I joined a line of women who had visitors. I knew it was someone from my family, probably my mother. My stomach ached with anxiety. Once I was arrested, it was inevitable that Mother would have to see me in jail. Now that moment had come. Here I was, her oldest child, standing in a wrinkled green prison dress, my hair nappy and knotted, a victim of the too thin plastic comb that was in the hygiene kit the guards gave me when I came in. Ironically, the comb must have been made for the hair of white people, though most of us in jail were black.

I walked into the visiting room, nearly frozen with dread. The room was more like a narrow hallway, with a thick glass partition down the middle. The prisoners stood on one side and the visitors on the other. We talked to each other through telephones. The guard pointed to a section of the glass, and I stepped up and saw my mother on the other side, her eyes red, her eyelids puffy, her mouth stiff and sad. She did not look like the mother who sang lullabies at my bedside when I was younger, when her soft, flawless face had reminded me of the moon.

I lifted my telephone receiver off the wall, and Mama did the same.

"Pat." That was all she said before her body began to shake from crying and tears ran down her cheeks.

"How's Andrea?" I asked.

"Fine. She misses her mommy."

"Wish I could see her." Tears dripped from my eyes.

Mother changed the subject. "Are you eating?"

"Yes. Sure."

She asked more questions about the food and conditions and how the other girls treated me. I tried to make her laugh, stepping away from the glass to show her my new dress and telling her about some of the funny antics of the women, about my new "bad" habits like drinking black coffee and playing cards.

Mama said she and Daddy had hired a lawyer who was trying to get my bond reduced. She questioned me about my arrest, but I refused to discuss it, fearful that someone was secretly listening to our conversation.

"I heard you had a pound of cocaine," she said.

"That's not true."

"Ben got out the day after the arrest." There was a "so there" tone to her voice. "He's back in Maryland."

I was surprised he hadn't tried to contact me, and I brooded over this for several evenings. But later I learned that the police, unable to hold Ben, since he hadn't had any drugs on him when he was arrested and hadn't sold them the marijuana, had ordered him out of North Carolina and threatened to arrest him if he ever returned. Meanwhile, James, like me, was still in jail.

"We can't do anything until they reduce your bond," Mama said. "I'm gonna stay in North Carolina awhile, so I can visit you. I'm leaving you some money downstairs." She paused. "Pat, when you get out, please leave that stuff alone."

I shook my head "okay," figuring no promise would sound convincing right now. When she left that day, I got terribly homesick, missing everything, but especially my mother's cooking. Her potato salad and fried chicken. Her collard greens and sweet potato pudding. A refrigerator where I could go to get food whenever I wanted. Saltshakers and pepper shakers. Sugar and cream.

I wanted spontaneity, delicate soap, bright-colored clothes, an Afro pick, sun and clouds and rain and rainbows. More books than I could read, five wristwatches on one arm. And tampons.

We were issued huge sanitary napkins and most of us in my cell preferred tampons. My cellmates, being ingenious, taught me how to make tampons: you cut a sanitary napkin in half, rolled it lengthwise, then inserted the rolled tube into your vagina so that the long tab of the napkin hung down like a string on a tampon. It was large and cumbersome, but because there were no virgins in jail, this method worked well for everyone.

The days developed a rhythm, and within the narrow confines of possibilities I chose my own routine. I got up when breakfast came, ate the food, and gave my coffee to Patricia. She drank it quickly and returned the cup so I could get water from the bathroom sink. We didn't get extra cups and we had to count aloud as we passed our plates and cups and spoons through the slot to the guards after we finished. If the count came up short, meaning one of the girls had kept an item, we would have a "shakedown," where guards came in to search the cell and then us. While I was in jail, the count in my cell came up accurately, so there were no shakedowns or punishment.

After breakfast, we cleaned up the cell. The guards brought us a broom, a mop, a bucket, cleanser, and rags. Twice a week we stacked our linen and nightgowns at the door to be picked up and laundered. But even these practices couldn't stop our bouts with lice and crabs. We were always scratching and begging to see the doctor. I tried to take my shower first because the hot water ran out quick. A shower lasted three minutes and you weren't supposed to take longer, though Tanya sometimes hit the button four or five times, hogging the shower. She didn't do it often, though, because Odessa would tear back the curtain and yank her out of there.

The first time I saw Odessa do that, I stepped back to wait for the fight. But Tanya, as it turned out, wasn't as tough as she pretended to be. Odessa reduced her to the bare truth. Tanya was a pathetic, lonely young girl, getting attention the only way she knew how—through intimidation and drama.

I generally took a nap at lunchtime, because the lunch was a gray mush that bore no resemblance to food. The first time I saw it, I asked, "What is it?"

"What did you have for breakfast this morning? What did we have for dinner last night?" Odessa asked. "That's what you got for lunch, honey."

When I heard them coming with the lunch, that was my cue to go to bed. I slept for an hour or so, then woke up and played more cards or read. Patricia liked to read and we exchanged books, mostly novels by black writers.

"You're gonna like the big jail," my cellmates kept saying to me, since they were so sure I was going to serve time in the state institution. "In the big jail you get to wear some of your own clothes and you can go to school."

"I'm not going to the big jail," I said. I had no idea how my case would be disposed, but I could not imagine months or years of a life like this.

About once a week we were allowed to line up and march down to get some of our money and then go to the vending machines. Visitors could leave money for us, so we each had accounts. We could get a few dollars at a time. On our way to the vending machines, we passed some of the male orderlies. The entire trip was our thrill of the week. The matrons, the females who guarded us, knew this and most gave us at least an hour's notice so we could primp and fix our hair before our stroll. As promised, the girls had altered my jail dress. Somehow they had gotten enough safety pins for each of us to have just the right number to hem our dresses to mini length. We passed those orderlies, strutting our ashy legs. The orderlies, not caring what color our dry, lotionless skin had turned, were just happy to see female legs, and they whistled their admiration.

None of us seemed to realize what we were doing, that even in jail we were performing for men, hoping to please them and exalting in our ability to do so. Most of us thought it was an innocent ritual, though the most wicked among us considered it a chance to taunt the orderlies, even if it meant they saw our faces as they whipped their dicks that night.

I learned to tell time by using the meals as a guide and by looking at the amount of sunlight filtering through the narrow, tinted slit windows. Also, there was a white woman in another cell who had a television set and we could tell time by the theme songs from our favorite programs, like *Concentration, The Edge of Night,* or *Perry Mason.* The rumor was that the woman was a madam who ran a large whorehouse popular with the town politicians and police officials, and that when she was arrested she requested a private cell and a television.

I preferred my cellmates to television; they were more entertaining. Before we went to sleep each night, we lay awake in bed talking about what we were going to do the next day.

"I'm going to Neiman-Marcus," said Patricia, who knew about the better stores because she had traveled more than most of us. Her boyfriend was a big-time hustler with lots of cash. Unfortunately, neither of them would be shopping again any time soon. He was going to spend years in jail for murder, and Patricia was expecting to do big time for her cocaine distribution charge.

"I'll meet you out in front of the store," I said. "I'll have on my orange miniskirt and a white silk blouse."

"Odessa and I are going to cop some smack, and we'll meet you at the Krispy Kreme," Tanya said.

We all cracked up, because it was a popular pastime in Charlotte to get high and then go to the Krispy Kreme for freshly baked, hot doughnuts. The parking lot was packed with cars full of people with droopy eyes, some of them hanging out the windows. Red-eyed patrons ran in and out of the store, hyped up on more than sugar.

"I want the honey-dipped," Odessa said.

"Get me a cup of black coffee," I said, and we all hollered with laughter.

We went on like that for twenty minutes or so, talking shit, embellishing tales, joning, until we couldn't stand it anymore. Then we fell asleep, exhausted from our lies and our longings. We fell asleep contented, too, in a way in which many of us had never been with our men. We gave each other laughter to help us through the night; we leaned on each other because we were all we had, and we discovered we were strong enough to hold up one another. Social and class lines disappeared; proper English rested comfortably in the air beside split verbs and dangling participles. We thought we had learned something that would last forever, but those of us who walked out of that jail shortly after that summer forgot those nights and those friendships. We returned to our men, to the world where we ignored our sisters and believed we were lonely and less if we didn't have a man.

Being in jail reminded me of high school and Ginny, before we lost our virginity and offered ourselves up to men, a time when we had been best friends. In jail we saw past the lies, clean through to the truths in each other, even the tough girls like Tanya. Our lives were at a standstill, and at that speed we could see the others' vulnerabilities and the ways in which we were alike; we developed compassion. We understood that visiting days weren't just happy and raucous, but also solemn occasions, when we were reminded that our children were out there beyond the bars—and our reach. We watched our sisters return from the visiting rooms so fragile we could see through them like spotless glass. We let them break into pieces in our arms.

Sometimes Patricia and I lay awake talking. Her bed was right across from mine. She talked about her three-year-old son, whom she

missed, and I talked about Andrea. At those moments, in the night
when only the light from the street lamps and the moon poured over
us, I forgot Patricia had been in jail most of her adult life, that she had
even been in jail when she gave birth to her son. There, in the bed,
talking about teething and disciplining, we were just two mothers
missing our children.

"I swear I'm never coming here again," she said, and I wanted
badly to believe her.

"I know I'm never coming back," I said bravely.

A few weeks later, Odessa got out. Before she walked out of the cell
we patted her on the back, kissed her cheeks, and warned her, "Don't
let us see your black ass back in here."

"You'll see ya mama here 'fo' you see me," she said.

She was back two nights later. About 3:00 A.M. the doors woke
us up with their clanking. We looked and there was Odessa stumbling in.

"Odessa?" Patricia was the first to reach her. "You'd better sit
down. You're drunk."

"Your mama." She reeked of liquor and she squinted her eyes.

Tanya grabbed her arrest papers. "Public drunk. Assaulting a police officer?"

"You got some nerve since you left," I said.

"Shouldn't have put me in his car," she said.

We laughed. Most of us were up now. "Better lie down," one girl
said to Odessa. "You can have my bunk. It's on the bottom."

"Don't want ya stinky bunk. I ain't catching lice."

"If any lice here, you brung um," the girl scoffed, walking away.

We encouraged Odessa to take the bottom bunk, but she insisted
on having her old bed, which meant a new girl, whom she didn't even
know, had to move. At first the girl argued. Then, seeing that no one
was going to get any rest until the question of where Odessa would
sleep was settled, the girl got up.

Odessa struggled to climb on top. She was on the ladder, leaning over the bed, with her butt hanging out the open back of her
nightgown.

"Dessa, you's a nasty bitch," said Tanya, who got out of the bed and used her shoulder to push Odessa over the ladder onto her bed.

"Yeah, and you'll do anything for a feel," Odessa said. Five minutes later she was snoring.

I woke up to an awful smell. Odessa had puked in her bed. Tanya got her up and took her to the shower. I pulled her sheets off her bed so we could ask the guard to take them out and give her some clean ones. Odessa was alert but irritable, partly because she had a hangover and partly because she couldn't believe she was back in jail.

At the breakfast table she told us what had happened.

"I remember I came out the juke joint. Some man was calling me, telling me to come back. You know me, though. Ain't gonna listen to no man. I knew I was drunk 'cause I had on one shoe. Couldn't find the other one, but I was ready to go home. Was gonna walk 'fo' I realized which juke joint I was at and it wasn't too near my house.

"So I decided to flag me down a cab. Only trouble is I flagged down a police car instead."

"You flagged down a police car, 'dessa?" Tanya spat out a mouthful of coffee and we all laughed harder than we were already doing.

"Sho did."

"What the police say?" I asked.

" 'Get in.' "

We doubled over in laughter.

Odessa continued. "He started off and a few miles up the road—see, at the time, I'm still thinking this is a cab—I said to him, 'How ya know where I'm going? I didn't give you my address."

"He's real slick. Hardly laughed. I know he was cracking up inside. Said, 'I'm psychic, lady. I know where to take you.' Next thing I know he's opening the door for me. I still don't get it. I'm getting out my money and saying to myself, 'This is the nicest white man I ever met.' "

"Stop it, 'dessa," Patricia said, laughing. "You're making this up."

"How you think I got that assault charge? He said, 'Keep ya money. You gonna need it to get a lawyer.' I looked up and saw this place again and commenced to beating him with my fist. Another cop ran out and they handcuffed me."

Odessa was our entertainment and we were glad to have her back.

We didn't laugh at her, but with her. We loved her for her sense of humor. We appreciated the way she stimulated laughter in us. When we laughed, while our bodies trembled from our breathless giggles, we could forget briefly where we were and who we were. I had always loved to laugh, but in jail laughter took on a new meaning. It was the closest feeling to being free.

Everybody knew Odessa. The police. The lawyers. The guards. The girls told me she used to be a cleaning lady at the courthouse, before her teenage son shot himself playing Russian roulette. Then her weekend drinking binges stretched into the weekdays. Now she was the kindhearted public drunk who never hurt anybody.

◆   ◆   ◆

I woke up one night to hear Patricia calling my name. Before jail, it took an extremely loud noise to wake me up, but now at the softest sounds I was up and alert.

"What's up?" I said, my feet already on the floor.

She pointed to Tanya, who was in bed writhing in her sheets and moaning.

"She's having one of them spells," Odessa said as she began walking about the cell waking up everyone else.

I was confused. "A spell?"

"Epilepsy," said Patricia. "We gotta make some noise and get the doctor."

Tanya was jerking more violently now. Her arms flailed about and she sounded like she was gagging. Odessa put a washcloth in her mouth. Tanya's eyes rolled back in her head and she looked pale.

We screamed, "We need a doctor! Get a doctor!" And five minutes later, when we were tiring, we just hollered over and over, "Doctor! Doc-tor!"

Someone pulled out an aluminum cup and banged on the bars. Every face was distorted by fear. Patricia kept a close watch on Tanya. At least ten minutes passed. Tanya stopped jerking.

"She's coming back!" Patricia yelled.

We all turned to look and saw Tanya's eyes opening and her body trembling only slightly now.

"She still needs to see a doctor," said Odessa.

We started yelling again, all kinds of things.

"We need help in here!"

"Muthafuckas!"

"Fight! Fight!"

Odessa yelled, "Fire!" and we all looked at her.

"What they gonna do? Arrest me?" she said, and we paused to laugh.

It was a half hour before a slot in the steel door opened and an irritated guard growled, "Whatdoya want?"

Tanya was sitting on the picnic table when two guards came in to escort her to see the doctor. They handcuffed her first.

"That girl don't need no handcuffs; she needs a wheelchair," Odessa said.

Tanya, walking slightly slower than normal, turned back and winked. "Take me away. A person can't sleep worth a shit in here," she said.

I was too tired to laugh. I fell asleep wondering if a person could fake an epileptic fit.

◆　◆　◆

I went to court two times before my bond was reduced. The night before my first appearance I couldn't sleep, thinking about walking outside and across the street to the courthouse. I imagined the warmth of the sun on my arms, the wind rippling through my Afro. How long could you stare at the sun without going blind?

I told only Patricia about my anticipation.

She whispered the truth as gently as she could: "Pat, honey, you won't get to go outside. They'll take you through the tunnel that runs underground."

I went to bed early, my face to the wall so no one could see the tears running from my eyes.

"Don't let it get to you," Patricia said. "Think about seeing your family there and being in a different room."

I lay there considering how my freedom was so limited that changing from one room to another was a major event. I swore I would never return to jail. Never. My life had to change. Nothing convinced me of this more than the day my mother visited me while Andrea waited outside with the rest of my family.

"Can you see outside?" my mother asked before leaving.

"What?"

"Do you have a window in your cell?"

"Yeah, long, narrow ones."

"What side?"

I can see the street and the courthouse."

Fifteen minutes later, I strained to peep out the window. My mama, my grandfather, my aunt, and my baby were out there, looking up, searching for me. I missed them more at that moment than I had at any time since I had walked into that cell. I missed my family so much I ached all over. My insides vibrated like a tuning fork. The hands inside that cell could not heal me of my pain. I longed to touch my family, to laugh and joke with my sisters about their corny boyfriends, to scream and run as my young brother terrorized us with his snakes, to ride through Rock Creek Park with my father driving ten miles per hour and a line of cars honking behind us. My family, like every family, had its own history, and I appreciated it more than I had ever realized before.

I looked outside at those relatives standing below with Andrea, all of them seeming to look in different directions as they tried to find me. My daughter looked so confused. Tears dripped down onto my dress. Patricia walked over and placed her hands on my shoulders to comfort me.

"My daughter can't find me," I said.

chapter seven

What's Freedom Got to Do with It

*J*ust before the Fourth of July, I went home with my family to Maryland. My bond was finally reduced from $100,000 to an amount my family could afford. My mother, an aunt, and some friends came to get me. I walked out of jail into the white sun, squinting to adjust my eyes to the brightest light I had seen in nearly a month. I paused, sucked in a deep breath, and rolled my eyes over everything I saw—a dark-skinned elderly black man with skinny legs and knobbed knees, wearing plaid shorts; the hot pavement, glistening as if it had cut glass in it; a battered green Volkswagen Beetle stalled at the curb.

My first stop was a doctor's office, where my mother took me so I could get rid of the crabs and itching that had plagued me off and on for weeks. In the mirror, a poor, scrawny, pale woman with a wild Afro and sunken cheeks stared at me. Once I got home to Maryland, I stuffed myself with food and sat out in the afternoon sun, trying to erase the telltale signs that I had been deprived of light, food, touch.

I arrived in Maryland just in time to be a bridesmaid in Ginny's wedding, feeling terribly out of place among college girls. I had talked to her a few months earlier, crying with her because her fifteen-year-old brother had died of a brain tumor. Now she was to march up to the same church altar where her brother's body had lain. I was still scratching from crabs and lice, and Ginny and her friends were still giddy over having just graduated from college. Ginny's new best friend from college was the maid of honor, a fact I viewed as evidence of the different choices Ginny and I had made. She had gone off to college and found a man there to marry; I had stayed home and followed a man to jail.

Within a month we were back in North Carolina for my trial. My mother and my Aunt Fannie, my father's sister, were with me. From the defendant's chair, where I sat next to my lawyer, I looked back at them. Their lips stretched into unnatural smiles. I wished that my father was with us, to sit tall and look like a soldier. But Daddy, the conscientious worker, had stayed at home so he wouldn't miss any more days on his job. I hated him for his absence, though at the time I didn't think it was hate. It was more like resignation, an acceptance of the fact that my father didn't care enough about me to take off work to be there when I received my sentence. To me then, it was one more act of negligence on my father's part. I gave it much thought, and it stayed with me for years, adding to the other dismissals and absences of attention that I felt from him until my hatred for him would amount to a flood and I would have to swim against the tide of my own pain to find my way back to the man he truly was.

I was stunned that my mother, my aunt, and I were the only black people in the room. It was then that I missed my father and wished that we had a man with us to make us feel protected. But there was nothing a black man could have done for me in that courtroom. The law was white: the judge, the lawyers, the clerks, the guards, the court stenographer, and the curious onlookers.

On the advice of my lawyer and the insistence of my mother, I wore my white look: conservative office clothes and long, straight hair. My mother had pressed my huge Afro flat the night before in my aunt's kitchen. My eyelids had swollen into huge lumps, which made my face look strange and monstrous and meant I could hardly see. The doctor diagnosed me as suffering from a nervous reaction caused by stress.

I was more frightened than I had ever been, more frightened than I was my first night in jail. Years later, when I was a reporter covering trials, watching defendants stand for sentencing, I was sure that each of them saw his life flicker before him, thought of what could have been, what should have been, how one good decision could have erased the present. It is a humbling experience to have to wait for someone else to decide your fate. Some people get over it in the next second, returning to their disposition and their crimes; others of us never get over it. We may not change instantly, because that's not how change occurs, anyway. We make up our minds to live differently, and then we do what we need to do to change all of the corners and crevices of our souls that need cleaning before we can reshape ourselves. Change is a monumental accomplishment, and it involves for each of us tasks that appear small, such as learning to put everything in its place in your house, or tasks that seem large, such as getting old friends out of your life and finding new ones. It is a long, difficult process that takes patience and perseverance, and along the way we stumble, but we never fall as low as we were before the moment we decided to change. I had my first moment at that window in jail; now I had my second—in court.

On my behalf, my lawyer had already negotiated a deal with the judge. I had been given two choices: go before a jury and present my case and risk receiving the maximum penalty of five years in prison, or plead guilty, passing up a jury trial, saving the state money and getting me five years of probation. I took the five years' probation, which also included a monthly fine, totaling $2,000, to be paid during those years.

As I sat waiting to hear the judge's words, my eyes fell on my own small, trembling brown hands and I realized where my real power lay. Even as a child, I had felt powerless. But as I was looking at these white men, it struck me that I had always given away my power—to my parents, to teachers, to men I loved.

It was as if I had been living in the dark with all of my belongings piled in the middle of what I thought was a tiny room. Then someone turned on a light and I saw floor and space and windows and realized I didn't have to live in a heap, that there might even be other doors leading to rooms in the house. And these little hands could open those doors.

❖   ❖   ❖

Before the disposition of my case, I had gone to Du Pont to pick up my paycheck, naive enough to think I could continue working there, at least until I was proven guilty. A company official, a white man in a wrinkled dark suit, had invited my mother and me into a small, stark office, handed me my last paycheck, and told me I was fired because I had not called in to discuss my absence with my supervisors. He shook my hand and wished me well. He reached for Mama's hand, but she ignored him and turned and walked out the office.

My roommate, Roberta, told me that rumors about me had flourished among my ex-coworkers. "So that's how she could afford to dress so well; she was selling that stuff," one woman said. "She looked like she was high. I bet she used to shoot heroin in the bathroom, because whenever I was in there she was in the stall," said another.

I felt a twinge of shame because my white coworkers, who had always considered me less because I was black, would point to my drug use as evidence to support their racism. But my shame was equaled by my anger at their already distorted views. It was more difficult for me to deal with the shame I felt because I sensed I had let down the elderly black people who worked at Du Pont with me: the man I spoke to each afternoon when he emptied my trash basket; the woman I ran into in the ladies' room, where she scrubbed toilets. When they smiled at me as I sat at my teletype machine, their faces were as bright as suns and their pride in me seemed to warm my blood. I did not want to see those eyes now, hurt and blank, staring at me as if they did not recognize or understand what they saw. Being fired relieved me from seeing them, though the shame I bore remained for years.

❖   ❖   ❖

Roberta had moved out of the apartment while I was in jail, obviously deciding that while she could be friends with people who did drugs, she couldn't live with someone who had been busted. I was disappointed, but I had already seen that we were too different to live together. Anyway, after jail, I wanted Andrea with me more than ever, so I searched for a job and prayed for a place to live.

As soon as I was out of jail, the black minister of a Presbyterian church I had attended occasionally introduced me to a black family he thought could help me. The Austins had two sons and two daughters, all tall and thin. They lived in a large, old one-story house with a big front porch and a creaking wooden swing. Mr. and Mrs. Austin were compassionate people, active in the community and serving as scout leaders and ushers in their church. Andrea and I went to live with them, sharing a room with one of their daughters, a quiet, pretty girl who was so shy she seemed to fold in on herself, her shoulders straining to press in closer to each other. She was slightly younger than I was, but we seemed years apart. She was usually on the bed reading when I crept in late at night, stumbling from my high. I was still finding drugs when I wanted them. While she listened to the Jackson Five, I played Jimi Hendrix with Buddy Miles or my worn copy of Iron Butterfly's "In-A-Gadda-Da-Vida," seventeen minutes of pure bliss for me and hell for her.

For a while I attended a community college, studying English and shorthand, with the goal of becoming an executive secretary or an administrative assistant. I had discovered that typing, by itself, would not earn me a good salary. But add shorthand and other office skills, and my worth rose. So I woke up before six o'clock each morning, dressed, then woke up Andrea, who nodded and went limp while I combed her huge Afro and dressed her. Mr. Austin dropped us at the community college, where Andrea attended a campus day-care center while I went to class. Some mornings I took her with me and she sat beside me in class, coloring in one of my old notebooks. In the afternoon, Mr. Austin picked us up and we went home.

I wasn't at all prepared for the rejection of being a convicted felon. On job applications I answered "yes" to the question: "Have you ever been convicted of a felony?" Then I explained the facts in the space offered. My thinking was that it was best to be honest, and that, anyway, it was just one mistake for which I had suffered already. But employers didn't see it my way, and once interviewers took a look at my application, they said, "I'm sorry."

I shrank with each rejection, shriveling into nothing, which was what I imagined these people who refused to interview me saw as they looked at my perfectly coiffed straight hair and my classic suits. I was being cast aside now not just because of my race, but because I had done something wrong that allowed employers to exercise all their prejudices. Their rejection transported me back to first grade, where I was hated by my white teacher, though I did all of my lessons perfectly; I was in high school, where my white teacher would not call on me, though my hand waggled in the air above the others; I was at home with my father, who sat silently before me each day, never hugging or kissing or even speaking to me. Each rejection in my life cut me where I had been cut before until my inner self was an open wound.

I was angry, too, that the world was so hypocritical. It asked me to be honest, then punished me for telling the truth. But I didn't know how to fight, so I carried my anger and pain with me—in silence, tricking myself into believing it was hidden and under control. Because I couldn't find a job, I hid out in school. In college the most important things I learned didn't come from my books, but from discovering I wasn't as dumb as I had believed I was.

College was enjoyable, too, because it was drastically different from high school in ways that mattered to me. There were no bells. No one to force me to go to class or to threaten to put me out if I didn't attend. I could do my homework, if I wanted to. Or I could fail. It was up to me. I didn't fully understand why, but not having rul or authorities hanging over me motivated me to do everything right. I went to class every day, on time, eager to learn.

After getting good grades on papers I wrote, I risked answering questions aloud. Teachers encouraged me to talk more and thanked me for my contributions to discussions. My confidence soared.

A semester later, my unemployment benefits ran out and I had to leave school. I was determined, though, to continue my education once I got settled. Mr. Austin got me a clerical position earning a little over one hundred dollars a week working with him at a nonprofit organization that trained people in various skills and then found them employment. The job was close enough to our house that I went home each day to have lunch with Andrea. No one cared that I was a convicted felon, because the program itself had been established to help people in transition, people who had experienced all types of failures in their lives.

Whenever they gave tests to the staff on the job, I earned the highest or second-highest score among the clerical workers, so a counselor there suggested I get a student loan and attend the University of North Carolina. I was excited about the possibility and decided to study social work. But I was greatly disappointed when a man at the admissions office told me I didn't meet requirements to even apply to the school; I needed to have graduated in the upper half of my high school class.

In a letter to my mother, I explained what happened:

> I rapped to the man for a while. I asked him didn't they take into consideration the changes a person has been through since high school or the work they have done. The result: He's sending my application before the board because they hold the power to make an exception. Meanwhile, I'm going to write the Dean of Admissions and if I'm turned down, Friday I'm going to set up an appointment with the board myself.

The board rejected my application. When I received the letter informing me, I read it fast then tore it to shreds and fell on my bed, sobbing. Now that I wanted to learn, no one was willing to give me a chance.

◆　◆　◆

Ben and I corresponded by phone and through letters, but our love had turned into a friendship, which suited us both. I didn't pressure him about being financially responsible for Andrea, because I still blamed myself for the broken bond between them. On the other hand, Ben was not the kind of father who was responsible on his own. That never bothered me, though, probably because I never expected much from anyone and didn't think I deserved anything. I forgot, it was Andrea—and not me—that he owed. When I visited Maryland, he usually picked her up and spent time with her.

After several months on my new job, I started dating Charles Williams, a manager at the agency who was a couple of years older than I was. He was a short, bony guy with amber skin, a medium-size Afro, sideburns, and a bridgeless nose on which he could barely keep up gold wire-rimmed glasses. Charles endeared himself to me by including Andrea on some of our dates. I considered him more like Phillip than Ben, though he was more mature than both, since he was already a college graduate at the beginning of a career. He made my heart flutter, which I interpreted as the beginning of love. But what I felt was actually fear. Deep inside, I believed he was too good and too perfect for me, so in his presence I trembled, afraid I would betray myself with some silly mistake and he would know that I was not really worldly or sophisticated, but just a stupid girl who was trying to be a woman. Sometimes I stuttered in his presence, though I had never before suffered from a speech impediment of any kind. When we went to bed, I was frigid.

Frigid was a word I had heard but ignored because I was a twenty-two-year-old sex machine. Yet when I crawled into bed with Charles, I was paralyzed, unable to think of one tender or erotic act. I lay stiff as a corpse with my brain searching for an explanation, while he did what he wanted or what he could with me. I have no idea what he thought, though I don't think he thought of me often, anyway.

I know that if I mispronounced a word he corrected me, which only made me more enamored of him and angry at myself for being so dumb. In the evenings, I sat on his porch waiting for him to come home and when he did I cleaned his apartment, washing the dishes encrusted with mold, vacuuming the corners thick with dust.

When we dated, which was never as frequently as I wanted, we visited his friends or went to nightclubs to listen to jazz. In retrospect, I believe he kept a healthy distance, standing back to look at us, to see if he wanted our relationship to develop. I plowed ahead, my feelings always just ahead of reality. We often went to a club owned by one of his closest friends, "J.B.," who sometimes kept the place open after hours for his favorite patrons.

J.B. was too much of a braggart, too full of himself, for me to want to know him. He was a charmer, though, a good businessman and a delightful host.

Roberta and I still hung out occasionally, and one night while we were together we dropped by J.B.'s club. I was hoping to see Charles—who I hadn't seen in about a week—but he wasn't there.

"He's supposed to come by my house later, after I close up," J.B. whispered to me. "He told me if I saw you to tell you to drop by."

It was Friday and J.B. was closing up about 1:00 A.M., so Roberta and I were at his house an hour later. Charles wasn't there.

"He should be here soon," J.B. said.

He mixed us drinks and we talked for about fifteen minutes. J.B. left the room and was in the back of the house for another fifteen minutes. Roberta fell asleep on the sofa.

I went to the hallway. "Hey, J.B., we're gonna go!" I hollered.

He stuck his head out of one room. "Before you go, come here. Let me show you something."

I went down the hall and into the bedroom, where he was sitting on the bed. The rest is blurry: I believe he was sitting on the bed holding a photo album and I went over to look at it. They were high school pictures, with some friends I knew in them. I felt dizzy and thought I was going to pass out.

"You can lie right here," J.B. said, standing and placing my legs onto the bed.

I lay back on a pillow and collapsed into asleep. I don't know how long I was out, but I woke up because J.B.'s fingers were tugging at my panties.

"No. You can't do that," I said. I wanted to scream, but my speech was slurred and it took all my energy to speak.

We struggled, but it wasn't much of a fight. I was weak. For the first time it donned on me that J.B. must have drugged me and Roberta, and I was terrified.

"Roberta." I tried to yell, but her name just fell out of my mouth.

My panties were down. J.B. had my arms pinned against the pillow, over my head. He was on top of me. I was weak and helpless.

"Roberta," I said, but there was no answer.

J.B. was inside me, I was sure, though I couldn't feel his penis or my vagina. He was on top of me, his chest on mine, his face turned to the side. When he got up, I fell asleep.

◆   ◆   ◆

I woke up about eight in the morning, groggy, trying to focus on furniture I didn't recognize. Then I remembered what had happened. I tried to jump up and run, but everything was in slow motion.

I stumbled into the living room. J.B. wasn't there. I woke up Roberta. She was too drugged to drive, so I drove. She didn't remember a thing about the night, and she was shocked when I recounted how J.B. had attacked me.

"What are you going to do?" she asked.

This was 1971 and there was no such thing as "date rape," or at least no term to describe what women knew to be an accepted fact of life. If a woman claimed she was raped, it was her word against the man's word, her reputation against his, especially if she knew him. J.B. had a reputation as a hardworking businessman; I was a secretary and a convicted felon, a single woman with an illegitimate child. Both Roberta and I thought what J.B. had done was immoral, but our minds did not venture to consider it criminal.

By the next day I had even convinced myself that I had not been raped. I had been "done wrong," but I had not been raped. J.B. was a no-good coward; a deceitful, sinful man, but he couldn't possibly be a rapist. Rapists were not people you knew.

Charles and I went out on several more dates, but he began to call less frequently. I considered telling him about J.B., but I didn't think he would believe me. And when I passed Charles in the office, I wondered if J.B. hadn't already concocted some lie that included my willingly sleeping with him.

Two months later, after I missed my period, I went to a doctor and found out I was pregnant. I had been taking my birth control pills irregularly, forgetting some days, tripling the dosage to make up on other days. It was foolish, but it was the way I handled all elements of my life in those days—lagging behind, doing extra in a scramble to catch up. People who feel they have very little control in their lives, anyway, use such warped logic every day.

Riding the bus from the doctor's office, I considered suicide. I couldn't live knowing I might be pregnant with J.B.'s child. Should I take an overdose of pills? Should I slit my wrist? Suicide was all I thought of—until I got home and saw my daughter.

She had on red corduroy pants and a striped red-and-white shirt. It was a plain, inexpensive outfit, but she was beautiful. When I walked into the house, she ran to me and grabbed me around my legs, holding me until I bent down and lifted her up in my arms. She had the fattest cheeks and I kissed her soft skin and knew I wanted to feel it for as long as God would allow. I always felt that way when I held her, as if holding onto her all the time could save me. She held me to this earth, kept my feet on the ground so I would not fly away. It was hard for me to lose my mind while I was braiding her hair. Or nearly impossible to think about drugs if I forced myself to read *Little Red Riding Hood* over and over, each time Andrea pushed it in my face begging for me to read it again.

But after I had tucked her into bed that night, my demons returned. I sat, haunted, listening to my forty-five of "One Less Bell to Answer" by the Fifth Dimension, playing it softly until it was warped, grieving for myself, for what I had lost and for the difficulties I sensed were ahead of me.

I told Charles I was pregnant and I asked him to give me $250, half the cost of an abortion.

"It's not my baby," he said.

"What do you mean?" I was shocked.

"It's impossible. I can't have children," he said.

"Then how did I get pregnant?" I sat in his office crying, not knowing whether or not he was telling me the truth. I hurt too much to ask. I wiped my tears with the back of my hand, stood, and, with my chin as straight ahead as possible, walked out of his office.

I seldom spoke to him after that, even over the next month, as I tried to arrange an abortion. On some level I must have realized I didn't know whose baby I was carrying. But it was easier to be a victim of rape than to accept the possibility that Charles, whom I loved,

could be lying. That would mean I was being rejected again by someone I had thought loved me at least enough to tell me the truth, especially when I was asking for so little. On the other hand, I had no
emotional investment in J.B.; I had never expected anything from
him. Within a year, though, Charles was dating another girl. Some
years later they got married and had a son.

◆   ◆   ◆

Abortions were illegal in North Carolina, but for $500 Dr. Shaw, a
gynecologist, would ignore the law. He was a ruddy, robust man with
graying hair and huge hands that swallowed my small fingers when he
greeted me with a handshake at his back door, after regular office
hours. He instructed me to take off my clothes and put on a paper
gown. My first clue to leave was his thick, slurred speech—was he
drunk? Still, I followed his instructions and sat trembling until he returned.

He appeared indifferent about what had brought us together,
speaking in a detached monotone, saying very little. He examined me
in a dimly lit room with cheap brown paneling, thrusting his gloveless
hands inside my vagina without one word of comfort.

"Dear, you've got to relax," he said. Then, after prodding my insides with his fingers, he added, "You're about four months. Why'd
you wait so long?"

I resented the question, and the tears that ran down my cheeks
were as close to an answer as I could offer. My legs were still in the
stirrups when he leaned over and whispered in my ear, "I can do it
next Saturday. Bring $500."

His breath smelled like liquor laced with mint candy.

"Okay," I said, knowing I would never return.

◆   ◆   ◆

In Washington, I learned, I could get an abortion legally if a psychiatrist said having the baby would adversely affect my mental health. I
resigned from my job, and two weeks later Andrea and I caught a ride

to Washington with a friend of mine. I had very little money, so I applied for Medicaid, which would pay for a psychiatric exam and the abortion. By the time my application was processed, though, I was more than four months pregnant. Another month later, dressed in maternity clothes, I saw a psychiatrist. After one visit, he recommended an abortion, saying I suffered from severe depression.

His diagnosis was accurate. The fatter I got, the more I withdrew from the world, passing mirrors without looking at myself, staying inside my girlfriend's apartment, trying to be invisible. I wrote long, self-indulgent poems about darkness and tears. It was an effort to get up each morning, to bathe and dress and to comb my hair. It was even more difficult for me to care for Andrea. My nerves were frazzled, and in my depression her normal mischievousness drove me crazy. We were together—alone. All day. Every day. Adding to this was the pressure of living with a girlfriend who was single and not used to children and didn't want Andrea touching anything in the apartment.

I sat on the sofa one morning, staring at the television but not really watching it. I had no idea what program was on, and I was only vaguely aware of Andrea playing around me. Maybe the kid wanted attention or maybe she was simply being a three-year-old. Anyway, she started playing with the control knobs of the television. I don't know how long I stared at the screen before I realized that there was no picture, only zigzag lines, and that Andrea was still standing there, turning knobs back and forth. This was a minor infraction, one for which I usually would have tapped her hand. But on this morning I grabbed her by one arm, held her in the air, and whacked her with the other, over and over.

I don't know how many times I hit her. I heard a shriek and recognized it was my child's voice. I grabbed her in my arms. I was shaking uncontrollably. I sat her on the sofa to check her for bruises, to make sure she was okay. She started gagging. I picked her up again, pressed her to my breast, and patted her back while I walked toward the kitchen to get her a cup of water. Before I got the water, she threw up, her vomit rolling down my back. I ignored it, got a cup of water, and let her drink it slowly.

When she was calm, I rocked her to sleep in my arms, whispering,

"I love you," in her ear and wiping her cheeks with the back of my hand. *What does she think of me?* I wondered. How could I hurt the person I loved more than I loved myself? This was my proof that I was sick, and after that day I vowed not to trust myself alone with my child until I was well again. I knew I would be unfit to care for her until after the abortion, after the depression lifted its dark cloak from my days and nights. I packed Andrea's clothes and took her to my mother, whom I begged to keep my child until I could be a mother again.

I had not recovered from Charles's refusal to help me pay for the abortion. In some way, his refusal was like being raped again. I had not asked him to love me, or to take care of me or the baby. Because I believed I had asked for so little, I was profoundly humiliated when he said, "No." I called Ben, Andrea's father, who listened to me, offered advice, and tried to cheer me. He was getting married soon, and he and his fiancée sometimes picked up Andrea to keep her for a day or two. When I needed to go to the abortion clinic, Ben gave me a ride. By the time I went for my abortion, I was six months pregnant.

The health clinic was in a decaying brick building that was once an elementary school. Though abortions were legal in Washington, they weren't widely or easily available. There was still a good-girls-don't-do-that mentality, and a woman like me, someone who would kill a baby after it had spent six months in her belly, was truly an abomination of the human race. Even the people who worked in the clinic, and therefore might be expected to be sensitive and empathetic, seemed to have made up personal rules for when abortion was okay and when it wasn't, and their beliefs had nothing to do with law. From the horrible way they treated me, I suspected some of the doctors and nurses were performing my abortion because they wanted to save the baby from me.

None of this surprised me; abortions were supposed to be horrid, it was the price you paid for your sin. I was willing to pay. I never allowed myself to regret the abortion, because if I ever did I feared I would go insane. In later years, as I looked for the blessing within this trauma, I concluded that a wonderful spirit, an angel, had traveled with me for six months and had seen me through the difficulties I had

created. But that spirit knew it would not be born into this world
through me and did not hate me or begrudge me that. It was a spirit
that had other work to do and would come into this world when it
chose. I will love it forever, for its sacrifice and forgiveness.

◆   ◆   ◆

"Who is the father?" a middle-aged black nurse asked me during the
preliminary exam before the abortion.

I hadn't expected that question. I sat in a chair next to her desk, my
lips tight, my hands folded across the bottom of my stomach.

"There *must* be a father." She craned her neck, leaned over to stare
into my face, and opened her eyes mockingly.

"I don't wanna use his name," I mumbled.

"Maybe next time you should go to bed with someone whose
name you can use. Better still, go to bed with somebody who will
marry you."

I began to cry. She looked at me with disgust.

"You can step into the next room and wait," she said.

I couldn't believe that I had been directed to a room where young
pregnant girls were watching a black woman show them how to
change a baby's diaper. I didn't want to be around pregnant women,
or care to see a child-care demonstration. But before a nurse came to
get me, I found amusement in the fact that all the young girls watching
were black, but the doll baby the woman was using was white.

A doctor whose face I do not remember injected me with saline
solution to induce labor, and they put me on a cot in a room with two
other black girls who were undergoing the same procedure. One girl
was thirteen, another fifteen. I was the oldest at twenty-two.

The thirteen-year-old screamed first. She hollered so much the
nurse brought in the girl's mother to hold her hand. Then they moved
me into a private room. I sweated and moaned. It seemed that hours
passed. I prayed for forgiveness and promised God sacrifices I would
not remember a week later. I cursed Charles and J.B. and then, finally,
all men. Occasionally, a female nurse peeped in the room, then turned
and left. Finally, she and the doctor came in. The two of them pressed

on my stomach and sides and told me to push. The nurse held an aluminum pan under my vagina, and the fetus dropped into it.

"Get some rest," she said as she and the doctor left the room.

When she returned, I asked, "Was it a girl or boy?"

"Why would you care?" she said, walking out of the room.

I was appalled at her question and yet I didn't know the answer myself. Another nurse came in minutes later. I asked her the same question.

"I'm not supposed to tell you this," she said. "It was a boy."

chapter eight

Only the
Child Is Sane

I walked out of the abortion clinic relieved, leaving behind the memory of a rapist—his face, his name, his hands. From that day I began to forget him, until he became such a blur that years later I nearly convinced myself that none of it had happened. But the wound would not heal until one day in a therapist's office I acknowledged its pain and I forgave the rapist and the young girl who was raped.

A couple of weeks after the abortion, Andrea and I returned to the Austins' house in Charlotte. I was my old self, a caring mother again, and our time together was a celebration of my release from depression. We played, running through the house and dancing until I was exhausted and begging for a reprieve. We curled up in my twin bed, and I fell asleep with her small, soft arms hugging my neck and woke up with her feet kicking me in the head.

Andrea, who was three, had grown like sugarcane, sweet and reed thin, reaching toward the sky. She had balloon cheeks and soft, thick hair that she loved to wear loose, hanging over her shoulders. When she talked she used her long, slim fingers to punctuate the air. She was born dramatic, mimicking everyone as soon as she could, pretending for months when she was almost four that she was someone else, introducing herself to strangers as "LaWanda Jones" and insisting I call her by that name, too. I reciprocated by enrolling her in drama classes for years, and she grew up wanting to be an actress.

I could not be sad around this child; her strong, chatty personality pushed through my sullen moods, and I laughed uncontrollably at her antics. When she left the house, it was usually in disguise: wearing sunglasses, a hat, a cape, or a pair of sparkling pumps. But beneath the disguise and the acting, she was always a dainty little girl, full of grace and sincerity.

She was my loyal companion, my faithful friend. I confided in her when she had no idea what I was saying, and she loved me without judgment. I wanted her to have what I grew up with: a house, her own bedroom, a yard to play in. What I subconsciously added to the list was "a daddy," though I wondered whether I had had a father any more than she did. My childhood family portrait seemed not to include him; nevertheless, there was a vacant place reserved for him, so he could step right in and complete the photo. It was a rule: every happy home had to have a daddy.

◆　　◆　　◆

For several weeks I went on job interviews, typing as fast and as accurately as I could, holding clever conversations with people who worked in personnel offices, filling out job applications in my neatest print. But nothing had changed since my last search. Each time I put the truth on paper, that I had been convicted of possession of drugs, the interviewer called me to the side and explained there was no work for me. I was weary from rejections, no longer strutting into buildings, but walking hunched over. At the Mecklenburg County Mental Health Center, I typed eighty-five words per minute with one error and got a perfect score on the spelling quiz. A white woman with salt-and-pepper hair accepted my application, then beckoned for me to come to her desk.

She leaned forward. "Honey, if you want a job you'd better take this off," she whispered, pointing to my words of confession. "Here; you take another application and fill it out. And leave that off."

I stared into her face, hearing Grannie's words: "You never know where help's gonna come from," at the same time thinking that this would even surprise Grannie, who was not particularly fond of white folks.

"You do want this job, don't you?" the woman asked.

"Yes, ma'am," I said.

"Well, you're the most qualified so far," she said.

She hired me to work as a billing clerk in the business office, taking payments from patients, sending out bills, and keeping up with the office petty cash. I was so touched by her courage and her faith in me that I made sure every penny of the money was accounted for and every day the records balanced perfectly.

The center, in a quiet rural area, was a cheerful place to work, a new building with lots of glass, carpeting, and towering green plants. Young therapists worked in blue jeans and sat cross-legged on the floor at meetings. People joked with each other in the office and socialized together after work. Barbara, the woman who hired me, was over the business office, too, and she became my friend and confidante. Andrea and I visited her often, the three of us sitting in the park across the street from Barbara's house. We may have been an unusual pair, an older white woman with a young, black woman friend. But Barbara slid into my life so easily—slid past my racist attitudes about whites, right by my distrust and bad experiences with them. The only way I could explain it to myself was that there had to be something inside me that responded to goodness and sincerity, no matter whom it came from.

◆   ◆   ◆

I was still in love with drugs, but it was hallucinogenics now including speed, my favorite. I knew the Austins were taking good care of Andrea, so I didn't have to worry about her; I was free to go out and get high with friends. Sometimes I went home and found I couldn't sleep, so I lay awake in bed, tripping while I played Marvin Gaye's "What's

Going On," over and over, softly, so I wouldn't wake anyone; then I got up early, and since Mrs. Austin was baby-sitting Andrea during the day now, I dressed, took more speed, and left for work.

In this souped-up state of mind, dressed in my favorite bright pink hot pants, I met a young man named John Harmon at a nightclub one evening. He was high, too, so the night had a bizarre air to it, as if neither of us were meeting a real person or, for that matter, being a real person. This would become a theme for our relationship until I was feeding myself barbiturates, dropping acid, and popping all kinds of pills just to be able to live with John. I had fallen into my lonely well again—and was drowning. Once I had sex with John, there was no rising to the surface. I could not separate sex from love. When his calloused hands touched me, loneliness stood back—at least for a while, staring just out of reach but smiling, too, because it was just a matter of time before it embraced me again.

John was not handsome and I was not sexually attracted to him; he appealed to that hollow part of me that was always open and empty. His hair was black and beady, except for an odd shock of white at the front, which grew curly. He was round like a panda and bounced on the balls of his feet when he walked. John embodied the absence of grace, bumping into the corners of tables, stumbling over his own feet, dropping everything his stubby fingers touched.

He was a low-level civil service worker, wasting the taxpayer's money every chance he got, sneaking off work early. I found him sitting at the bar drinking one beer after another. Everyone who walked in knew him, and he kept them laughing with his jokes and banter. He bought a lot of people drinks, and one day, much later, I would think that what people really wanted from John was not friendship, but whatever he was giving away free that day. Still, that night in the bar, he became my friend, too.

We dated for a year, spending most of our nights high on pills and smoke and our days working and recovering from our nights. John sold marijuana and stolen goods as a side hustle to his legitimate government job. He wasn't a big-time hustler, selling just enough marijuana and "hot" goods to keep enough money to satisfy his longings for material goods. He wasn't a flashy guy, his most lavish habits being purchasing a new car each year, staying in good hotels, and eating at expensive restaurants. For all his flimflams and drugs and late bar nights, what he yearned for most was respectability—that he and his family, his mother and four siblings, be permanent members of the middle class.

Six months after we started dating, I began imagining him as my husband. This was a bad habit of mine. I imagined myself married to men I should never have even looked at once. Still, after somewhere between three and six months I would look into their faces and see H-U-S-B-A-N-D written across their foreheads; then before I went to sleep that night I saw a house and me cooking and this guy, who wasn't ready to be anyone's husband, coming home from work, running to the kitchen, and kissing me.

John's family was similar to Andrea's father's family, which should have been a major red flag. John, like Ben, had replaced his father as man of the house. John's father lived with the family, but he drank a lot and sometimes spent a night or two away from home. He had little education, which meant he worked in low-paying jobs while his oldest child, John, earned a good salary. John supplemented the financial support his father provided to the family and each year, when John bought a new car, he gave his mother the old one. While his father was a shadow of a man who moved through the house hardly noticed, John was worshiped and adored, the reigning king of the household.

I sympathized with John's father and wondered what it felt like to be replaced by your son in your wife's heart. From where I watched I saw the toll Mrs. Harmon's affection took on everyone, particularly John. She had raised her boy to be a stand-in for her husband, which meant manipulating John to make sure he possessed the proper amount of sympathy to make him provide for her. Yet all the time Mrs. Harmon hated John, too, because she didn't really like needing him. What she would have preferred was a husband; it was just plain easier to make a boy be a man than to make a man be a man—even if the boy wasn't ready to grow up. Mrs. Harmon was high-strung and nervous around me, the person who threatened to take away her man-son, and John was cheated out of the experiences in life that teach you that love is worth too much to be bought. In some ways, John was very similar to my own father, in their insistence on providing, financially, for the women in their lives.

Unlike my father, who loved very young children, John wasn't comfortable around them. There would come a time when I believed his discomfort existed because children are the most honest human beings—that, before adults ruin them, children have vision that extends beyond what they see with their eyes. They saw John's real self and reacted with stiff bodies and pouts. He was uneasy playing with Andrea and more comfortable buying her things, so he gave her more clothes than she needed, more toys than one child could ever play with. I, a person who had once shouted to her father that love was more than material things, now interpreted John's actions as love. Andrea did not; she saw the truth.

Mrs. Harmon knew John could not head up two households, so she tried to wish me away by ignoring me, just as she did her husband. She was kind to Andrea, though I was suspicious of her affection. Despite her grumblings, John and I forged ahead with plans to marry. A couple of months before the wedding, we moved our things into a rented duplex. John purchased most of the furniture, heavy, expensive, traditional pieces. I bought a bed and chest for Andrea, a wrought-iron dinette set for the kitchen, draperies, and curtains. John and I agreed that until we were married he would stay at his cousin's and Andrea and I would live in the duplex, a place that represented all the comfort and security I longed for, and wanted for my daughter.

About this time, John began to act as if I belonged to him, as if I were just another piece of furniture in the duplex. He pouted and threw tantrums when I didn't do what he demanded and when I disagreed with him in public. I donned my curly dark brown wig one day when he was driving me and one of my sisters, who was visiting from Maryland, to the store. He stopped the car and ordered me to take off the wig. I refused. He opened the door and pushed me out. My sister—in shock—got out with me, and we caught the bus. I tried to laugh it off, but I was angry and humiliated. Yet after John came downtown, found us, and gave us a ride home, I forgave him.

I had second thoughts about marriage, but I let the fact that I had already sent out wedding invitations tilt the scale in favor of proceeding. One day I would look back and laugh at that, that I allowed a life-altering decision to be influenced by seventy-five dollars' worth of pink paper squares.

My girlfriends planned a bachelorette party for me at the duplex a couple of days before the wedding. On the eve of the party, a friend jokingly told John we were going to have a male dancer. John stormed into the apartment, ranting to me about how we couldn't have the party at our duplex and declaring that no matter where it was held, I couldn't attend if there was going to be a male dancer. I laughed because I knew there was no male dancer and because I thought John was feigning rage, since I couldn't imagine someone getting so upset over something so insignificant. But John rushed into the kitchen and pulled from the cabinets the black wine glasses I adored, and had paid eight dollars apiece for. He threw every one of them against the kitchen wall, while I screamed at him and cursed and cried.

I called people to announce that the wedding was canceled. My mother and a girlfriend, in town for the blessed event, were pleased. From what she heard in rumors and saw for herself, my mother knew John was short-tempered, selfish, and childish. She and my girlfriend quickly packed my things, pulling down curtains, hastily wrapping dishes in newspaper, and emptying the clothes from my drawers into a trunk.

"We prayed John would stay away until we finished," my mother told me months later. "We knew if you saw him and he started crying and begging you'd give in. You were always a sucker for a sad story."

It happened just as my mother feared: John came to the house. We went into the bedroom to talk. He started crying and begging and promising, and I relented. The wedding was on again. I insisted against the odds in my head that this was the marriage that would bring the happy home with the bedroom, the yard, and the doting daddy for Andrea.

My mother, who thought John was mean to Andrea and that I had chosen a man over my child, cried through the entire wedding. We held the reception in a dimly lit nightclub that was normally packed with young black professionals and the older black bourgeoisie. Mama and several friends of mine sat on one side of the cool, expansive room while John's parents and friends crowded together on the other side. We couldn't get our parents close enough to take the traditional photo with the entire bridal party. Anyway, the picture would have been incomplete without my father, who did not come and had told Mama, "She doesn't know the boy well enough. I don't want no part of it." I have wondered over the years if my life would have been different if my father had spoken these words to me, personally. But that gulf between us was widened by secondhand messages.

After the reception, as John and I were headed to the mountains for our honeymoon, we stopped at Mrs. Harmon's because I wanted to take the cake with us. "I hope you're satisfied now," my new mother-in-law said to me as I walked into the house.

"What do you mean?" I asked.

"I guess you're satisfied you got him," she said.

"John?"

"Who the hell you think I'm talking about, hussy."

I laughed, a tired, nervous titter.

"Yeah, laugh," she said.

I reached for the cake and she picked it up. She walked through the living room, out the front door, and onto the porch, with me following close behind. John was walking up the steps.

"I want you to take her out of here and don't bring her back!" Mrs. Harmon screamed.

"Give me my cake!" I hollered. I tugged at the box, then gave up.

"Here's your damn cake." She dropped the box.

The bride and groom figures toppled over; the top layer of the cake now had a jagged split through the middle.

"Your mother is a fucking maniac!" I screamed as I passed John. At the car, I turned and yelled out the window, "And I didn't take your son! He gave himself to me!"

John picked up the cake and followed his mother into the house. He came out a couple of minutes later, still carrying the cake in the box.

"I don't want that thing! Give it to your damn mama!" I screamed.

Later, Mrs. Harmon told my mother the cake had slipped accidentally from her hands. I didn't believe her, nor did my mother.

Over the next year, John provided for my material needs, just as he had been taught. But he was difficult to live with, verbally abusive and prone to severe mood swings. He was a scared little boy in a man's body, afraid to grow up to be a father or a husband. When we were high, our house was peaceful; he laughed and joked and I relaxed. When we were sober, considering what we had gotten ourselves into drove him to temper tantrums and me to the brink of depression and starvation. I lost twenty pounds.

John's meanness fed my insecurity. I wondered why he told me Andrea preferred staying at his mother's house. It hadn't occurred to me, though, that she stayed there because John had turned our house into a maze of chaos and confusion. He played with Andrea one minute and the next he teased her until she cried.

He picked her up from the day-care center one evening, and when they came into the house my daughter was hysterical.

"John said you were dead!" she cried, running to me.

"You told her what?" I snapped.

"She just kept asking me, 'Where is Mommy? Where is Mommy?' I was teasing her. I told her you were dead," he said, as if it were a natural answer.

John stayed out late most nights. I suspected he had girlfriends, though I didn't fret over the issue. Before long, I'd decided that if someone else wanted him, she could have him. He told me he was taking care of business, selling drugs or the trunkful of stolen goods he kept in his car. Soon our rantings woke up Andrea in the middle of the night and, scared, she'd run to me, crying. Instead of letting me comfort her, John made her go back to bed.

"You'll never be the cook my mother is," he said to me after dinner one evening.

He had said this before, and generally, I sulked over it and let it go. But this evening I answered, "If the bitch is so perfect, why are you so fucked up?"

I was closing the refrigerator when he slapped me so hard I fell against the refrigerator door. Before the sting left my cheek, I was planning my departure. A few days later, I sat in a free legal clinic getting information on filing for a divorce.

"If you leave the house your husband provides for you, under North Carolina law you get nothing," the lawyer said. "Nothing."

His words brought tears to my eyes, then down my cheeks. He passed me a box of tissue, his hands shaking worse than mine. He rattled on, delivering one piece of bad news after another, advising me to remain in the house with John while I filed for a legal separation.

"Are you kidding? He'd kill me if he knew I was trying to leave him," I said.

The lawyer perked up. "Well, if he hurts you, then we can do something."

I returned home, hoping to see things differently. Maybe John wasn't so bad; maybe I didn't understand him. But the arguments became more frequent, and after each one John bought Andrea toys and me gifts and took us both to dinner. He confessed his love for us, and for a few days we would live a fairly normal life. Then his behavior turned erratic again and Andrea begged to spend nights at his mother's house. I withdrew, not eating, not paying attention to my personal hygiene, half-combing my hair and wearing no makeup, which gave my face a blank look, as close as I could get to being invisible.

The alarm went off one morning, and when I rolled over to turn it off I discovered I couldn't lift myself from the bed: I was paralyzed. Every time I tried to move, a sharp pain shot up my spine. John dressed me and called an ambulance. At the hospital they admitted me for tests.

"Are you under a lot of stress?" a doctor asked me the next day.

"Some," I said.

"We can't find anything physically wrong with you. I believe your illness is caused by your mental state."

"What do you mean, 'mental'?"

"Stress, anxiety. Something has you wound so tight your muscles aren't relaxing. As long as we give you tranquilizers you're fine, but that's not natural. You should be able to live without tranquilizers. I suggest you see a psychiatrist."

I didn't hear the rest of his explanation, because I was mulling over the idea that a twenty-three-year-old woman could worry herself into a state of paralysis. Could I kill myself with my mind? I was intrigued and frightened by such power.

The paralysis of my body set me into action—I had to get out of my marriage. But I didn't have any money. John always paid the major bills, since he made more money, while I paid Andrea's day-care center and took care of my personal expenses. Subconsciously, I used my money to try to buy happiness, splurging on expensive clothes for Andrea and me and taking trips to see my family as often as possible. Everything I owned could be used up or would be outdated within a year; there was no savings account. Also, John and I were shopping around for a car for me. My plan was to save money and get a car first, then leave. But my plan was shortsighted and rooted in concerns about material items, when what I needed to think about was the mental health of myself and my child.

A therapist at the mental health center agreed to see me—at no cost—twice a week on my lunch hour. Meanwhile, I was having a recurring dream: I was alive in a grave. I looked up and saw an opening in the ground, a circle of light. John was standing at the top of the hole looking down at me. I didn't see him; I felt him. The light got smaller and smaller, as someone threw dirt on the hole. I always woke up, sweating and choking, before the opening closed totally.

In addition to my dream, there was my daughter, who through her innocence and honesty nudged me to leave John in a hurry. She and one of her friends were playing in Andrea's bedroom one afternoon, growling loud like beasts.

I walked into the bedroom. "What are you doing?"

"We're playing monster," Andrea's friend, Regina, said.

"Yeah. The monster's name is John, and we're running from him," Andrea said.

I meant to tell them to keep down the noise, but instead I shut the door and left the room. "They named their monster John," I repeated to myself.

A half hour later my daughter ran into the living room with a toy camera. I was watching television.

"Smile, Mommy," she said as she pointed her camera at me.

I flashed a phony smile.

"No, Mommy. Smile the way you smile when John isn't here," she said.

I looked at my child, her big eyes full of love and pity for me. Had I heard her right? Was my sadness so obvious that my daughter, who was not yet four, could see it on my face? Could she pinpoint when I smiled and know why my smiles disappeared?

"I'm leaving you," I told John when he came home.

"You can't do that," he said.

He pleaded with me to reconsider, and though I knew I wouldn't, my concession to him was to take Andrea to his mother's house so we could go out to dinner that evening and talk. It was a bad idea from the beginning. By the time we got home, my head was throbbing from too much listening and explaining. We were both so exhausted we fell asleep immediately.

A loud noise woke me up around eleven. John was standing next to the bed holding the phone, which he had yanked out of the wall. Now he threw the phone out of the bedroom and locked the bedroom door.

"What the hell are you doing?" I asked.

"I want us to talk. I don't want anybody disturbing us," he said.

He had gone off the deep end, I thought, but I wasn't scared, because he looked like a worried, weary baby. I stretched out across the bed, and he sat down next to me. He talked for nearly two hours, his sentences pouring out until he sobbed. I was so tired that my body ached. The phone in the living room rang. My girlfriend, I found out later, called the police when I didn't answer. She knew this was the night I was announcing to John that I was leaving, and she was afraid he had hurt me. Eventually, two police officers banged on the front door and yelled our names for about five minutes, then left.

John held me in the bedroom while they were at the door. "Don't say a word," he ordered, his big hand pinning my shoulder to the bed. I didn't fight, but I was getting scared now. I thought of the rifle John kept in the closet.

After the police left, John opened the bedroom door and went into the kitchen. I tried to open the bedroom window to escape, but I couldn't get it up. By now it was 2:00 A.M. Trembling, I opened the closet door; the rifle was still in the corner. I went into the kitchen.

John stood at the sink, his face contorted, beads of sweat dripping from his forehead to his wet undershirt. He held up a shaking hand, clutching an empty bottle normally filled with tabs of mescaline.

"What's wrong with you?"

"I took an overdose," he said.

I forgot about being angry. "John, why?" I cried, hugging him.

"I can't live without you," he sobbed.

"I'm calling help," I said.

"Not the police."

I called a drug rehab program that had counselors on call twenty-four hours a day to deal with overdoses. I patted and hugged and stroked John until a young white woman knocked at our door. She talked to him, gently, then forced him to throw up. We dressed and she accompanied us to the hospital.

Neither John nor I could see what was coming. We both thought he'd get a checkup and then they'd release him. But shortly after our arrival at the hospital, a counselor whispered to me that people who try to commit suicide are kept in the psychiatric ward for observation for a few days. I was shocked, and I knew if John discovered their intentions he would run. I kept quiet.

They put him in a wheelchair and rolled him upstairs. I looked at him and saw the fat, boyish face I had seen the night we met. He acted bewildered and frightened. They rolled him into a padded room, and I followed. John squirmed. Now a nurse explained that he would be treated for the drug overdose and also counseled in the psychiatric ward over the next few days.

John's disposition changed. He grew visibly angry, instantly possessed, and his body appeared to swell to twice its normal size.

"I'm not gonna stay in here. You got the wrong guy. There's nothing wrong with me," he snapped. As he stood, several men in white coats grabbed his arm.

The nurse spoke to him gently: "Please lie down."

One of the men held a syringe. They were just starting to wrestle with John, to make him lie on a cot, when I stared into his eyes and saw hate and fear, but mostly hate. I backed away.

"I didn't really take those damn pills!" he hollered. "I was faking!"

"Faking?" I screamed, my concern for him turning instantly to a hate I was sure matched what I saw in his eyes. "You put me through all this shit and you're playing? You selfish muthafucka!"

I was crying. John flailed his arms wildly, but the men subdued him, pinning him down.

He screamed his last order: "Call them off, Pat!"

I backed away and wiped my tears.

"Fuck you, John!" I ran from the room, headed home to pack my clothes.

chapter nine

Fall and Rise

Because I wanted to be fair, I only took the wedding presents my friends had given us. I divided the gifts from mutual friends, leaving John half of them, along with presents from his relatives and friends. I parked his shining new 1972 canary yellow Grand Prix with the black vinyl top in the driveway of his mother's house, knocked on the door, and gave his brother the keys.

To forget my troubles, I kept busy, working and going to school two nights a week to learn shorthand. I had a theory that despite all of the errors and tragedies in my life, if I just kept going to school, training for the next job, learning new things, one day it would all pay off for me and my child. I couldn't see exactly how education could be a bridge, but I believed it nevertheless.

Andrea and I moved in with my friend Sabrina until I could afford an apartment. I bought a very used car, a white 1960 Rambler Ambassador. In the evenings I sat up in the bed with Andrea and read her a story. Then we nestled up snugly against each other, thankful for the chance to sleep together again. She seemed happy about our move. To keep the disruption in her life minimal, I traveled across town each morning to take her to the same day-care center. On weekends we returned to the old neighborhood so she could play with friends.

On several evenings when I got off work at the mental health center, John was waiting in the parking lot. Each time I saw him his rage at me was more visible, etching angry lines across his face, creeping into his voice until it boomed, then wavered uncontrollably.

"How can you take care of a child and work?" he asked, as if it had been easier, or different, when I was with him.

"I'll take that baby from you!" he yelled in desperation one day.

"Not after I tell the police what you do for a living," I said, stunning myself with my boldness. He stared at me, his bottom lip quivering.

I was scared he might hurt me—even kill me—while he was in this highly charged, angry mood. Whenever I was away from home, I was looking over my shoulder, afraid John was lurking around the corner. My coworkers took turns walking me to the car and waiting to watch me drive off. But John would wait a block away in his car and tail me. Once he drove up beside me and gave me the finger; another time, he just stopped beside me at a traffic light and stared menacingly.

One evening during a snowfall, I looked in my rearview mirror and there he was, his car dangerously close to mine. Terrified, I sped up. He dropped behind. A moment later, he sped up close enough for his bumper to tap mine. Then he dropped behind. He repeated this, the second time ramming my car harder. I screamed. In my rearview mirror I saw him laughing. The road was slick and I saw a curve, so I eased up on the gas pedal, but John barreled toward me. I tried to think: Where could I go? I drove fast, watching the road, yet keeping my eye on the mirror. John kept a gun under his seat; I watched to see if he ducked low.

We entered a sharp curve. I hit the brakes to slow down and the Rambler obeyed, but the wheels spun, turning the car into an oversize sled as it careened off the road into a ditch. My first thought was: *Will he open the car door and shoot me?* But John kept going. Two other drivers stopped to help me, but neither had witnessed John ramming my car. If the car had been going faster or the ditch had been deeper, I could have been seriously injured. As it was, I had a badly bruised shoulder, a knot on my forehead, some aches, and a tremble through my body that I thought would never leave. A tow truck pulled the dented Rambler out of the ditch, but the car never ran well again.

The next day I went to the police station to get a restraining order that forbade John to come near me. For a few weeks, I occasionally saw him sitting in his car on my route home. He never did follow me again, and eventually he stopped harassing me. But I remained wary, unnerved, both for myself and Andrea, long after my shoulder stopped hurting.

I coasted through my days on prescription tranquilizers, which took the edge off my fears, not just of John, but also of the possibility that I was destined to repeat the same mistakes over and over again. I was a perfect victim for men: I thought of myself as incomplete without a man, and I had no self-esteem. I attracted black men already struggling to find a way to rid themselves of the rage they felt because they believed their choices in life were limited by their color. They hated this white-run America, but how could they fight a whole country? It was easier to exert what power you could, to at least proclaim domain over something or someone. I was that kind of someone. Where was the power for a black woman? I could not see it. I didn't see power in my mama or my grandma. What they had they got through marriage, through taking care of a house and children for a man. I had heard stories of how my grandmother, as a single woman, had worked hard to provide for my mother, but those stories were lost on me because I clung to what I saw.

What people thought of me was important to me. For years I bent too much and leaned too low simply to win friends. I did not know yet that life was a series of lessons and that you have to study your mistakes to succeed. I plowed ahead. What my life was missing was the wisdom of an older man—a father, even an uncle. My father had been absent even when he was present, emotionally AWOL from my family. My grandfather was from another generation and I revered him so that I would never ask him questions about sex or the behavior of young men. I did not know how men loved or why or when. What did they want from women, or life, or themselves?

◆　◆　◆

A couple of months passed without any sightings of John, and I felt safe again. As if on cue, Gabriel appeared, wiggling into my heart like a worm digs into a fresh apple. He was the cousin of a woman I knew vaguely, because we had mutual friends and I had seen her at parties. I knew way too little about Gabriel when I slipped between his arms in bed.

From appearances, we were so different that if life were a mathematical equation, we never would have been in the same set or subset, or related in any way. Blinded by my loneliness, I could not see what everyone else saw: that Gabriel was a two-bit hustler who lied through his gold teeth.

Though I was to know him a short time, he left an indelible mark upon my soul. When I was an older woman, a psychic took in her hands a ring I wore and called the name, "Gabriel," and I nearly fainted; I had forgotten about him. "I only knew him a short time," I told her. "That may be true," she said. "But he was important in your life; he left a deep impression." I wonder if Gabriel is only embedded in my jewelry, or if he is some part of me I cannot remove.

He was a dark man with skin like velvet and the short, muscular build of a pit bull. He sold marijuana and drove a five-year-old gold Cadillac Eldorado. On our first date we sat in his car outside a movie theater smoking herb, drinking tequila, listening to the O'Jays, and talking for so long that we nearly missed the start of *Cleopatra Jones*. When Gabriel spoke of what he wanted in life, he detailed the interiors of six cars and described each of the seven bedrooms his house would have. My list did not intersect with his; I wanted a good marriage, a country house that smelled like trees, and three children.

Gabriel's looks were marred by his bad taste. Two top front teeth were covered in gold, and he wore wide-brimmed hats in unusual colors like mustard, lime green, and tomato red, always cocked so sharp on the side of his head that they defied the laws of gravity. I overlooked the hats as I did his entire wardrobe, the gold teeth, and the broken-down, dip style he had of walking.

It was never my intention to keep him around for long. Besides, he always talked as if he was headed back home to New Jersey soon. He was pleasant enough, soft-spoken, gentle, and helpful: he paid my daughter's day care, bought my groceries, and took me wherever I needed to go, since the old Rambler only ran sometimes.

We had dated for nearly a month and gone to bed at least six times before I discovered who he truly was. I had just put Andrea to bed one evening when Gabriel asked me to ride with him to his friend Robert's house.

"Got a surprise for you," he said.

On several dates we had dropped by Robert's house, a large brick rambler in a nice community with well-tended yards and tall, old trees. We generally let ourselves in with Gabriel's key. Robert worked nights and he and his wife were separated, so it wasn't unusual for Gabriel and me to go to the house to have sex. When I met Robert, he was arrogant and brash and I immediately disliked him.

At the house, Gabriel left me in the living room for a few minutes to go downstairs to the basement, where I could hear him talking to Robert, though I couldn't make out what they were saying. When Gabriel returned, he poured us each a glass of wine, and we sat in the living room for a while drinking and smoking herb.

"Come on," he said. He grabbed my hand and led me down the hall to a familiar bedroom.

When we stepped inside, he turned to me and said, "Take off your clothes." His tone was demanding and cold, which startled me. He was a gentle lover, and it wasn't his manner to rush.

"What's wrong with you?" I moved back against the door.

He walked toward me slowly. I thought he was teasing and wanted a kiss. I extended my arms to hug him. He reached behind me and locked the door.

"What are we gonna do now, Gabriel?" I used my best seductive baby voice.

"Take off your clothes, Pat."

I giggled and unzipped the front of my top and pulled it down. I stepped out of my pants.

"Take everything off."

"Anything you say, baby." I was playing the role of obedient whore, and he smiled, flashing his gold, pleased with himself. I waited for him to make the next move.

He walked over to a chest, opened a drawer, and pulled out a black leather horsewhip.

"Gabriel!"

He moved toward me, gripping the handle.

"Turn around, whore!" His voice was flat and icy.

"No, Gabriel! No! Please!"

He shoved me around with one hand and I fell on the bed. I saw him draw back the whip. The lash wrapped around my arms and hands, as I tried to protect myself.

"You're mine!" he yelled. "You'll do anything I tell you to do."

He tackled me and threw me on my stomach. The lash snapped again. It burned across my back. I rolled over and scrambled to stand on the bed. The whip sank into my thigh, and I screamed.

"You belong to me!" he hollered.

I jumped up and down, screaming. The whip stung my hips and cut my legs. I was on fire. I leapt off the bed, ran to the door, and shook the doorknob. The whip dug into the flesh of my back again.

"You're making it worse!" he yelled. "You're mine! You hear me?! You're mine!"

How long did he beat me? The police would ask me that, but I didn't have an answer. Before the beating ended I lost all sense of time. I was one large open wound, my entire body pulsating the way my thumb had once after I slammed it in a door. I couldn't hear my own voice, yet I knew my mouth was opening. I could almost see my words spurting out like vomit.

He beat me until he was too tired to continue and the lash fell limp on my skin. I thought I was dead. My body was numb. No burning. No stinging. No pain. Then in some way—I don't understand even today—I was out of my body, floating near the ceiling. Below, Gabriel arranged my body on the bed the way a child would a rag doll, so that I lay flat on my back. I saw tears roll out the corners of my eyes and across my cheeks.

I saw Gabriel spread my legs apart. I saw the bloody welts on my legs.

He unzipped his pants.

He climbed on top of me.

He shoved his penis inside me.

He humped up and down on my body.

I looked at myself with such pity. But then, quickly, my sorrow for myself was replaced by an overwhelming sympathy for my mother. *They are going to tell her that I was found naked and beaten to the death,* I said to myself. I will always believe that at that moment, on some level of consciousness, I made a decision not to die.

I can't recall putting on my clothes or getting in his car or returning with Gabriel to my house. What I remember is being back in the apartment where I was living and seeing Gabriel sleeping on my sofa. I was standing, looking down at him, and a thought came to me, *Go get a butcher knife and stab him in the throat.* I walked into the kitchen, chose the biggest knife, one with a long, jagged edge, and walked back into the living room. He was still asleep. I stood over him, lifted the knife, and held it in the air so that the point was right over his throat.

Time must have ceased, because while I held the knife suspended in the air I remembered my daughter sleeping in the bedroom in the back. If I killed him, the police would come with their white faces and blaring red lights and they'd take me away. My daughter would wake up to see her mother being taken away in handcuffs by police. *What will happen to her?* I asked myself. *Will they put her in a foster home until my family comes? Then what?*

How could so much time pass while I held my arms over my head, ready to kill a man? How could so many thoughts pass through my mind? I went to bed, tucking the knife under the mattress beneath me. I pulled my daughter close to my chest. When I woke up later, Gabriel was gone. I dressed my daughter and dropped her at the day-care center, as if nothing had happened. But instead of going to work, I went home and back to bed.

When it was time for Andrea to come home, I got out of bed, and in the same clothes I had worn earlier and then slept in, I went to pick her up. It was Friday, so she and I went to our old neighborhood, to spend the weekend at my girlfriend Betty's house, where Andrea could play with Betty's daughter and I could talk.

We were drinking tea when Betty spotted a welt on my swollen hand and gasped. "How in the hell did you get that?"

I looked at my hand as if I had just seen it for the first time. Betty told me later I was like a zombie and that I described the beating as dispassionately as if it were a bad movie.

"Pat, you are going to the police," she insisted.

It hadn't occurred to me to go to the police for help. What could I tell the police Gabriel had done to me? Had he raped me? I was his girlfriend, and I had willingly slept with him several times before. Betty wasn't even sure it was rape in the legal sense, but she considered it rape and she was outraged about it and about the beating.

"He beat you like this?" she asked, as she lifted the back of my blouse. "You have to go to the police."

As far as I was concerned, the police were men who didn't believe in rape. Not much would have changed since I had been raped by Charles's friend. Rape was not a charge that men easily understood, and they understood it even less when a woman claimed she had been raped by her boyfriend. Everything I read and saw on television confirmed for me that the courts believed the definition of rape didn't relate at all to boyfriends who forced girlfriends to have sex, or husbands who forced wives. Rape was a crime committed by strangers.

Besides, I was still an ex-convict, a former heroin user, someone a defense attorney would call a "loose woman." I would have been too weak mentally to go to the police, if Betty had not been so determined and sent her cousin Jimmy to escort me.

At the police station, I was not a convincing victim. Neither sad nor angry, I described the events in a cool, detached manner. Also, as the police pointed out, I had waited more than twenty-four hours, which, they insinuated, said something about my credibility.

"Would you mind stepping into a bathroom with one of our women and taking off your clothes so she can see your injuries?" a male officer asked nonchalantly.

I had purposely worn a long-sleeved shirt and long pants. In the bathroom, I let my top fall off my shoulders so the woman, a matron from the jail, could see my back.

"My God," she said. "What kind of animal . . ."

Before I stepped out of my pants she said, "Wait." She left the room and returned with a Polaroid camera. As I stripped, she took pictures of every inch of my body. Later, dressed, I walked out of the room to face three officers with their eyes glued on me.

"We've got a sicko on our hands. We want you to tell us everything you know about him," one of them said. I believe it was the beating that impressed them, because they asked me to recount the whipping over and over and to describe the whip. They issued a warrant for Gabriel's arrest.

Betty and her husband insisted that Andrea and I stay with them, because they were afraid that if Gabriel found out about the warrant he'd try to hurt me. I went back to work, my legs and hands still swollen and my body scarred, but I was healing; my blouse could touch my back without making me wince.

◆ ◆ ◆

Just before lunch Gabriel called. "I'm gonna kill you and they'll never find me," he said.

My hands shook so badly I could hardly put down the phone. Someone in the office dialed the police so I could report the call. The next day Gabriel's cousin called to say he had left town. She could have been lying; I wanted to believe her. "I'm so sorry," she said. She told me that Gabriel once had prostitutes working for him. "I guess he was trying to turn you out," she said.

That explanation for his brutality had never entered my mind because I thought it was obvious, from the way I carried myself, that I was not the kind of woman who could be a street prostitute. It wasn't that prostitution seemed so terrible, but that if I were going to sell my body, it would be in high-class places, under the cover of a dating service, and for hundreds of dollars that I didn't run home and give to a man. I didn't pause to consider what about me would make Gabriel think the possibility existed.

I was afraid to close my eyes at night, getting up to check and recheck the doors, waking up startled at the slightest sound. I didn't go out at night, and I never went out alone. Whenever I left the house I was uneasy, constantly looking over my shoulder, never sitting with my back facing a door. Though I wanted Gabriel punished, I prayed he would not be caught. A trial would crush the mustard seed of strength I had left inside me. I imagined Gabriel's lawyer holding up my mistakes for a jury to see: a drug user, a woman with an illegitimate child, a felon. He would add "liar" to the list. He would convince the jury that a woman like me could not be raped. So each night, I prayed Gabriel would not be found.

Andrea and I moved to a cheap apartment in a complex of plain white, fading buildings that looked like one-story military barracks but were unmistakably homes for the poor. It was a cheerless place with grass worn bare by the shoes of children who wished for a real playground. My apartment was nearly empty. When I called John to beg again for Andrea's bedroom set, his answer was: "Come home."

The women at Andrea's kindergarten and day-care center gave me a cot for her to sleep on, the kind kids used for their midday naps. I slept next to her on the hardwood floor, on a pile of blankets friends had given to me. A couple of weeks after we moved in, the man next door, who was a single parent with four children, gave us his old, rickety kitchenette set because he was getting a new one. Friends gave me curtains and helped me buy food and other items I needed. Andrea and I ate at Betty's house a couple of nights a week. It had taken all my money to put down a deposit, pay the first month's rent, and get the utilities turned on.

My old Rambler sighed its last breath, and the car salesman, who did not appear surprised, gave me what he called "a deal" on a bronze-colored Ford that looked exactly like an undercover police car. The car caused near hysteria among some of my friends, who upon seeing it drive up bolted their doors and flushed their drugs down the toilet.

Andrea and I spent a lot of time visiting people, because we found our own home depressing. It was a colorless box of rooms with no pictures or plants or anything that stamped our personalities on it. That type of transformation cost money and I didn't have any; all of my money was spent surviving—on gas and day care, on food and clothes and going to the laundry. But Andrea and I, the girl-child and the woman-child, were happy because we had escaped the mean tyrant John.

I was nearing the point where I could afford to buy some small items for the apartment when the mental health center gave me a month's notice that my job was being abolished. I felt like a punch-drunk fighter, reeling from a barrage of hard blows. I wanted to give up, but I didn't know how. "I admire you because you always bounce back," my friend Betty said to me. I could not appreciate the compliment; my head was spinning from the bounce.

The evening news featured stories on the Watergate hearings. I knew that two *Washington Post* reporters were responsible for uncovering the story of a break-in at the Democratic Party headquarters. I knew events were unfolding that might lead to the impeachment of President Nixon. But I didn't care about the news; none of it had anything to do with me. I was trying to figure out how to feed my child, how to pay for day care, where was I going to find a job. It didn't matter to me whether President Nixon resigned or was impeached. Would it put one morsel of food in my child's mouth? I was consumed with surviving, and could not imagine that one day one of the reporters who broke the Watergate story would interview me for a job; it was even more inconceivable that I would become a *Washington Post* reporter.

I went on several interviews a week, but two months after my job at the center ended, I was still unemployed. I was also practically penniless, because my unemployment checks had not started. Since my parents had six children at home, I never considered asking them for money. Besides, I was their oldest child, the one who should set an example for the others. Still, a couple of times Mama sneaked me ten or twenty dollars out of the grocery money my father gave her. I was never sure exactly how much he knew about what was going on in my life, since I left it up to Mama to tell him what she wanted. Andrea's father, Ben, was married, had a new family to support, and still had long periods of unemployment himself. He sent money for Andrea periodically.

Every day I ran to the mailbox expecting to see my unemployment checks, but all I found were bills. When there was only a carton of milk in the refrigerator and I didn't have enough money to go to search for a job, I turned to my last resort: the Department of Social Services.

The evening before I went to the county offices, an incident occurred that still had me shaking the next morning. I had yelled for Andrea to come in for dinner and she did not answer. I knocked next-door, and no one was home. I searched the complex and could not find her. I sat on my small stoop and cried. Just as I was going to go inside to call the police, I saw her skipping up the street. She had walked off without my permission, following some kids to the 7-Eleven store, three blocks away.

I spanked her for the first time since that day when I was pregnant and depressed and waiting to have an abortion. But I didn't hit her hard; I knew I could get carried away again, my hands propelled by fear this time. I was afraid we would always be poor and that she would become a disrespectful child with an old woman's face, like the girls she had followed to the store.

By the time I walked into the Department of Social Services the next afternoon, I was brittle from worry. It was near closing time when I arrived; I had spent most of the day trying to think of an alternative to begging, which was how I viewed my being there. A white woman counselor told me I was eligible to receive surplus food. This was in the days before food stamps, when the government gave you basic food like cheese, powdered milk, powdered eggs, beans, and lumpy peanut butter in a can with all the oil at the bottom.

"Your food will be delivered in two weeks," the woman said.

"Two weeks? I need food today," I pleaded.

"We can't help you today. You have to wait until the first of the month."

My lips quivered uncontrollably and tears ran down my face. It had been no small feat to come to that room to ask for help. I had laid aside my pride and, feeling naked, had gone to beg a system I despised. And it had refused me. I stood to leave.

"Maybe there is something I can do," the woman said. "Wait."

She left the room and was gone for about ten minutes before returning with a man. "Follow me, miss," he said.

We walked down a long hall. He opened a door with a key, and we stepped into a storage room. "There is just you and a child?" he asked.

"That's right," I said.

He pulled down an empty box and started filling it with food. "How old is the child?"

"Four," I said.

By the time the woman joined us, he had filled a box and two grocery bags. I was very thankful, but I was also still ashamed and scared because my life was so much out of control that I had to depend on strangers to give me food. A couple of weeks later, I began receiving my regular monthly shipment of surplus food. Andrea and I did not like the taste of most of the food, even when I improvised on the recipes that came with each supply. When my unemployment checks started, the money was barely enough for me to pay bills. There was no money for anything extra; I still didn't have a telephone and had to give prospective employers my neighbor's telephone number.

I found a job as a teletype operator at a printing company, making half the salary I had been paid on my previous job. It was a horrible place, where most employees were mistreated because they were uneducated and felt lucky to be working at all. All of the supervisors and managers were white, and the people in lower-paying jobs were black. I tolerated the job, of course, because I needed the money. But a month after I was hired, the owner called me to his office and fired me. He had gotten the results of my police check, which showed my record. He handed me my check and escorted me to the front door.

I was enraged. "You have your fucking nerve!" I yelled as he opened the door. "This is the worst job I've ever had! You treat people like shit!"

I was mad at the hypercritical world and all of the white people in it, because as far as I could tell, they made up all the rules. If I lied on my job application, I got fired. If I told the truth, I never got the job. I wanted to go to college, but I couldn't. It didn't matter that I was changing, because white people kept changing the rules to suit them. Why try at all? Why play by the rules?

This was what I was thinking when I met Pauletta Jackson. I spotted her playing outside with her children, laughing like a kid herself, hugging her son and daughter often in her delicate arms. She was a short, small-boned woman with ringlets of naturally curly hair and skin the color of caramel candy. Her children were just as fragile-looking as their mother, well mannered and loving.

Pauletta, whom everyone called "Letta," turned out to be a book lover, too, so we visited each other regularly, talking about books and exchanging our favorites. I took a break from job searching, weary from the rejections and fearful of the police checks. Letta and I ran back and forth from one apartment to the other each day, carrying pots of food, combining the meals we cooked, eating breakfast or dinner together. Her husband, Hassan, worked two jobs and went to bed when he got home, so we put the children to bed and went over to my apartment to listen to Earth, Wind and Fire, Roberta Flack, and War. We also smoked a lot of herb.

Letta gave me a nice floral sofa, and I bought a new kitchenette set. Friends gave me two full-size mattresses and box springs, which I set on the floor, not even caring about bed frames. Letta made my curtains from sheets, painted pictures for me to hang on my walls, and macraméd plant holders for the small plants she gave me. She was the most generous person I had ever met, but I wondered how she could afford the things she gave away.

I knocked on her door one day, and when she answered I knew something was wrong. Her face was harsher, her eyes were wild and wide, and as we talked she continuously scratched her arm. I recognized a guy at her kitchen table as someone I knew from the days when I shot heroin, before I went to jail. I looked at his face and then at Letta's, and then I saw her arms, which—as I had not realized until that moment—were normally covered by long sleeves. She had blue-black scars, the tracks of needle marks, up and down her arms. Delicate, pretty Letta was an addict.

If she had been a recreational user, I would not have been stunned. If she craved heroin in her darkest, lowest moments, I would have understood; we seemed so much alike. It was hard for me to believe that Letta was that different from me, that she was regularly and severely strung out.

I spoke to the friend in her kitchen. Letta was surprised that I knew him. Seeing them together made my stomach churn. "I'll come back later," I said.

Over the next few weeks, Letta told me about her habit, how Hassan, who was a Muslim, forbade her to use drugs. He had learned to accept her smoking marijuana, she said, but he was outraged whenever he discovered she was using heroin. Letta said she quit for months at a time, but she was never able to give it up totally. After she confided in me, I would not get high at her house, scared that if we smoked herb she might want to get higher and pull out her heroin and her works and shoot up in front of me. My sense of reality had been shattered already by the discovery that she was an addict; I could not bear to watch her use the drugs. Coupled with this fear, though, was a worse one: that if I saw her shoot up, I might shoot up, too.

I was running out of cash again, so I took Andrea to my parents' house in Maryland to stay for a while. It was a difficult decision; I didn't like being separated from Andrea. When she was out of my sight, I ached for her presence. I was no one without her; I was lonely and consumed by my own brutal, unrelenting thoughts about my inadequacies and faults. But I didn't want to wait until we were eating surplus food, or until there wasn't enough money for me to buy a ticket to take her home.

Back in Charlotte, I grew angrier each day I couldn't find a job. In addition to hiding my police record and worrying about it being discovered, I now had to explain months of unemployment.

Then Letta suggested I start "boosting," stealing from the department stores, to earn a living. This was how she made her extra money and got things she could not afford, she said. She could walk into department stores wearing her finest clothes and leave with two dresses, a sweater, and ten pairs of stockings hidden under her midiskirt. She sold her stolen goods to friends, or if she couldn't sneak the things past Hassan and into her own house, she sold them all to Bettie Mae, who ran a boutique out of her house. Bettie Mae's bedrooms were shops, two for women and one for men, featuring clothes stolen from some of the best stores in Charlotte.

I was a little hesitant at first, not because I thought stealing was wrong, but because I wasn't sure I could boost well enough to earn a living. What I was sure of was that I wanted to be able to afford to bring my daughter home and have a savings account for the first time in my life, so that when some white person fired me because of my past I could still feed my child until I got another legitimate job. I dreamed of everything I could do with the money I would make—the same kinds of dreams other people have when they're planning how to spend their paychecks.

Stealing from a store didn't seem like such an awful thing to me, anyway. I had grown up in communities where thieves openly sold their stolen goods on street corners and in the beauty shops. Also, stealing from a store was not personal; I didn't know the owner, so I could convince myself that I wasn't hurting anyone, that no one felt the loss.

While Letta's children ate their pancakes one morning, I watched her walk across the living room, demonstrating how to snatch a dress off a hanger, roll it into a neat bundle, and stick it up between your legs. She showed me her oversize bloomers and the coats and jackets with special inside pockets. I practiced walking with a dress and blouse stuffed between my legs, taking measured steps until I reached a shopping bag. Leaning slightly over the bag, I spread my skirt, then let the items drop from between my legs and into the bag.

At some time or another most cons have to wrestle with their own greed, and Letta and I, amateurs that we were, were no different. We got greedy in K-Mart one evening. It was our habit to go out on our excursions every Saturday and at least once during the week. Sometimes we walked around a store together, and at other times we split up, agreeing on a time and place to meet in the mall or parking lot. Letta drove her Toyota; we always cursed it, because we could have packed so much more into a larger car.

Under Letta's tutelage, I graduated to stealing household goods, all kinds of linens, and miscellaneous items like clocks, pictures, small lamps, and toasters. Inflated by our successes, we were overconfident now and careless. We giggled at our "finds" before we left the stores and foolishly went to the same stores too many times. On this day, we repeated another one of our stupid habits: going to the car with one load, then entering the store again to steal more. We were headed out with our second load and had just stepped out the door when two male security guards in plainclothes grabbed us both by the arms.

"What the hell . . . leave me alone!" Letta screamed indignantly.

I looked around to see who was watching and felt a twinge of genuine embarrassment. I was quiet, thinking for the first time about the fact that I was still on probation and could be returned to jail to serve the remainder of my probation term.

They took us to a room in the back of the store, where they explained that they had hidden cameras that had filmed us stealing. Then they made us empty our bags. Letta had a five-inch brass elephant, two sets of king-size sheets with the pillowcases, five pairs of stockings, a set of steak knives, a set of bath towels, and a clock radio. I had ten pairs of earrings, ten pairs of stockings, three musical jewelry boxes, three sets of double sheets, and two sets of bath towels.

"Where's your car?" one guard asked.

We pretended not to hear.

The police arrived and took us to jail. We still refused to say where the car was because, of course, we knew it was filled with stolen goods. "We'll find it when the parking lot clears," the guard said.

Letta couldn't reach Hassan until late that night. He wasn't able to get a bondsman until early the next morning, and we didn't get out until shortly before the awful jail lunch was served. I didn't sleep at all while we were there, worried that the police would discover my previous record and keep me locked up. Every time I heard a footstep, I thought my secret had been discovered. I wept softly into my pillow, considering the possibility of being separated from my child again. Letta cried all night, too, only she cried really loud, aggravating everyone. Like most criminals, we had sincerely thought we would never be caught.

As it turned out, no one ever found out about my night in jail—not my probation officer or my mother or any friends, other than the few I told. I was given another chance, a reprieve to straighten out my life. I had taken my last shopping spree with Letta.

"Letta, I don't have the heart to do it anymore," I told her once we were released.

We received a letter from K-Mart telling us the store was dropping the charges against us, but instructing us never to enter a K-Mart again. We never found out why they dropped the charges. I chalked it up to divine intervention. Letta could use up all her chances, if she wanted to; I was retiring.

I renewed my job search. A few weeks later I found a position as a secretary-receptionist. Within a month, I had my daughter back home. My new employer, Rainbows, Inc., was a business management consultant firm owned by a black woman and her father. I had never worked for a company owned by black people, or even met a black person who owned a business and I was extremely proud to be associated with Rainbows.

With me working, Letta and I didn't see each other as often, and eventually, over the next year, we drifted apart. I started dating Betty's cousin Jimmy, the man who had gone with me to the police station when I filed charges against Gabriel. Jimmy was a regal man over six feet tall with ebony skin. The winter of 1973, when I met him, he sported a dark gray leather maxicoat that made him look even taller and more elegant.

He had moved south from Connecticut after someone snitched to the police about his cocaine dealing. According to street justice, he could have killed the person who dropped the dime on him, but Jimmy wasn't callous enough to do that. He was feeling lonely and homeless, searching to belong, so we found refuge in each other.

Cecilia Cummings, the woman who owned Rainbows and was its president, was a few years older than I was. Her father, a major investor and vice president of the company, was in his early sixties and dressed more like a country preacher than a business executive. Shortly after I started working at Rainbows, Mr. Cummings invited me to dinner, which didn't interest me at all until he offered to give me some money.

I had come to believe that some men should pay for my company. It's not a quantum leap from being raped to using your body to gain money or favors. Two men had raped me, had taken my body by force and left me feeling powerless and useless. I thought the way to turn that around was to demand money from men for sexual favors, which gave me some power. I wasn't going to be pimped, the way Gabriel had hoped.

I dated Mr. Cummings for several months, traveling with him on

business trips, staying close to the hotel room so neither his daughter
nor his associates could see me. He gave me money, bought Andrea
and me clothes, and helped me buy my first new car, a Toyota Corolla.
When we had sex, I closed my eyes and tried to imagine someone else,
though I was never successful at it. His hands trembled with excitement, his penis was almost always soft, and my consciousness
throbbed with the reminder that he was married and had a wife who
was bedridden.

But with Mr. Cummings's help, I crept out of poverty. Jimmy and I
pooled our money; he went to New York City twice to buy cocaine
and sell it at a large profit before he returned. It wasn't long before we
were able to move into a two-bedroom garden apartment in a complex where there was a swimming pool, a clubhouse, well-tended
lawns, and several playgrounds. We packed the place with new furniture: a big furry brown sofa and black-and-brown-striped chair, a
brass bed for Andrea, and an imitation bamboo bedroom suite for
Jimmy and me.

Andrea didn't like Jimmy. It wasn't personal; she didn't like men
being around her mother. She preferred our life when she and I were
alone. A man was an intruder, someone with whom she had to share
not only my time, but my affection. As far as she was concerned, there
was only enough of me for her, and her way of protecting her part was
to be as obnoxious and disrespectful as possible to any man who
dared enter my life. When Jimmy, who was always playful and kind to
her, tried to discipline her in any way, Andrea reminded him, in an
indignant tone, "You're not my daddy. You're too black to be my
daddy."

She knew Ben, her real father, though she had seen him only a few
times since he and I had separated. But her argument with Jimmy, of
course, really had nothing to do with her longing for or even caring
for her father. At age five, she was not fooled by men. Once on a bus
ride from Washington to Charlotte I befriended a young white college
student. We flirted a little, that kind of funny, innocent flirting that
exists only to boost two egos for the short time they're in each other's
company. The guy played the guitar and sang to Andrea and me. At
one stop he hopped off the bus and returned with a huge stuffed dog,

which he presented to her. She refused to accept it, so I took it for her.

When we got home, she said, "You keep it. He didn't buy it for me."

When she acted her age, almost five years old, she was a kindergarten chatterbox, rattling off questions nonstop: "Why is the moon white? Why does it follow us around? Where is God? Why can't I see Him?" She still had her flare for drama, but now she preferred dressing up in my old clothes, sticking her tiny feet in my platform shoes, wearing my sunglasses on her nearly bridgeless nose. She sang the words of a Helen Reddy song: "I am woman; hear me roar," then always screaming her favorite line, "I am in-vin-ci-ble!" She brought home from school gifts made from Popsicle sticks, paper plates, and egg cartons. I cried over them, then filed them in a box labeled "Andrea," which I still have.

I took her to swimming lessons at the YWCA because my mother had passed along to me her fear of the water and I didn't want my daughter to inherit it. Andrea and I took a ballet class together. I told her my thoughts and ideas before I told anyone else.

◆   ◆   ◆

I traveled with the staff of Rainbows to Chicago for PUSH Expo, a huge convention featuring exhibits and workshops by black entrepreneurs from all over the country. It was the first professional trip I had ever taken and the farthest I had traveled from home. It was a historic event, partially because of its connection to Rev. Jesse Jackson, revered as a former confidant to Martin Luther King and the founder of People United to Save Humanity (PUSH), which sponsored the annual expo. But even without Jackson, PUSH Expo would have been successful. It captured the hope and excitement blacks felt in the early seventies, when legislation seemed capable of toppling over all racial barriers like lines of dominoes, until the past was flat enough to walk over and economic parity and equality were within grasp. The hope showed in the way we strutted proudly past booths advertising new black businesses and in the excited chatter of people in the lobby of the black-owned hotel. At the Expo, blacks could find out how through entrepreneurship they could lay claim to some of the wealth predicted to be headed toward black people who were educated enough to accept it.

Even those attendees like me, who held no entrepreneurial interests, were transformed by seeing men and women who not long before could neither vote nor eat at a lunch counter gather to discuss the businesses they owned. I had stepped onto the pages of *Ebony* magazine: Quincy Jones was eating at a table next to me in a restaurant, Gladys Knight walked past our exhibit booth, and Roberta Flack was talking to someone backstage while I sat with a friend who was interviewing Jesse Jackson for a radio program. In our hotel parking lot, my girlfriends and I ran into Harold Melvin and the Blue Notes, including at that time Teddy Pendergrass, who later became a solo balladeer. They invited us to accompany them to a nightclub where they were performing, and we did, swooning madly while they sang, dancing and drinking with them during the break. After the performance, we hugged our good-byes and we women returned to our hotel rooms alone, which seemed to suit everyone.

As we dismantled our booth on the last day, I felt like Cinderella. The clock had struck midnight and I had to step off the pages of *Ebony* and return to my wretched life. But the weekend had shown me that the people I saw in magazines were not untouchable. There was a commonality to our lives that I had to hold fast to on my darkest days, when my life seemed separated from everyone else's by an uncrossable gulf of misery.

◆　◆　◆

Not long after my return to Charlotte, Mr. Cummings figured out Jimmy was living with me and, in an act of jealousy and revenge, told his daughter about his affair with me. At least he told her his version, which included a story about a loan he had made to me for the down payment on my car. Of course, this wasn't true; he had given me the money. But my boss, being a dutiful daughter and probably seeing me for what I was, a conniving slut who wanted nothing from her father but money, said she'd deduct the money out of my paychecks. Before she got the chance, I quit, which was probably what she really wanted anyway. Instead of being ashamed of sleeping with her father and luring money out of him, I was angry at the daughter and wrote her a scathing letter, attacking both her and her father.

It was a classic move. I was really ashamed of what I had done but didn't want to show it. I was the child in class who misbehaves and terrorizes everyone else because she is in pain and afraid, yet doesn't know how to ask for help or forgiveness or even how to explain what is wrong.

Nevertheless, my dishonorable relationship with Mr. Cummings helped me end up in a job that would change me for the better. A couple of weeks after leaving Rainbows, I was hired as the only black secretary at the *Charlotte Observer,* the city's morning newspaper. I lied on my job application, answering that I had never been convicted of a felony. Since my last firing, I had stopped putting my criminal record on job applications. I rewrote my history because that was the only way employers would stop judging me by who I used to be. I didn't even think of it as lying anymore, because the years were passing and I believed I was no longer the young girl who had been convicted.

Discovering I was the only black secretary at the paper didn't make me angry, as it would today; it boosted my self-esteem—at least as much as I would allow. Even though I loved to write, I wasn't excited about working for a newspaper; I didn't have any desire to become a newspaper reporter. I wrote short stories and poetry, not journalism. I had written enough poems now to fill a book, which I kept tucked in my underwear drawer. I wrote short stories with a heavy moral message. One story was about three soldiers killed in Vietnam, their bodies destroyed beyond recognition by a grenade. Their remains were shipped in one casket, and the families—Jewish, Baptist, and atheist—had to hold one funeral. One soldier was black. I wrote a poem about the attention paid to pregnant women and the lack of care given the environment. It ended: "Would things have been different if the fathers of this country had been mothers instead?"

I wrote about matters of the heart and I couldn't see yet that journalists did this, too, with more skill and sense of communication than

I could yet muster. Still, if there is such a thing as fate, it had acted on my behalf, to put me in a place where when I woke up I would have before me what I had wanted all the time, where, even though I hadn't been in the upper half of my graduating class, I could still learn to be a writer and, perhaps, have a chance to excel.

My new boss, Peter, was a white guy barely a year older than I was. We immediately struck up a comfortable friendship. He was a member of the new, young, white South, those who tried to build the bridge between the Confederate tradition of Jim Crow and the more integrated future of Martin Luther King, Jr. I became Peter's close confidant and assistant, in many ways no different from the scores of secretaries who in the course of their office duties compose personal as well as business letters, serving as human calendars, remembering flights and meetings, birthdays and anniversaries, covering for bosses who sneak off to play golf. Secretaries can be like members of the family, and with most of them being female, they often become the nurturing mother-wife and sister-friend. It was a position that suited me well for many years, and Peter was as near-perfect a boss-mate as possible.

He arranged for me to have my first chance to write for others, a position on the monthly employee newsletter, which I helped write during my extra time. This was a big deal to me. It was as close as I could get to imagining myself as a writer. Becoming a reporter was too big a dream; just writing for the employee newsletter frightened me to near paralysis.

My first story was about pets—talking birds, big snakes, and show dogs. The editor returned my draft covered with red marks, noting misspelled words, slang, wordiness, and whole paragraphs that needed to be rearranged or dropped. Accompanying his critique was a note: "An ego is too big to fit into a typewriter." I understood immediately what he was saying and dropped my initial feelings of embarrassment and disappointment. I stayed awake that night fretting, but by day my normally oversensitive self, who hurt at any hint of not being accepted, wrote with the attitude that every red mark was an opportunity to learn.

I discovered I thought differently when I wrote; I was smarter on paper. I saw where the mistakes were made and I corrected them. It took a while—maybe six months—but eventually there were fewer red ink marks and among the lines of criticism were a few compliments. For me, it was nothing short of magic to string together words in a way that made people notice and care. This was the answer to my prayers, to be able to touch people in a way that I had not been able to with my actions or the words from my mouth. As my relationship with Jimmy lost its pizzazz, he wrote me one last love letter, baring his heart a final time. I was a woman who now needed a man like Jimmy less. Disinterested in what the letter was really saying, I read it, circling the grammatical errors and misspelled words with my red pen before crumpling it up and throwing it away.

chapter ten

Making Home

I was tired of men. Andrea and I reveled in our maleless world. I kicked off my shoes as soon as I stepped inside the apartment each evening and stripped to my underwear. No cooking dinner every day or stepping over some man's funky tennis shoes. Andrea rode her tricycle through the living room, whooping and yelling because she only had to obey one person. I slept sprawled over my bed. Andrea and I showered together, running to the bedroom, squealing, dripping wet, as we wrapped ourselves in towels. Girlfriends dropped by and we cooked meals together, letting the children eat at the kitchen table while we ate in the living room, listening to Jon Lucien sing love songs on the stereo.

Andrea graduated from kindergarten, but she couldn't attend first grade that fall in North Carolina because she would still be five years old when school opened. A child had to be six to enter first grade in that state. So to avoid having Andrea repeat kindergarten, I decided to send her to live with my parents again in Maryland, where the laws were different and she could start first grade that September, in 1974. I packed her clothes and toys and drove seven and a half hours to deliver her to my parents' house. The next day I cried almost uncontrollably for five miles down Interstate 95.

Over the next nine months of the school year, Andrea and I fell into a pattern where I called several times a week and visited at least two weekends a month. But at her age, she was nonchalant about talking to me, so that sometimes she preferred to keep playing outside rather than come to the phone. Meanwhile, I missed her so terribly that I seemed a little out of my mind; the time I spent without her is still fuzzy in my memory. I brought her home as soon as school ended and began looking for a new place to live.

At the home of an artist friend I met a woman named Judy, a single mother with a daughter about a year or so older than Andrea. I had gone to the friend's house to buy an abstract painting I had seen at one of his exhibits; Judy had gone there to pick up that very painting and had paid for it only moments before I arrived.

"You've got my painting," I said to Judy, as the artist wrapped the picture.

"No, I got *my* painting," she said.

I liked her immediately. She had my kind of in-your-face, handle-it-if-you-can humor. We talked, discovered we both were looking for roommates, and agreed to get together the next day to talk more. We spent that next afternoon together, laughing and drinking tea, talking about our children, and smoking reefer. By the time the day ended, we were steadfast friends, the beginning of a relationship that would affect both of us profoundly. We would become like sisters, each of us influencing the other's direction. We were the perfect complement to each other: she made me more confident and spontaneous, while I encouraged her to be less brash, more thoughtful. Together, we sought what we wanted and how to rid ourselves of those fears that held us back.

Judy had an infectious passion for life. It was in her smile and the way she gave in to laughter. The way her ample breasts and hips would move, not shaking so much as swaying to her own rhythm—and you had to join her, laughing even when you didn't understand why. There was no in-between for her: it was love or hate, hot or not, good or bad. She couldn't talk without her hands, slicing the air, flut-

tering and waving them. At about five-seven, s|
big-boned; for dress clothes she favored soft
and silks that floated around her as she walk
like the college student she once was, don'
with messages and symbols, peace signs, an
"street" attire, huge flowered earrings, and tight, ug
was wearing comfortable clothes, too—loose jeans, tie-dyea
and Earth Shoes.

The only immediate flaw I saw in Judy was that she was a bitch when she was broke. Later, when we became roommates, the kids and I tiptoed around the house and made ourselves small whenever Judy, who was a counselor at a financially strapped drug rehab program, announced that her check was late. She drove a purple Gremlin, the ugliest car I had ever seen. Though you couldn't hide that car, some guys stole it once to use to rob a bank. Of course they were caught.

One morning during our search for a place to live, Judy and I and her daughter, Michelle, spotted a sign outside an elegant old brick building on a tree-lined street. One of the four units was for rent, and there was a woman's name, "Edna Spann," and a number. We called, and Mrs. Spann agreed to meet us at one o'clock in front of the building.

"We'll be in a purple Gremlin," Judy told her.

"I'll be in a gray Cadillac," said Mrs. Spann.

Shortly before one, we were parked in front of the building in the Gremlin when a gray Cadillac pulled up just across the street. A white woman was driving and a girl about seven sat in the front seat. We walked toward the car, smiling. The woman looked right into my eyes; then, when we were about six feet from the car, it sped off.

Judy and I looked at each other.

"The bitch saw that we were black and left," Judy said.

"Naw," I said, because I really didn't want to believe that.

We knocked on the door of one of the apartments, and an old white man in a bathrobe answered. We asked how to get in touch with Mrs. Spann and he gave us the address of her office, which was located in her home. We headed there, neither Judy nor I exactly sure why, but both of us knowing that we couldn't make it through the day

question hanging in the air: had Mrs. Spann driven off be-
e didn't rent to blacks?

drove down a long driveway and pulled up to a brick rambler,
e of the smaller homes in a neighborhood we knew was upper-
middle-class and all white. A teenage boy with long, stringy hair came
to the door. "My mom's not home, but you can come in and wait for
her," he said.

It was a warm, sunny day, but the shades were down, the curtains
closed, and the dark living room seemed airless. The boy reared back
in a lounge chair, watching an old black-and-white movie on television, while Judy and I sat on the sofa. A half hour later we heard a car
drive up.

"That's my mom," the boy said, not moving from his chair.

"Would you tell her we're here?" I asked.

He got up and went outside. Within seconds, Mrs. Spann was in
the living room screaming, "What are you people doing here!"

I started to explain, but she wasn't interested. She screamed at her
son, "You let these people in here?"

Judy and I were not afraid but ready to give her a mind-fuck. "We
even came in the front door," I said, interjecting some humor in what
was turning into a scene from a macabre play.

Judy topped me. "We used your bathroom," she said.

Mrs. Spann gasped, as if she was having difficulty breathing. "Get
out of my house! Get out! Get out!" She raced to the kitchen.

We followed, trying to explain. "I'm calling the police," she said,
picking up the phone.

We looked at her son, who shrugged, sighed, and said, "I'm really
sorry."

"Hello, police. I came home and found three coloreds in my
house," Mrs. Spann said. She rattled off her address, then slammed
down the phone.

Judy and I fled that house, but we didn't want to leave the property, because we feared the police would search for three black burglars. We waited outside next to the purple Gremlin. Michelle had
gone with Mrs. Spann's daughter to the backyard to see the Spanns'
horses. The two girls were returning, holding hands, when Mrs.

Spann came out, snatched her daughter, and ran into the house. About the same time, three police cars, their sirens blaring, lurched to a halt in front of us. Before the officers jumped out, they saw their three burglars, one of them a six-year-old black girl with tears streaming down her cheeks, crying, "Mama, I don't wanna go to jail."

Two officers knocked on the door while one talked to us. Minutes later, the two who had gone into the house came out to say, "All she wants is for you to leave her property."

The next day Judy and I went to the NAACP Legal Defense Fund to file a housing discrimination suit. Ironically, I had more faith in this court process than Judy. The system had worked well against me; I was ready to find out if it could work as well on my behalf. This was my first time in court as a plaintiff, my first time putting my trust in the system and believing justice would be served. My new faith in the law came from the fact that I did not see myself as the same young girl who had stood before a white judge waiting for a verdict. I had a good, respectable job, a respectable prospective roommate who even worked with police officers sometimes. I was older, more mature, the mother of a first-grader. I believed I deserved to be treated better than Mrs. Spann had treated me.

A year later, while Judy and I were roommates, our case went to trial. Our law firm had hired a detective who came back with evidence showing that all of Mrs. Spann's properties, some sixty-two units— houses, duplexes, and quadruplexes—were occupied by whites until after our suit was filed. A chart presented in court also showed that Mrs. Spann still did not rent any of her thirty single-family homes to blacks.

I thought Mrs. Spann herself was our best witness. When questioned she referred to "colored people" by their first names, regardless of their age, while all white people she addressed as "Mr." or "Mrs.," using their last names. This didn't prove she was racist, but it showed she at least internalized this racist practice, how she looked at "colored people," as she still called them in 1975, as being different. Judy's daughter, Michelle, cried in court as she recalled how scared she was when the police zoomed up to Mrs. Spann's house.

But Mrs. Spann's attorneys portrayed her as a mother and widow, a woman who had inherited her husband's business and was doing the best she could with it, someone who wasn't prejudiced but didn't know the sophisticated ways in which business should be handled. They painted a picture of us as fortune seekers who deliberately set up Mrs. Spann so we could sue her and win a monetary award.

After three days of testimony, the trial ended. The foreman stood and proclaimed, "Not guilty!" Mrs. Spann, who had been wearing her right arm in a sling since the trial began, jumped to her feet, swinging her injured arm, yelling, "God is good!" I looked at Judy. She was crying and pounding her fist on her knee.

After the verdict, our lawyer wanted to question the jurors; I wanted to help. Judy couldn't bear it. There were two black jurors, a woman in her late thirties who had been the first black salesclerk at the most expensive department store downtown and a man in his sixties, a retiree who had worked all his life as a messenger for a small white-owned jewelry store.

None of the white jurors would talk to us. The black woman said, "I felt sorry for the woman; y'all were trying to take advantage of her," and then ran off. The elderly black man said, "I believed y'all, but I was the only one."

The lawyer explained to the man that if he had held to what he believed, the jury would have been deadlocked. "The verdict had to be unanimous," the lawyer explained.

"It had to be what? No, sir, I didn't know that," the juror said, looking baffled.

The judge even considered overturning the verdict but later informed us that he did not want to set such a historic precedent. And so we had to live with this unjust resolution, one I felt connected me to an awful history, to all of the blacks before me who had not received justice in a courtroom.

Judy stayed in bed most of the next week. She broke into tears at unpredictable moments—after picking up the telephone to say, "Hello," to some unsuspecting person, while reaching across the dinner table for the saltshaker, in the middle of listening to a record of Malcolm X speeches. I couldn't stop talking about the case, telling strangers at the most inappropriate moment, once at a party in the middle of a funny conversation, another time at a bus stop, where most of the people were white. I wanted something, though I wasn't sure what I could get now that would satisfy me. Somebody to validate my anger? Somebody to empathize? I wanted as much of America as I could get to acknowledge that racism throve and that I had been its victim again.

The rage I felt was like the pain I would feel years later after a series of deaths in my life. Each death would reawaken my mourning for all the preceding deaths. It was the same with this verdict. It opened an old wound that went back to Virginia, when a white woman had called the dog pound to take away my little dog, lying, saying he was vicious and had snapped at her child, when she knew the truth was that it was me she wanted them to pick up, so I would stop playing with her daughter. It was a wound that was probably older than that, an ancient wound I was born into. This time it came just when, for the first time, I had willingly given myself over to the mercy of the system that was supposed to give me justice.

For weeks I felt as if I was a little out of sync with everyone else, on the edge. I choked back hysteria. I considered making a Molotov cocktail and hurling it at the courthouse, even going so far as to drive past the courthouse at night to see if there were security guards around. A month later, I was too exhausted from my thoughts to do anything. Also, I was afraid that if the courthouse burned to the ground, I would still feel dissatisfied.

◆   ◆   ◆

Judy and I and our girls had ultimately settled into a large, old, one-story frame house with a country kitchen, a fireplace in the living room, a formal dining room with French doors, and a charming kitchen with a breakfast nook. The children scattered their toys across the wide front porch. On warm evenings after the girls had gone to bed, Judy and I sat in the swing, talking for hours. Together we had an enviable record collection, featuring a little bit of everything: jazz, soul, folk, orchestrated movie scores, speeches by Malcolm X, and experimental recordings that defied placement in any category, not just pulsating beats that moved my feet, but also soothing melodies and piercing avant-garde riffs. There was always music playing in our house, even if it was just to serve as background to our conversations.

Neither Judy nor I dated for months at a time, which allowed us to spend more time with ourselves and with our children. I had some poems published in a literary magazine at Johnson C. Smith University, including one called "Father," which continues to haunt me because it verifies that my relationship with my father troubled me throughout my life. At the time I wrote the poem, doctors had discovered a growth on his spine. Eventually, they removed the growth and determined it was not malignant. My father was well again, though he walked with a limp the rest of his life. We returned to our regular routines, and I ultimately forgot that I had ever written this poem or had had these thoughts.

> My father never really meant anything to me.
> Now at the slightest hint that the could be dying
> be it one year, two years, or five years from now
> I'll cry
> Oh, how I'll cry!
>
> How could you miss love you never knew existed?
> Search for something that has always surrounded you?
> Why did I pity him when, perhaps, I should have pitied
> myself,
> for never recognizing his love,
> never allowing myself to bathe in its warmth,
> never being taken in by its sweet odor.
> Why should I pity him?
> It is not his fault that he suffered,
> but mine for letting him.
> For if he knew not how to express his love,
> I should have shown him by expressing mine.

Andrea and Michelle were inseparable, sharing a bed and secrets and God only knows what else. They got in trouble together, and, generally, suffered the consequences in unison.

Where once I had been bleak and downtrodden, now I was beginning to believe anything was possible. The change didn't come overnight, but because I was not searching outside myself for someone to
make me happy, there was time to turn inward. Together Judy and I
nudged each other deeper into our own selves, sharing books and
holding long conversations about what we read and how we interpreted it.

We read all of Carlos Castaneda and books like *Zen and the Art of
Motorcycle Maintenance*. When "positive thinking" became the pop
psychology of the seventies, we bought everything we could that mentioned those two words. At yard sales we bought used school texts,
psychology books, writings by Aristotle and Freud, and scientific
books about the mind. Next we read religious writings, the Hindu
Bhagavad Gita, the teachings of Confucius and the Hare Krishna. We
turned our attention to metaphysics, reading about psychic energy,
reincarnation, and ESP.

We went to a psychic, who told us things about ourselves that we
believed no one else but God knew. I was more interested in asking
the woman questions like: "What is time?" and "What is death?"
than in knowing what was going to happen to me tomorrow or next
year. Judy and I began to have psychic experiences of our own,
dreams that came true, but more frequently, the ability to pick up
each other's thoughts or send each other telepathic messages. Either
that, or we were simply beginning to know each other so well.

"There is a dress downtown you should buy," she said when she
came home from work one day, launching into a description.

I had just come home from a shopping trip, and when I pulled my
dress from the bag Judy gasped, recognizing it as the one she had
wanted me to buy.

We lived together for two years and came to accept such occur-
rences. Our house took on a calmness that engulfed everyone who
walked through the door. People seemed drawn to our home,
whether to sit and talk or to listen to music. When one of our friends
went on a talking fast—at least, that's what Judy and I named it—and
didn't speak for over a year, he still dropped by our house because he

knew we wouldn't try to make him talk. He'd sit for as long as he wanted; then he'd wave good-bye and leave.

Overall, I was feeling good about myself for the first time in years, proud of my job and myself as a mother and a friend. Judy and I and our children created a family in which we all flourished. The children set up a lemonade stand in the front yard in the summer, selling glasses of the beverage for a dime each and gingersnap cookies, three for a nickel. We invited friends over to watch the girls perform in plays. We rigged up draperies that could be drawn and closed in the doorway leading from the living room to the dining room, which was their stage. Then we presented flowers to the actresses and held a reception with herbal tea, lemonade, cookies, and ice cream. The home Judy and I and our children created was the first safe haven my spirit had had since I left my parents' house. Perhaps in some ways, it was even safer than my parents' home, because this was *my* place, and with ownership came freedom. The two years that Judy and I lived together was also the longest period I had lived without a steady boyfriend, and the significance of that was not lost on me.

I had outgrown my job as a secretary at the *Charlotte Observer*. Boredom wreaked havoc on my work, and I fell asleep in the middle of typing letters. When I told Peter I was quitting to return to school, he got me a part-time job in the newsroom so I would still have an income. Three mornings a week, I transcribed the telephone calls of people phoning "Tell-It-Line," a column that published the answers to trivia questions and helped people with consumer problems. In the afternoons I attended Central Piedmont Community College, taking all the English and writing classes time would allow, as well as other courses marked "college prep." It was my intention to get my associate's degree and then transfer to a four-year college to major in English. Beyond that, I didn't know exactly what I'd do except write novels and plays.

Even while I was sitting in the newsroom, it didn't hit me that here was a place where people actually earned money writing. I figured I would write breathless literature while working at some other job to make a living, maybe teaching or working for an employee newsletter. Becoming a reporter was not a consideration, because I didn't want to write about the real world; I wanted to create my own. Also, I considered reporters just representatives of the System, touting the same messages, chewing up whatever the State Department said and spitting it out in palatable form for the public. I wanted to write fiction because it would allow me to write the truth. But watching a newspaper come together, knowing what will be in it before anyone else does, is tantamount to time traveling, seeing what tomorrow will bring. I was sucked in by my awe of the process. Even before I saw my name in print, I felt I was a part of that newspaper. And when I read "Tell-It-Line" in print, I saw the questions I had transcribed and could remember the anxiety in the voice of the woman who had ordered three chicks through the mail, only to receive a box of dead birds; she wanted a refund. I knew that the man having a problem with his new 1977 Chrysler New Yorker had tears in his voice when he asked if the anonymous people of Tell-It-Line could intercede and talk to the makers of his dream car.

Knowing these small, human details made me feel powerful in some strange way; I knew the secrets. I saw the faces of reporters and columnists, people known only as names to most readers. The noises in the newsroom blended to form a constant hum, as if the air were electrified, and when you walked into the room you not only heard it; you felt it. Before I considered writing journalism, I fell in love with the newsroom, with the hum, the secrets, and the creative clutter.

◆　◆　◆

It was probably inevitable: first Judy met a man; then I met one. Her beau moved in with us for a short while, but then they decided to get a place of their own. So my new boyfriend, a musician in a popular band based in Charlotte, was going to move in with me. Judy and I were happy that we were both in love at the same time, but we mourned for our friendship, because we knew it could never be the same again and because it was painful breaking up the home we had created together.

In so many ways, that house had been our bridge from girlhood to womanhood. We had grown more peaceful, had stopped the harried dating game to delve into our own selves. Each of us had provided the other with what men had not given either of us thus far: unconditional love and genuine friendship, a place where we could peel away our insecurities and strip down to our real selves and not feel raw.

As a going-away gift, Judy gave me a poem she composed about sisterhood and our life together. She had handwritten it in beautiful calligraphy, painted a flower on the side of one verse, and put a paper frame around it herself. I hung it on the wall in my bedroom. Near our last day together, I helped her pack up the small things in her room: perfumes, her watercolors, her photos, the beads she would string together to make jewelry. There was one photo that I wanted to keep, a color shot of Judy dressed in a T-shirt with a large peace symbol on the front of it. She was standing with her arms draped around two grinning white police officers, whom she probably had met when she went to the police department to fetch one of her clients from the drug rehab program. Anyway, the picture was a perfect depiction of everything Judy was: a charmer who could talk two police officers into dropping charges against a young, troubled drug addict, a healer who cared enough to get out of bed in the middle of the night to get someone else's child out of trouble. I held the picture between my fingers, knowing that I wanted to cut out the image of Judy and place it under the flower on the poem she gave me. But the artist in me said that to put the photo on the poem would mean altering someone else's expression. I dropped the photo back into the box I was packing and went to the bathroom.

When I came out five minutes later, I went to my room to get a marker to label the boxes. I glanced up at my poem on the wall. My eyes filled with tears and my knees shook so hard I had to sit on the bed. While I had been in the bathroom, Judy had cut the image of herself out of the photo and had pasted it in the exact spot where I wanted it: under the painted flower on the poem.

◆　◆　◆

Ziggy was a gentle man, with a voice both soft and gravelly, like the sand-swept breezes of Key West, a place I adored. This was 1977, and he made my mood ring glow a warm turquoise. In the evenings, we snuggled up in the corner of the sofa, sipped wine, and listened to jazz: Herbie Hancock, Chick Corea, and Weather Report, while I fell asleep like a baby nestled against her father's chest.

Ziggy was gorgeous: a beautiful full beard, bronze skin, a funny nose that puffed at the end, and nice, big lips. He played saxophone in a popular jazz-funk band. A woman like myself, who loved music nearly as much as she loved life, or maybe even equated the two, found it easy to love a man who seemed to create notes with his breath.

As a musician, Ziggy possessed the discipline I wanted for myself, practicing his horns daily and always writing new songs, regardless of what else intruded on his time, or whether or not he had a gig. But from the beginning there were discords that I should have dealt with and did not. For one, Ziggy did not work a nine-to-five job. If he couldn't earn his money as a musician, he was just broke. Even the hustlers I had dated had worked hard, doing whatever was necessary to keep money in their pockets—and they had shared their earnings with me. Ziggy had a daughter just over a year old, who, as far as I could see, he made no attempt to support financially. He picked up the child regularly, bringing her to spend the day with us, but he didn't have that I'll-do-anything-to-feed-my-child attitude that had gripped me since the day Andrea was born. I had grown up in a household with a man who always took care of his family financially. That unconsciously influenced what I expected from a man.

After months of working on my mind and spirit, I believed I was wise enough to see through bullshit and detect the faintest possibility of trouble. I thought too much of myself, basically. Meditation, reading, and studying had made me perfect; I was so smart that I was blind again, as much in the dark as I had been before my months of inward searching with Judy. In some ways, maybe I was even in worse shape now, because at least before I knew that I needed to search for truth. Now, I had stopped looking. Not recognizing that life is a constant journey, I believed I had arrived.

Everything I thought I had learned fell aside in one swooping incident. Ziggy and I went out one night with his best friend, Richard, who was the vocalist in the band, and Richard's girlfriend, Regina. After a movie, we stopped at Regina's apartment, where we talked, smoked a couple of joints, and drank wine. I went to the bathroom, and when I came out, Ziggy motioned to me to join him in the bedroom. He immediately planted a hard kiss on my lips and his hands roamed my body, over my breasts and in my crotch. Within a few minutes we were in the bed, naked, our bodies entwined. In the middle of this, when we were both hot and excited, he abruptly got up and left the room.

I was lying on the bed with my legs apart when, seconds later, Richard came into the room, leaned over me, and kissed me hard on the mouth. I froze. What was going on? Where was Ziggy? Should I scream? Should I be cool?

From the living room I heard Ziggy and Regina moaning, obviously having sex. It hit me then that this was what Ziggy wanted, for us to swap partners for sex. In the next moment, I made a decision that erased everything I had learned. Instead of yelling, "Stop!" as I wanted to, I was silent, to please Ziggy. I cut off my own tongue and did not utter a word of objection on that night, or on any of the painful nights that followed over the years. Though I enjoyed immensely the sex Ziggy and I had together when we were alone, I never totally enjoyed the sex we had with anyone else. There were flashes of pleasure, fleeting moments of ecstasy, but generally, my mind was in combat with my body and both lost.

I would know Ziggy intimately for nine years, would marry him and eventually love him as a brother rather than a husband. Yet whenever I look back over the relationship, I point to that night, probably two months after I met him, as the beginning of the end, the sign that our relationship was doomed. Something inside me died that night. It had nothing to do with my sleeping with his best friend, or his sleeping with another woman. It had to do with my choosing to be dishonest, with swallowing my own needs and holding them inside me, where they festered until they spoiled all the love I had for Ziggy and nearly all the love I had for myself.

After Ziggy and I were divorced, though, and the self-deception had ended, I asked myself: what would have happened if I had said "no" that night? The truth was, he probably would have accepted my "no," with some fuss. And if he had not, the relationship would have only ended sooner—and without a divorce.

On that crucial night when I chose silence, I returned to my old self, the woman desperate for a man. Ziggy never knew how I felt. When Richard and I finished in the bedroom and we went into the living room, I smiled at Ziggy and Regina writhing on the floor.

I developed a series of warped rationales to support my relationship: at least Ziggy told me who he was fucking; our relationship was better than most because we didn't sneak behind each other's back like so many other couples I knew; all men cheat because a man is gonna be a man; if I could handle this, I would be a better person because I would have rid myself of jealousy.

I could not see that I was like my old cellmates who said that life in the big prison was better than life in the city jail because in the big prison you got to wear your own clothes. I could see so clearly in jail what I couldn't see now with Ziggy—that a jail is a jail, but the greatest imprisonment of all and, therefore, the greatest freedom, too, is in your mind. I would not even consider the fact that I could have a man who was honest and who did not sleep with other women or want me to sleep with other men. I was obsessed because Ziggy was the best man I had ever had, because he did not physically abuse me; he was gentle and affectionate. So I accepted life in the big prison when I didn't have to live in prison at all.

As the months passed, Ziggy and I became each other's best friend. Moving like a lot of 1960s Americans from counterculture politics to Earth Shoe establishments, we searched for a way of life we felt was more congruent with the natural order of the world, deciding to become vegetarians, baking our own bread, growing our own herbs and sprouts, making our own yogurt. I took yoga and weaving at the community college and wove small mats and wall hangings while Ziggy played his horn. In my new job as researcher, I was one of three people who answered the inquiries from callers, helping them solve consumer problems and looking up answers to their trivia questions. Then I wrote my answers up for the column, though no one would ever know, because we didn't get bylines; we were anonymous. I couldn't wait to get home from work to tell Ziggy about my day, a new person I met or a funny call to Tell-It-Line. I told him everything, except the obvious: that I did not like our sexual escapades.

Ziggy helped with the bills when he had money. Sometimes the band played regularly, and at other times engagements were rare. Meanwhile, our house turned into a rehearsal hall. Musicians, most of them young men, set up their instruments in our dining room and jammed late into the night. Andrea and I loved having music in our house, though most of it was jazz and my daughter would have preferred pop or rhythm and blues. I diced up vegetables for homemade soup and washed dirty dishes left by guests while Ziggy blew long, high notes on his soprano sax; I slapped the broom across the hardwood floor and wiped the dust from our furniture while a drummer improvised, beating slow, then fast, skipping and brushing across the skin of his instrument until my heart was faint.

We had parties that started late on Saturday nights, after the clubs had closed, so the musicians and vocalists could drop by our house and perform. Women in sparkling sheer materials hugged the microphones set up in front of our fireplace and belted out their velvet ballads. Sometimes we had poets performing at the same time, à la "Last Poets" style, rapping verses to music or to the beat of an African drum in our kitchen.

Ziggy and I had long, wonderful conversations, so satisfying that later, when I had fallen out of love with him, our exchange of ideas replaced sex for me. I was contented and, therefore, I could look beyond my own front door and see that I was connected to the rest of the world and responsible for it, too. I held a Halloween party for children from Easter Seals at my house, recruiting friends and neighbors to give out treats and roam about as fortune-tellers, magicians, and clowns. With friends, Ziggy and I organized a group that sponsored festivals to showcase black visual artists and musicians. Ziggy and I were politically active, traveling to Washington, D.C., with Helen Chavis, a woman I befriended briefly, to participate in a march in front of the White House to free the Wilmington Ten. Helen's brother Ben was a member of the group, ten civil rights activists accused of igniting riots in Wilmington, North Carolina. (Ben would later become the executive director of the NAACP, succeeding Benjamin Hooks.) We taught Andrea about each cause we supported and tried to involve her whenever we could. She wrote a letter to the governor of North Carolina asking for clemency for the Wilmington Ten.

Ziggy came home one day and told me he had met a Jamaican guy who wore his hair in a style called "dreadlocks," which the guy said was the natural hairstyle for black people. We learned more about dreadlocks, that they had been worn in ancient Africa and were the style of the Rastafarians of Jamaica. We decided to dread our hair, too. Ziggy stopped combing and brushing his hair, and when he washed it he separated the clumps into thinner, long strands. Within a couple of months, he had two-inch long ropes of hair, even where he had been balding. I followed him, though I never thought my dreads were as pretty as his, because my hair separated into thicker, more diversified shapes of ropes. For work, I wrapped my hair in scarves and other materials.

Hair is often considered an expression of politics by blacks. The illusion is that blacks who hate being black imitate whites by wearing their hair in an unnatural state, perming it to make it straight like the hair of white women. Other blacks, those who are proud of their heritage and promote everything African, wear their hair natural, nappy, unpermed, in braids, an Afro, or dreadlocks. I had wrestled with these beliefs most of my life, from the time when I was a child and thought nappy hair was "bad" hair until my days of dreading, when I thought I finally knew myself and had chosen for one last time how to define me. Dreading my hair would tell white people that I didn't want to be like them; it would assure my black brothers and sisters that I was no house nigger, particularly since many of them questioned the politics of any black person working for a white-owned paper. Our dreadlocks embarrassed Andrea, who as a preteen wanted nothing more than for herself and her family to blend in with everyone else.

◆　◆　◆

"Pat, Daddy beat Mama and locked her out the house last night," my sister Carol said on the phone to me long-distance. "He put the dead bolt on the door and she tried to climb in the window."

My parents had never appeared to be in love; at least none of us children ever saw any physical expressions of their love for each other, no touch of the hand or kiss on the neck, not even a pat on the butt or a brush against each other while passing. Daddy gave Mama cards on special occasions and holidays and gave us money to buy her gifts from him on those special days, too. This was the way my father treated all of us: he did the proper thing; he did not go one step further. As I grew into a woman, I noticed that my mother, like me, longed for more. But I am not sure she ever asked, and so perhaps we were alike in our silences, too.

In the beginning of their relationship, I imagine Mama was more true to herself, smothering Daddy with expressions of her love. But as time passed, Mama became more like Daddy, holding back, reciprocating only what she received. The Women's Movement affected Mama's life in the same way it affected many who were never activists or marchers. It swept her along gently, the way a hurricane passing a hundred miles away sends gusts of wind through a city not directly in its path. Mama read about women working in professions once the total domain of men, women fighting for equal pay, housewives demanding respect for the work they performed each day. The gusts of change blew her way and nudged her to do something her children and husband thought she would never do: She got a job outside the house. She went to work at a day-care center.

It became increasingly obvious that Daddy defined himself in large part by his ability to take care of his family financially. If Mama worked and made money, too, how would he define his role as a man? Meanwhile, his health was deteriorating. He had an operation for what doctors diagnosed as a pinched nerve in his left leg. He already limped on that leg; after the operation, he dragged the leg. This was difficult for the proud marine used to walking ramrod straight. He cut back on his activities and stopped playing golf, a move that struck us all deeply because we worried it was an omen that he was dying.

But Daddy was nowhere near death. There was a void in his life, because there were no babies around anymore and he didn't know what to do with older children. This void added to his anger over Mama's working and his mourning about his useless leg. Together they all created a bitter man, who grew more bitter each day.

The image of my dignified middle-aged mother trying to crawl through a window enraged me so much that I got in my car with my child and my pocketbook and headed straight for Maryland. Seven and a half hours later, I stormed into my parents' house.

"Daddy, if you ever lay another hand on Mama I'll kill you!" I screamed at my father, who was sitting in his lounge chair in the basement. I spotted the pint of McNaughton whiskey beside him, just where my sisters had said it would be.

He barely blinked and didn't seem at all shocked to see me. "You've always been on your mother's side," he said.

I talked to Mama, whose lip was busted, puffy, and red where Daddy had hit her in the mouth with his fist. She explained that she had been coming home from a recreation committee meeting and was a half hour late when Daddy hit her and locked her out.

Over the next year they fought many times, and I usually jumped in the middle, playing protector to Mama, whom I considered a helpless victim. My role as policewoman strained even more the fragile relationship between me and my father. The fighting between them stopped only after Mama went to a shelter for battered women and got the nerve to take out a warrant on my father. When Mama returned home, she slept alone in the master bedroom and Daddy moved into the bedroom downstairs. She carefully decorated his room and cleaned it faithfully, until one day when he forbade her to ever set foot in there again.

He so often accused her of being with other men that one day she must have decided to live up to his accusations; she started dating someone. I thought she deserved to be happy; it had been so long since she had smiled. But some of my siblings were appalled when they learned about her affair; for years they disliked Mama because of it.

Mama graduated from a beauty school and began working as a cosmetologist. "You think you're so smart," Daddy told her, not realizing that his anger betrayed the real meaning of his words. *He* was the one who thought she was so smart, because he thought of himself as dumb. She had gone to college, and he had dropped out of high school. He didn't give himself any credit for the fact that he had dropped out because his family was poor, so he could join the Marine

Corps and his parents would have one less mouth to feed. He didn't pat himself on the back for studying and receiving his GED while he was a workingman and a husband with half-grown children. But I didn't give him credit for any of this either. When he was finally near death, I would realize that one of our greatest similarities was that most of our lives we had belittled ourselves.

◆   ◆   ◆

The word *marriage* came up casually in a conversation between Ziggy and me. It dawned on us one day that marriage seemed a natural step in the progression of our relationship, so without much discussion, we donned our jeans and went to the justice of the peace.

When Ziggy wasn't out of town with the band, he was a house hus-band, cleaning, washing the laundry, and cooking. Most of the time, this suited me, because I didn't like housework and I was enjoying my job. Also, Ziggy was a better cook than I was, folded the clothes neater than I did, and could iron rings around my wrinkles. It didn't bother me that I paid most of the bills, bought our clothes, and paid for vaca-tions and trips. Only periodically did it matter that sometimes the band or most of its members spent the night at our house in between out-of-town gigs. Generally, both Andrea and I adjusted. Once she hung a sign scrawled in her writing on the bathroom door: "Do Not Enter. Little Girl Taking A Bath." Most of the time she brought some of her girlfriends into the house and they watched the guys rehearse, their mouths hanging open in amazement at the sounds. If the music was funky enough, they danced in the living room.

Ziggy still told me about the women he slept with. Sometimes, in-stead of getting jealous, I actually got hot and we ended the conversa-tions having passionate sex. He introduced me to Janice, a woman he had dated before he knew me, and she and I became close friends. Ziggy had sex with her occasionally, and the three of us climbed into bed together at other times. But Janice and I developed the kind of special relationship that two women who are wives to the same man must have. We respected each other, each admiring the other's intel-lect, artistic talents, and compassion. We were like sisters, but more. I was never jealous of Janice's relationship with Ziggy because I was sure that all she wanted was sex and not my husband—forever.

The three of us were lying in bed one night, after having sex. Ziggy had climaxed during intercourse, but I hadn't. Generally Janice and I looked out for each other, making sure that Ziggy satisfied us both; this time I didn't care about Janice.

"I didn't come," I announced angrily.

Ziggy apologized. I jumped out of the bed and ran to the bathroom. Janice followed. She closed the door, and I started crying. Janice knew my tears had nothing to do with sexual satisfaction. She pushed me for the truth.

"He fucks whoever he wants and he doesn't even work," I blurted out.

Janice had heard me talk about my frustration with Ziggy for not working while I struggled to pay all of our bills. She had encouraged me then to issue him an ultimatum, leave him or accept him as he was. But she really didn't believe he was going to change.

"Whenever you two argue—no matter what you're fighting about—you're always arguing about money," she told me more than once.

It was more than sex and more than money, too; it was the entire lifestyle I had chosen, the steps I had taken away from the traditions and values I believed in. But I couldn't say this out loud, because that would be tantamount to admitting that my life was a lie. Besides, I was ashamed of the fact that this was my third marriage. No sensible person got married three times. If this one didn't work, I would always be a failure.

A few days after my crying spell, I cut off my shoulder-length dreadlocks.

"You're crazy," said Ziggy. "I swear I'll leave you if you cut them."

"You don't work a regular job where people have to conform," I told him. "It's hard. People assume certain things about me because of my hair. They're put off. And my hair is stopping me from getting positions and raises."

This was only half the truth. I could have lived with other people's assumptions and fought for positions and raises. But the bigger truth was that I dreaded my hair for the wrong reasons: not for a philosophy or belief or because I wanted to, but because Ziggy dreaded his. Now I was being just as dishonest. It was easier for me to cut off my hair and blame it on someone else than to say, "I don't want to wear dreadlocks."

Ziggy stormed out of the house and didn't come back that night. He was at home when I came home from work the next day. For the next month or so, whenever I made a mistake, he taunted me. "You have strength in your hair," he said. "Can't you tell? You've been stupid since you cut off your locks."

He lied. I was getting smarter, though it was happening slowly and in spurts and not on all fronts at once. At work, I wrote occasional short features, my first one a prelude to a performance of the Negro Ensemble Company's production of the musical *Raisin*. I wrote weekly features about local people.

When someone told me about a summer journalism program being held at the University of California, Berkeley, I applied because it was free and because I had always wanted to see California. I got a letter, which I stuffed in my pocket and carried around for half a day before opening. After reading the first word, "Congratulations," I sat down and cried. For the first time in my life, I had won something.

Ziggy was ecstatic for me. He was going on the road with the band, so we made arrangements for Andrea to stay with my parents. Just after my twenty-ninth birthday, I headed for Berkeley with my vision of California as home of *American Bandstand,* the Black Panthers, Yippies, and Angela Davis. I found an enthralling carnival of life around the campus: sidewalk vendors, teenage panhandlers, street performers, and all kinds of information plastered on every telephone pole.

It was a poignant summer. I heard Joan Baez sing "Blowing in the Wind" at a rally on campus for a Soviet dissident, stared misty-eyed at my heroine Angela Davis at a "pro choice" meeting, danced at a Bob Marley–Peter Tosh concert, and saw the controversial play that defined black womanhood in 1978: *For Colored Girls Who Have Considered Suicide When the Rainbow Is Enuf.*

The students of the summer program put out a weekly newspaper, which meant we covered local and national stories, the issues of the day: reverse discrimination, Gov. Jerry Brown's administration, the battle over Proposition 13, a state constitutional amendment that reduced property taxes. We went to government meetings in Oakland and covered fires and murders. By the end of the summer, my soul was wrapped in newsprint.

The newspaper that was supposed to hire me dropped out of the journalism program. A friend of mine, who had been an editor at the *Charlotte Observer,* agreed to hire me at the *Miami News,* where she was now managing editor. For ten years I had been either a typist, a teletype operator, or a secretary, and now, at twenty-nine, I was going to be a reporter who wrote stories read by hundreds of people.

chapter eleven

Seething in the Sun

Rose Smith, the only other black reporter at the *Miami News,* invited me to stay with her until I found a place to live. Ziggy and Andrea waited in Charlotte. We all thought it would be just a short while, but we didn't know this: many property owners in Miami did not want to rent to people with children, anyone with a foreign accent, or anyone who was black. I fit two of those categories.

Here I was in another state experiencing the same form of racial prejudice I had faced with Mrs. Spann in Charlotte five years earlier. In Miami, property owners made appointments with me by phone, obviously thinking I was white. When I met them, they told me they had just rented the property. Less tactful owners simply ran or hid behind curtains, refusing to open the door. One woman told me, "I would rent to you, but I'm moving and I have to think about my friends who will still be living here. They don't want black people on the property."

My search stretched into weeks and then into months, until I was angry, frustrated, missing my family terribly, and crying each day I

returned to Rose's. When my white coworkers tried to carry on normal conversations with me, I was abrupt, offering few words and no
explanation. I was angry that life required I be discriminated against
by some whites and then come in, sit down, and act normal next to
other whites. My imagination magnified the smiles of my coworkers,
and I saw what I wanted to see: people with no problems.

By this time, I had saved enough money to buy a house. People
selling houses were more compassionate and friendly than those rent-
ing them, perhaps because the sellers understood clearly that the only
color that mattered was green. I found a small two-bedroom banga-
low in North Miami Beach with a so-called "Florida room," a large
room with more windows than walls, so the sunshine filled the room
most days. The house was set on a large corner lot with two orange
trees and aloe vera plants in the front yard.

Ziggy came down to see it and to sign his name at settlement, then
went back to Charlotte to return again with Andrea and a U-Haul,
packed with furniture and household goods. He didn't stay in Miami,
though, insisting that he had commitments in Charlotte. But we both
knew he hated the city, having determined that when he lived there
ten years earlier. Andrea was excited, looking forward to warm win-
ters and neighborhood beaches. Ziggy was definitely disappointed—
and stalling. He was still living in our old house in Charlotte with a
couple of friends as roommates.

In Miami, Andrea had the cosmopolitan experience I had hoped
for all of us. She and her new friends, who were white, Haitian, and
Jamaican, spent hours at the neighborhood swimming pool or at our
house, listening to music and dancing. I got to know their parents, but
our busy lives kept us from socializing. My favorite neighbors were
the Paseos, an elderly Italian couple with a big, fat female cat they had
named "Boy" before either of them realized he was a girl. Mr. Paseo, a
short, balding man with thin strands of white hair and thick, muscular
arms, had mango trees in his yard, and we traded the oranges from my
trees for his mangoes. But he preferred to invite us over to eat the
mangoes at his house, where he and Mrs. Paseo kept the fruit
chopped up and stored in Tupperware bowls in the freezer. At least
once a week, in the evening after dinner, I went across the street to

their house for desert, eating chilled mangoes and drinking Italian wine at the kitchen table.

Early on, Mr. Paseo made me an offer: "Pat, take me to the barbershop every Saturday and I'll take care of your yard." I figured it was a good deal. How long could he be in the barbershop with so little hair? So at the age of eighty-three and with an artificial hip, Mr. Paseo became my gardener. He had trimmed the trees in his yard until they looked like Disney creations, squat trunks wearing green square tops, too perfect for my liking. Of course, he trimmed my bushes into smaller versions of his treetops, perfect green boxes that rested on the ground.

◆　◆　◆

The shift I worked changed from time to time. I was the night police reporter, which required some creative juggling at home. When I worked from three o'clock to midnight, I cooked dinner just before I left home. Andrea heated up the food, if she had to. I spent a lot of time at work nervous or on the telephone talking to her. My next-door neighbors checked on her before she went to bed. When I worked from 7:00 P.M. to 3:00 A.M., I was even more nervous. Sometimes I had a baby-sitter, but it was hard to find a teenager willing to stay all night and I couldn't afford live-in help. Anyway, Andrea begged to be left alone and she didn't want to spend the night away from home with one of my friends. When I got home I was usually wired from the anxiety of deadline, or still struck by the profound eeriness of following police, walking into a silent house just after bodies had been removed. Sometimes unable to sleep, I stayed up until just before dawn, and when Andrea got up to go to school I was fast asleep, unable to move.

My child poured herself a bowl of cereal or boiled an egg and fixed toast. She put a notebook on my nightstand, logging in each day what outfit she wore so that if anything happened to her I could describe her to the police. This only compounded the guilt I felt and the tape inside my head that repeated throughout my workday: *You're such a bad mother.* On weekends, I tried to make it up to her, the two of us skating in the streets in Coconut Grove or in Biscayne Park beside the water; or we went to the beach, where most of the time Andrea swam while I stretched out on a blanket and read a book. If I was feeling particularly guilty—perhaps I had to work overtime that week or she had to eat leftovers one day—then I took her shopping for expensive, faddish clothes. Of course, she knew the weeks I felt my guiltiest and she used me, not maliciously but intelligently, the way children often use adults. At those times, in addition to shopping we ate at a seafood restaurant on the bay, where Andrea had her favorite "all the crabs you can eat" special. To give us more time together, I volunteered to be the "class mother." A couple of times a week, whenever the teacher needed me, I went to the class to help correct papers, make copies of materials, or assist in any small task I was asked to do.

When Andrea was older, she would say of this period, "I thought I was going to be a juvenile delinquent." Everything she saw on television told her that children left alone ended up in trouble; therefore, she waited for the inevitable to happen. As for the log of what she was wearing, it eventually evolved into a listing to make sure she didn't wear the same outfit in a two-week period.

I began to appreciate my new career as a chance to see life in a way few people get. I saw human beings at their most fragile moments, and to my surprise, there was a beautiful by-product: At that moment when people are reacting from what seems like sheer emotion, they are most honest. There is no time to think of lies or deceptions, no will to even try. When I questioned a mother whose daughter had been murdered in a park not far from their home, a couple whose son had hanged himself in the front yard, they did not have the time or forethought to edit what they said. Any barriers that normally divide us—race, sex, social status—all disappeared. What came out of their mouths were the most beautiful, simple truths about life and love and death. I felt terribly fortunate to hear them. It was an opportunity to learn from other people's tragedies and mistakes, when I was so used to learning more painfully, through my own. I tried to show the people I interviewed that I respected this privilege, that I understood that the gift they were giving was much more than words, and that if they trusted me, I would prove to them I was worthy of their trust.

People seemed to open themselves up to me so freely that I developed a reputation for being able to get people to talk to me even in the most sensitive situations. If a family had slammed a door on one reporter, the editor might send me out to the house to try again. I muttered to myself all the way about how what I was doing was wrong and an invasion of privacy, but before I drove up to a house, I also prayed that the people I was going to talk to could see that I respected them, that we could quickly find our common ground. Usually, people trusted me. A mother sat and talked to me about her agony; her small son had walked away from his day-care center and been killed when a car struck him on the nearby highway. A teenager talked while he waxed the already spotless truck that belonged to his older brother, who had been killed the night before in a car accident.

They were not all sad stories, but the saddest ones are hard to shake, like shrines in my memory to people I never knew. It always struck me when writing about the dead that I was meeting them after they had left this earth; that in some way I was the last person to meet them, to see the rooms where they slept and to talk to the people who loved them. This was a weird blessing that caused me sorrow, of course, but also a painful happiness, that I should have an opportunity to learn from the dead. Mostly they were common people, but each one was divine. I surmised that the world around me was constantly changing in some profound way, each time one person died.

I paid for these stories, lying awake for hours some nights, unable to shake the images: The skinny young girl who reminded me of my sisters and myself, lying in the hospital room with tubes in her arms and nose and her head bandaged because she had chosen to love a man who ended up firing a bullet into her head. The mother my age weeping over the school pictures of her dead son, her only child. A man who died because he overworked his weak heart helping neighbors prepare for a hurricane that never came, and how he hid his heart condition from his family just as he hid the Purple Heart and other medals awarded for his unselfishness in military duty. I questioned God about all of these things while thanking Him for letting me live twice, through my own life and through the lives of others.

I witnessed the reuniting of Cuban families, watching as people thrown out by Castro arrived in Miami to see for the first time in years the aging faces of brothers and sisters who fled with the first wave of Cuban refugees. Then I reported on the arrival of the Haitians, who had not been exiled but who, by their own accounts, were fleeing political persecution or life-threatening poverty. Yet our country did not grant them the political asylum refugee status they gave to the Cubans, so the stories I wrote about the Haitians were completely different from the happy stories of reunion I wrote about the Cubans. I saw frail, hungry Haitians landing in rickety boats run by greedy captains who charged them more money than most of them made in a lifetime in their native land. And these were the Haitians who made it alive, who were not tossed into the sea by more ruthless captains or did not die from illnesses while on the ocean. Sometimes I wrote about the dead Haitians, too, whose bloated bodies washed ashore, ruining the lunches of diners in the restaurants lining the ocean.

No matter how many times I inserted in my articles quotes from State Department officials explaining that Cubans were political refugees, but Haitians had left their land on their own accord, I swallowed my true feelings of disgust and disbelief. While the rest of the country read about the Haitians, we in Miami saw the government's policies in practice. For blacks, particularly, it was difficult to see the Orange Bowl Stadium, a symbol of one of America's most loved traditions, used as a temporary home for Cubans, while Haitians were detained in barbed-wire camps resembling prisons. It was as simple as this to blacks: the Haitians were dark people like us, but most of the Cubans looked white, and Americans had a history of mistreating people with dark skin and loving people with white skin. For me, each Haitian voyage was like staring at the horror of my history: I saw slaves packed on slave ships, my ancestors tossed into the ocean as food for fish or thrown in pens like animals. And yet, with furiously trembling hands, I wrote as objectively as I could.

◆   ◆   ◆

I missed my husband. But in our long-distance phone conversations he said, "I have a few more gigs and then I'm coming." Our conversations got shorter and our arguments about money grew longer. As I approached age thirty, I was thinking more about material wealth, a decent car, nice clothes for my daughter, and a college education for her, too. The new mortgage was taking a hunk out of my budget. Ziggy wasn't helping, spending all of his money on rent and his other expenses in Charlotte.

Some days the stress of responsibilities weighed heavily on me and I snapped at my child, usually about money. We stopped at the grocery store early one morning and I went in with twenty-dollars to spend and a grocery list that had to be cut in half. Andrea begged for a bag of potato chips.

"We don't have money for things like chips!" I screamed. "You said you need two dollars for school today! You think I'm made out of money?"

She ran out the store in tears. I bought a quart of milk and a dozen eggs, then rushed to the car. "I'm sorry," I said.

She didn't say anything, but when we stopped in front of the school she hugged me as she got out of the car. "Keep the two dollars, Mama," she said.

I ran after her, trying to stuff the money in her shirt pocket, but she was fast, inside the school and down the hallway before I could give her the two dollars. I walked toward the car, crying; I was supposed to be the parent, the one who made sure the child had food and clothing and was happy.

That guilt stayed with me for years. When Andrea was a teenager later and I bought her a blouse for $120 or boots for $250, she thought it was because I had the money; actually, it was because I didn't have it when she was ten. More accurately, it was not only because I didn't have it then, but also because I believed later that I didn't have it because of my choice in men, that I had somehow chosen Ziggy over my child, that I had supported him and she had suffered because of it. When I see children today dressed in expensive attire, I wonder whose guilt they're wearing.

One night I was talking to a friend long-distance when my phone went dead. At work the next day I called the phone company and was told that the service had been disconnected because a phone bill in my name in Charlotte was overdue. I called Ziggy and he told me his roommates had run up the bill and failed to pay it on time. I hung up.

Six months had passed since I had moved into the house, and Ziggy was still in Charlotte. I counted each day as evidence that my husband–best friend had betrayed me. When I rushed home from work, anxious to tell someone about what had happened to me that day, there was no one to tell who could truly understand. My respect for Ziggy faltered; my anger and loneliness multiplied. In this frame of mind, I dated other men. First, casually, as escorts to fancy receptions or as my dance partners at nightclubs. I didn't sleep with them. But what made the relationships different—wrong, in a way—was my secrecy; I didn't tell Ziggy about the dates.

I was angry with him, and so I did something I never imagined I would do: I had an affair. The man was a community activist, married, with two children. Of course, he said he was unhappily married, and there was probably some thread of truth to that, just as there was some truth in my saying, "My husband and I don't get along." But what we were actually having was a fling, an escape for two people not ready to do the hard work of changing what was wrong in their relationships. We had wonderful, easy times together, the kind of fun you have when a relationship is based on nothing more than romance and fantasy and minus the struggle that is necessary sometimes when you're committed to each other forever.

This is not to say we were not serious; on the surface, we considered ourselves madly in love. And the surface was what we were dealing with, because all we saw in each other was what we wanted to see. Whenever I felt guilty about cheating on Ziggy, I dredged up the reasons I was angry with him. In my rage, I dressed for another date. I met my beau outside my house so I could keep my philandering from my daughter.

Though I didn't then think of it in this way, I was doing what my mother had done. I had found a convenient out, an escape that delayed my having to make any truly hard decisions. But I didn't feel the way I had felt for my mother. I had patted her on the back, if only mentally, and basically said, "Good for you. Have a good life," which was like saying, "Don't worry about why you don't get along with Daddy. Don't even try to figure it out or resolve the problems within yourself; you can't change anything, so just go on and escape." Now I was walking in her shoes. I was torn and anguished. No matter how long the delay, the day would come when I would have to face Ziggy and our differences.

That day came sooner than I thought. Ziggy announced he was moving to Miami. I wondered if he had been ushered into action by the tone of voice I now used in our conversations, my sustained bitch pitch. I told my lover that my husband was coming home. For a couple of weeks we grieved over the end of our affair, both still as unhappy as we had been before we met.

At first I ignored Ziggy. I was going to work at 7:00 A.M. and getting off about 3:00 P.M., unless I had to work overtime. At home, I cooked, we ate, and then I studied writing. I had fallen into the habit of spending a couple of hours each evening reading newspapers, tearing out articles I liked so I could figure out what made them move me, writing words and phrases I admired into a large loose-leaf binder. After I finished my studies, I showered and went to bed. I left no time to talk to Ziggy, for us to get to know each other again. That was my way of punishing him. It went on for weeks until he knew what I was doing and why. "If you want me to leave, just tell me and I'm outta here!" he said.

I didn't want him to leave; I just wanted him to hurt. Seeing that my goal was accomplished, I began working on being a supportive wife and friend again. Ziggy got a job at a construction site, but when his boss made him angry, Ziggy quit, his usual response to discomfort on a job.

"Don't you think I've wanted to quit jobs?" I argued. "I tell myself I can't because I have to support the family. You chalk it up and you go on, Ziggy. You don't quit."

Deep in my bones I must have possessed my father's spirit. He ran away from home, lied about his age, and entered the Marine Corps; he dug graves, cleaned office buildings, and chauffeured generals to earn money to take care of his own. I didn't tell Ziggy any of this because I still didn't see the relationship between my family past and my personal present. But the pieces of the puzzle were waiting to be put together.

Ziggy got a paper route, which actually was a job that suited his needs and his personality. He needed not a career, but a job he could quit if a band wanted him to go on the road. Also, the paper route gave him a sense of independence and freedom, since he didn't take orders well, particularly from white people. I thought my father bowed too low to white people, cleaning their toilets, driving them around in luxury cars. But here I was with a man who would not bow or even learn to psych people into believing he was bowing. In some ways, I was still with the boy who cocked his hat to the side and shunned the rules because he was angry with white people. Only now I didn't recognize the tough boy, because he didn't have his hat or his pimp walk. I thought I had moved on to a different kind of man. I didn't realize I was still fighting the images of my father and his friends. But I was beginning to want something different, something more in the middle, a man who could do both, who could have my father's work ethic without bowing low, a man who could pimp and play the game and still keep his head high.

◆ ◆ ◆

In December of 1979 the *Miami Herald* ran the first story about a black man who had died under suspicious circumstances while in police custody. Before I arrived in Miami, there had been several highly publicized suspicious incidents in which police had beaten or shot blacks. In one incident a young mentally retarded man was killed. After I arrived, police stormed into the house of a popular black teacher, beat everyone present, and ransacked the house, while the teacher and his family tried to tell the officers they were not at the address on the search warrant.

Blacks in Miami complained about police brutality, but nothing changed. Then the startling details unfurled about the death of a man named Arthur Lee McDuffie. The police spotted McDuffie, a thirty-three-year-old insurance executive, doing daredevil stunts on his motorcycle one evening. After a high-speed chase, they stopped him. About a dozen officers encircled him, and for twenty minutes they beat him with nightsticks and flashlights. Four days later, after slipping into a coma, McDuffie died. He was the father of two daughters.

His ex-wife, whom he had planned to remarry, was on duty in the hospital when he was brought in with his face bleeding and his head swollen with bruises.

The police wrote up an accident report saying McDuffie had sustained injuries when his motorcycle hit a curb and went out of control. But the medical examiner became suspicious, and eventually his suspicions and rumors prompted the police department to begin an internal investigation.

Some things you never forget, and still, whenever I hear that police officers have beaten someone to death or near death, I remember Arthur McDuffie. I remembered him when I saw the video tape of Rodney King being beaten by police in Los Angeles. When I watched them whale at him with nightsticks, as if he were a beast, I recalled that the medical examiner in Miami had said McDuffie's skull was hit so hard it looked like a "cracked egg"; that the killing blow crashed into his forehead at ninety times the force of gravity; that the weapon was probably a heavy-duty flashlight swung two-handed like an ax. They beat him while he was handcuffed. A blow cracked his skull clean in half, from front to back. When I watched the Rodney King tape I understood why a Miami police officer, at a loss for words, could only describe his fellow officers who beat McDuffie as "frenzied." The feeling, said another, was that McDuffie "was a nigger who was running from the police, and he deserved everything he got."

People in Miami's black community said early on, "They killed the wrong man this time," meaning that the death of McDuffie, an insurance executive and clean-cut ex-marine, stood a better chance of getting investigated than the death of a criminal. McDuffie had run that night because his license had expired and he had already received one ticket for driving without it. Five officers, four whites and one Cuban, were charged in his death. Like all of the blacks in Miami, I watched closely to see what would happen next.

There is nothing so unifying as persecution. The beating death of Arthur McDuffie reminded me in a bold, public way that regardless of my job as a reporter, I was still a nigger to some people. I knew that if I managed to assimilate into the white world, neither my brother, my husband, my nephews, nor any black men in my life could ever follow me, because America feared a black man more than it feared anyone or anything.

Through some of my contacts I was able to convince McDuffie's ex-wife, Fredericka, to be interviewed. This was a coup, since she had refused everyone else, and members of the media from all over the world who descended upon Miami wanted to talk to her.

She was demure, almost childlike, though she must have been in her late twenties. Her eyes were still young, dark and round, with long, curly eyelashes. The first time we met she sat on her living room sofa, barely moving, her eyes misting once when she talked about how her baby girl still ran to the window when a car passed, yelling, "Daddy!" Later, Fredericka would tell me how she was working as a nurse at the hospital on the night when her husband was brought in and how she could hardly recognize him beneath his swollen, bruised skin.

I rode the bus with her to Tampa, to the trial of the police officers. I watched tears drip down her cheeks as her ex-husband's bloody clothes were shown as evidence. When they rolled in his motorcycle, one she remembered as shiny and immaculate, and she saw it was dented and smashed, she rocked back and forth in her seat and held her arms tight across her chest, as if to keep herself from flying away.

"My God, look at that," she said, shaking her head.

I left her side only once, on the Saturday when the jury, all of whom were white and male, went into deliberation. I was so sure it would take them at least a day to reach a verdict, long enough for me to go home for clothes and a quick visit. I still believed people wrangled over evidence, so they could reach justice; I was wrong. It took the jurors two hours to find the officers not guilty. I was in my car driving to Miami when I heard the news on the radio. My first thought was: *Oh my God, where is Fredericka?* This was not the reporter in me talking; it was that other part of me, the side that reporters are supposed to ignore, though they never really can. I cared about this woman, what she was going through, the pain she would feel, to varying degrees, all of her life. I called her hotel room. A friend answered; in the background I heard a howl, a noise that sounded half-animal, half-human, a kind of guttural wailing. It was a noise I had never heard before, but it reminded me of the wailing of foreign women that I heard on the nightly news reports of war in the Mideast.

"Is Fredericka there?"

"She can't come to the phone right now," a woman's weak, exhausted voice answered.

"What is that noise?" I asked, still not understanding.

"That . . . is . . . Fredericka . . . crying," the woman said between sobs.

I hung up the phone and fell against the side of the phone booth, crying for Fredericka and her husband and their children, for all the black men who had been lynched, burned, maimed, and shot. I cried because until that moment I had been a polite, professional Negro who tried to separate her collective history from her personal self so she could survive the story she had to write. I cried because I was too tired and weary not to cry.

At home, I did not know what to do with myself, so I went to work. It was May 17, 1980, two days before my thirty-first birthday, during my prebirthday period when, annually, I would ponder the meaning of my life. But on this day nothing mattered but the present. I went to the Dade County Justice Department and saw several hundred people had gathered, some with signs like: "Who's Going to Police the Police?" and "Remember McDuffie!"

These were the invisible people, I thought, the ones who usually appeared only in the voting booths not on the streets. These were not the professional protestors, those who made public demonstrations an art; they were not the young rabble-rousers who taunted police regularly. Those people were there, too, but this time they were outnumbered by the normally silent ones: the housewives usually too busy coordinating their own households to protest in the streets, the fathers who worked, then coached their sons' softball teams, then worked again. The crowd was young and old, middle-class and poor, and for the early part of the evening it was black and white. But the white people fled when it was obvious that they had stepped into an incinerator of rage, with flames that instead of simmering and dying, as was the normal procedure, were growing, fanned by old, unsettled anger. Even those Negroes who normally seethed below the skin were exploding, popping off obscenities here and there in the crowd. They were the ones who generally saved the good white people. Who would save them now?

I myself had underestimated the rage. On the steps of the Justice Department building just before dusk, after some people had joined hands to sing "We Shall Overcome," a black man who was a community leader called for prayer and someone in the crowd yelled, "We're tired of praying! Let's march in the streets!" That voice was the spark that ignited the anger that was so alive it crackled in the air. I ran around with my pad and paper, at times thinking that I was absurd, that the revolution had come and instead of carrying a gun and shooting bullets, I was armed with ink and scribbling. But it is exactly in situations like this that I feel blessed to be a reporter. I roamed the streets as a witness, seeing what I would not have otherwise: A group of teenage black boys hurling rocks like baseballs at a carload of whites—the startled and frightened looks on the faces of the young white boys and girls in the car, the anger and hatred on the faces of the black boys tossing stones. A middle-aged black man throwing a Molotov cocktail at a neighborhood gas station owned by another black man and the glee of this arsonist, as he jumped up and down, laughing as he hit his target.

During the three days of rioting, I went back and forth between two worlds. I felt torn and strained. On the street, I let a few guys know I was a reporter so they could guide me through the neighborhood and look out for me. To the others I was just a visitor, an outsider who showed up for the battle between police and the community. But in actuality, few people were fooled by my attempt at invisibility.

"You're not from around here. Are you an undercover cop?" a boy about fifteen asked one evening.

I was insulted. "Do I look like a cop?" I snapped.

One of my guides explained, "Naw, man, she's a reporter. Be cool."

Over those three days I was forced to realize I was now different from the people out on the street. *Can you ever go home?* I kept asking myself. Could I be "street" again, or had I assimilated into the white corporate world so well that I was forever different from the people I was once "down" with? Where did I belong? The thought that I was more white than black scared me, but I didn't have time to ponder the question then. I wanted to scream out that I had been a victim, too, that I understood the rage because before Miami I had dealt with it in my own unhealthy way. I wanted to match their stories about blatant discrimination; tell them that though some whites accepted me while I had my press credentials hanging around my neck, when I took them off, I became a nigger, too.

I was in a crowd of blacks who saw me as a traitor. I was unprepared for this attitude from my own people. The first time I noticed it during the riots was when I was running down the street with a white male photographer. (There were no black photographers on staff.) A group of black men and women yelled, "Go home with that white boy! What you all doing down here! Go back to your white newspaper! We don't want you!"

Their words stabbed my heart, but I stood there in front of them, trying to ignore their taunts as I took notes. Later, I watched as a group of young boys rocked a car back and forth until a young black television cameraman and his black female companion jumped out. Then the boys stripped them of their cameras and equipment. Another man opened the trunk of a car, took out a gun, and pointed it at the couple, shouting, "Now get the fuck out of here!"

For the first time in my life, I was afraid of people who looked like me. What frightened me most was that they were scared of me, too. I was the enemy. Each night before I fell asleep, that fact weighed on me, as if a redneck police officer were standing on my chest, the toe of his heavy boot pressing on my Adam's apple. Before I left work each evening, I stood on the roof of the newspaper building with other reporters, looking across Biscayne Boulevard, over the palm trees and the pastel-colored homes to the flaming orange sky lit by burning buildings. I looked at the faces of my white coworkers and saw compassion on some, fear, disgust, and sheer amazement on others. I choked back tears. All I could think was: *My people are hurting.* Standing on that roof was a metaphor for what my life had become: I could stand up high and look down on the pain of other blacks, watch it from afar—and yet I was still a part of it. Again, I resented my white coworkers because they did not have two drums beating counter-rhythms inside their exhausted chests. When I drove home on Interstate 95, around Liberty City and the blocks of fire, glancing constantly in my mirrors to avoid trouble, I saw a traitor staring back at me, soaring on her magic carpet to her safe castle.

At home, I found the Paseos too frightened to venture into the yard, even though all we saw of the riot from our neighborhood was an occasional billow of smoke in the distant sky. I continued my habit of leaving the newspaper on their doorstep each night, but the head-lines screaming details of the riot probably reinforced their fear. Mr. Paseo, who loved to question me about my assignments, never mentioned one word about the riots. His silence fed the grief I felt that week.

By the third day, the riot had dwindled down to a large group of children, mostly boys in their early teens, aged by anger and bitter-ness. After everyone else had exerted their anger and gone home, the riot whimpered along on the backs of these young men, who threw smaller stones and ranted to passing cars and television cameras, try-ing to get the attention they had never gotten in all their young lives.

President Carter came to Miami to meet with leaders of the black community. Crowds of black people lined the street outside the build-ing where the meeting was being held. The members of the media were inside the building, waiting in the cool air-conditioned hallways. Then the crowd, already frustrated, grew restless and people started chanting, "Come out and meet with us!" and "Meet with the peo-ple!" The press ran out to capture the scene. The National Guard lined the middle of the street, to keep people from the building. Someone in the crowd threw a soda can at the building, and I watched it arc high, its path streaking the air like an exclamation point at the end of a giant scream of frustration.

On May 19, my birthday, the city looked like a closed carnival: the horror show was over, the lights out, the people gone. The city, under curfew, stopped to look at itself, to see what millions of others had seen on the nightly news. Under the circumstances, I didn't expect a birthday celebration, but two friends came over with lobsters and champagne and we all ate well, recounting riot stories. The riot had raised so many disturbing questions and doubts inside me that I needed time to clear my head. Ziggy and I decided to take a trip to Bimini in the Bahamas.

It seemed the Bahamians walked straighter, more erect than any black people in the United States. Straighter than I walked. It was a relief to see people my color running businesses that catered to white tourists. Ziggy and I gorged ourselves on conch fritters. When word spread that Ziggy was a musician, he was invited to sit in with a band at the most popular hotel on the island. But all too soon, it was time to return home.

I had been in Miami two years. For the last one I had wanted some small reason to leave; the riots gave me more reason than I wanted. I had already considered moving back to Washington, since my grandmother was sick and I had made a couple of trips to see her and to help my mother. But I was afraid of Washington. I had been a different person there, a woman battling against drugs, stealing, running from one man to another, uncomfortable with her family. Most of my girlfriends back home had moved or I had lost contact with them. The men I knew were in jail, on drugs, or fighting other monsters.

Yet something was calling me to return. Ziggy was not excited about the prospect, but he thought anything was better than Miami. Andrea seemed indifferent about the decision; she would miss her friends, but she was excited about returning to my large family.

The *Miami News* gave me a substantial raise as an incentive to stay. The money kept Ziggy and me in the city for three more months, until we realized no one could pay us enough to stay. I ran from Miami, not just from a city of racism, but also from myself. From the hatred sparked inside me when I was forced to *see* racism daily, not just in local practices, but in how America treated its darker immigrants. I fled from more personal questions, like whether or not I, a black person, could work for a major newspaper and still respect myself.

chapter twelve

Going Home but Not Back

Shortly after my grandparents had their Washington row house sold out from under them, Grannie stopped making her mouth-watering baking-soda biscuits. It was an omen. They had lived in that row house for all of my memory, but they couldn't afford to buy it when it was put on the market. They moved to a box-shaped garden apartment in Seat Pleasant, Maryland, where the windows looked out onto a parking lot.

Within a year of the move, Grannie had her first stroke, which left no noticeable effects except a little difficulty with her memory. A few months later she had a more serious stroke. Now she spoke haltingly, her sentences broken by long pauses, thoughts left hanging in midair.

By the time Ziggy and I moved to Maryland, it worked perfectly that we could live with my grandparents and help care for Grannie while my grandfather was at work. Andrea lived down the street with my parents, with the plan being that we would unite under one roof as soon as Ziggy and I found jobs and a house. I signed up with a temporary agency and got assignments as a secretary. At nearly every business I was offered a job, but I turned them down. Though I still felt conflict about being black and a journalist at a white-owned paper, I missed the excitement of the newsroom. Also, given time to think, I had replayed the riots in Miami over and over in my head, including my feeling like a traitor. But when my mind fell on the issue of race, it always returned to this one fact, too: that it was a white reporter who had broken the story about the McDuffie beating, a white woman who had told us all that white police officers had beaten a black man to death. That didn't resolve my conflict. On the contrary, it told me there was no easy answer to what was troubling me, that I would probably always struggle with the question of being black and a journalist. But I also considered for the first time that perhaps that struggle in itself was not a reason to leave. I applied for a reporter's position at the *Washington Star*.

Four months after moving to Maryland, I went to work at the *Star* as an education reporter in their suburban Montgomery County Bureau. As pleased as I was, I was also scared, my confidence faltering sometimes as I wondered if I could really compete with the other reporters, many with much more experience. I was also dissatisfied with my assignment. I wanted to work in Washington, where I could write about inner-city problems and black people. But the bureau I was assigned to was in the suburbs, surrounded mostly by wealthy and middle-class white communities. In Miami I had discovered I didn't like covering one beat but preferred to roam the city, looking for stories everywhere. Writing about education in a predominantly white community bored me, and my attitude blinded me to stories unfolding right before my face.

I had worked for seven months when Time., Inc., owners of the *Star,* announced they were closing the paper. By the last day I had figured that my lesson was to know that a job does not belong to you; it can be snatched away. If this was true, I reckoned, I needed to have something no one could take from me. So I decided to return to school to study writing, a skill I could use to create opportunities for myself.

I enrolled in the University of the District of Columbia and majored in English, taking creative writing, English composition, and playwriting as well as some basic required courses. Ziggy and I lived on the money we made from the sale of the house in Miami plus any odd jobs we picked up. I managed to write a few freelance articles in between studying and going to PTA meetings.

We rented a two-story brick house with a fireplace in the living room, three large bedrooms, and a basement where Ziggy and his new band could rehearse. I was relieved; spending time with Grannie was increasingly more difficult because she was getting more irritable and paranoid. Still, as I packed the last of my things, I was overwhelmed by sadness.

My grandfather announced in a flat, empty voice that he was retiring from the job he had held for more than twenty-five years. I thought of how we were at different places in our lives—how I rejoiced at losing my job because it opened up other opportunities for me; how he was willingly giving up his. With me moving, he knew he would have to be home full-time. My grandmother choked me with her bear hug when I leaned down to her wheelchair to kiss her goodbye. As I drove off, headed for my new home, I looked up at their window and saw my grandfather waving, as if I were going away forever. Before I reached the end of the parking lot, I burst into tears.

Andrea was in junior high, sporting expensive tight jeans and using her own separate telephone line in her bedroom. Ziggy and I didn't have the wild social life we had had in Charlotte and Miami, mostly because we didn't know anyone and I was so busy being superwoman. I got up at five o'clock each morning to work on short stories and, eventually, a novel. I went to school, wrote freelance articles, and worked short-term jobs like teaching writing and serving as a public relations consultant.

Ziggy played band gigs and occasionally worked odd jobs. But when Andrea and I came home from our busy days, he was often lying on the sofa watching television or napping. He and Andrea bickered—regularly. Her teenage hormones urged her to be daring and Ziggy was stricter than I was, so their arguments seemed unavoidable to me, which was why I ignored them at first.

Ziggy wasn't himself, though, more lethargic, not exercising like he used to. My resentment of him grew as our money dwindled. At first, I believed I could change everything by getting the band some steady gigs. I became the band's promoter and manager. I would have written music and lyrics, played an instrument, and sang, if I could have. It never occurred to me that there was nothing I could do to fix someone else's life or, in this case, intercede in an entire band of lives. What I overlooked was how my own life would suffer, how I was ignoring my own well-being—and paying too little attention to my child.

When Andrea came home from school each day she rushed to her bedroom and shut the door. I thought this was natural behavior for a teenager, especially since Andrea had everything in her room a kid could possibly want: the latest electronic games, her own telephone, privacy.

Eventually, I had to stop school to go back to work full-time. My resentment of Ziggy began to feel like hate. I had supported him while he studied his music, but he had failed me when I wanted to study writing, I thought.

We stopped talking to each other. I was wrestling with the relationship inside my head, and that took all of my energy, draining me so that I had no desire to open my mouth. I wondered if Ziggy was depressed because he no longer believed his talent would one day win him respect and fame. The fiery hope I used to hear in his music, the spirit that had attracted me, was gone. He lay on the sofa the way my father sat in that chair in his basement. For months Ziggy and I were silent most of the time when we were together. We seldom had sex and never made love. The months turned into a year and I was still pondering whether or not to leave, not realizing that I had already left. I had separated from Ziggy emotionally, a slow but steady detachment that cut a path for me to walk away.

◆　◆　◆

Mother and I alternated cooking dinner for my grandparents. Some of my sisters pitched in where they could, but some of them wouldn't help at all. There were siblings who said they couldn't bear seeing Grannie in her faltering health and others who felt it was my mother's responsibility to care for her. We argued about what I viewed as their selfishness, until one day I met a woman in the waiting room at a hos-

pital. I complained to this stranger about my family. She listened intently, then said, "Isn't it marvelous that God saw fit to put you in this
family? Each of us has our own strengths. Now, this has shown you
that you're a healer. One day your siblings will discover their
strengths, too."

Her answer was not at all what I wanted to hear. Yet long after I
had forgotten her face, her words reverberated in my head, until the
day came when I understood that there are no accidents or coincidences, that wisdom could come from a child or a teenager, from a
fallen leaf or a television program. Or from a stranger, a fat white
woman who sat beside me in a hospital waiting room and then disappeared, leaving me with a lesson that would stay with me forever.

Then my grandmother had another stroke, which left her in worse
condition, barely able to speak, her left arm limp and useless, its hand
a ball with knotted fingers. We started thinking about the end.
Mother and I searched for Grannie's bankbook and important papers. All her life, my grandmother had fretted over money, saving
pouches filled with silver dollars, pennies, and Kennedy fifty-cent
pieces, speaking of money in a whispered tone, as if she had fortunes
to hide. But when I found her bankbook stuck between the mattresses
of her bed, there was only $353 in it. I cried, staring at its entries,
trying to understand how a woman so consumed by money could die
with so little.

Grannie came home in her wheelchair with a paper bag full of medicine on her lap. She communicated with her eyes and facial gestures;
we learned to read them. Forced to watch her more closely, I saw the
mole on her lip that I had never noticed, how she squinched up her
nose when she didn't like a particular food, how my bottom lip was
full like hers.

Grannie's illness was my diversion from the troubles of my marriage. Whenever I returned to my own life, I felt like a sister to my
husband. I cared greatly about him but had no desire to have sex with
him. During the years when he was sleeping with other women I had
slowly shifted my feelings to protect myself: A sister did not have to
mourn each time her brother slept with a woman.

In our last attempt to save our marriage, we went to a counselor at a government agency that allowed us to pay what we could afford, which was nothing. I made the appointment originally because a counselor at Andrea's school suggested my child might need to see a therapist. Andrea, I discovered, had hooked school one day and had talked disrespectfully to a teacher. Something was obviously bothering her, I was told, because she was not herself. In the therapist's office she admitted she didn't like being at home and specifically she didn't like Ziggy, whom she described as lazy and demanding. "My mama works all the time and he doesn't do anything," she said.

I thought she was exaggerating, as teenagers are prone to do when describing the sins of their parents. But I couldn't deny the pain and resentment I heard in her voice, or the nagging truth I knew was in what she said. The therapist said Andrea was depressed and suggested the entire family receive counseling. Ziggy went to two sessions, then refused to return. Andrea and I went several more times; then we stopped, too. A few months later, Ziggy and I separated.

On the day that I left the house, Ziggy and I sat on our living room sofa, weeping in each other's arms. He said that he could not imagine life without me. I had no answer for him because I knew that for over a year I had imagined life without him. I wept because it was profoundly sad to me that two people who once had loved each other so much could end up like this.

Ziggy moved in with a friend, while Andrea and I moved into a two-bedroom apartment closer to my grandparents. My child blossomed, not overnight but slowly and noticeably, first talking to me more often, then going places with me again. She became her old self, and when I saw who she used to be I realized how blind I had been to her depression. That fall she was a tenth-grader, entering high school. She plastered her bedroom walls with pictures of Prince and Michael Jackson and blasted the radio every morning. Her grades improved; she joined school organizations, got a job at McDonald's, and talked about college.

I was still freelancing, writing mostly for black magazines but also articles for the *Washington Post*. I returned to school part-time and took whatever writing workshops I could. When I heard that author Gloria Naylor was teaching a free fiction writing workshop at George

Washington University, I submitted what I had shaped into the introduction to my novel—and I was chosen. Still, I was in a funk because I was thirty-six and had had three failed marriages and not one published novel. Several weeks later, my depression disappeared, chased away by gentle encouragement from Gloria and by my classmates. It was magic walking into that classroom, hearing the stories that people had woven from their hearts. When I listened to them read aloud, their words healed me.

I completed a one-act play, and my playwriting instructor, who directed a theater company, chose my play to be read professionally on stage. It astounded me that people paid five dollars to sit in the audience and listen, but it also boosted my confidence. When the fiction writing class with Gloria Naylor ended, I was not the same person who had walked into class dejected and hopeless. I now worked on my novel daily, believing it would be published and knowing that regardless, I had no choice but to write. Writing was saving my life as much now as it had when I was younger, writing bad poems to survive the pain.

A friend told me about an artists' retreat in Saratoga Springs, New York, called Yaddo, a place where visual artists, writers, and musicians worked at their craft in peace, on a wooded estate separated from the world by a stone wall. I had never heard of such things, but I applied, sending the improved introduction to my novel. I was accepted, and for two weeks I lived and wrote in a small sunny bedroom on the top floor of a mansion, mingling mostly with writers, artists, and musicians better known and more accomplished than myself.

Back home, I searched for full-time employment. Because I had written so many articles for the *Washington Post,* I applied there first. My application languished on one desk or another for six months, and I dropped by different offices trying to find it. Finally, I approached the assistant managing editor for the local news section and asked for an opportunity to prove myself as a reporter. He agreed to a three-month trial that would give me a chance to show editors that I could still meet daily deadlines. I was not awed by the fact that the *Post* was considered one of the best newspapers in the country or that hundreds of reporters applied for jobs there each year. This was where not growing up wanting to be a journalist helped me. I had admired the writing in the *Post* when I was a reporter at the *Star,* but mostly I was driven to get a full-time job by my determination to earn enough money for my daughter to go to college.

I applied for this job, carrying significantly fewer philosophical questions. After I lost my job at the *Star* and the status that comes from being a reporter, a friend told me to remember that no job could define me. A reporter was a small slice of me, a wonderful part but, nevertheless, not the sum of my being; it did not tell people my life's story or my degree of black consciousness. I had also concluded that there is no such thing as objectivity, though there is fairness. To judge no one or nothing, to be able to look beyond perceptions, is a goal that is worked on an entire life.

My family was extremely proud of my new job, though my father often asked, "Why don't you work on TV?" Or he advised, "Get yourself a good, secure government job."

Three months after I started at the *Post,* my mother called me at the office to say neighbors had heard my grandmother screaming and found my grandfather lying on the kitchen floor. I rushed from the office to head for the hospital, my hands trembling as I held the steering wheel of my car. Somewhere along the way, I noticed how bright the sun was shining and, simultaneously, knew my grandfather was dead. "This is a beautiful day to die," I said. It was March 26, 1985.

We went to the apartment to tell my grandmother, but when we walked in she looked at our faces and let out cries that sounded like some wounded animal. In the kitchen I found the chicken my grandfather had been cooking for my grandmother when he had his heart attack. *I want a man who would die wearing my apron, cooking me something to eat,* I thought. The chicken was still warm. I picked up a wing, trying to decide what to do with it. How long could I keep it?

I went to the dining room table, sat in the armchair that my grandfather had always sat in, and sank my teeth into the meat. I chewed slowly, taking in the warmth, closing my eyes.

Grampy was my mother's stepfather, though no one—not even Mama—thought of him that way. Mother was about twelve when he married Grannie, yet he was the only father she had ever known. It must have been a common perception during her childhood that step-fathers raped their stepdaughters, because Mother kept repeating proudly to anyone who would listen, "He never tried anything." All of us, her children, shuddered, agreeing that this was tacky behavior on Mom's part. At the funeral we stretched across the pew, all seven of Grampy's grandchildren, with our heads bowed and tears drip-ping, until the minister asked, "Would anyone else like to say any-thing?"

My mother sat up straight and put her hand in the air to signal she wanted to speak. Her seven children stopped crying to look at her, all of us with horror on our faces, all of us thinking the same thing: *Mama wants to tell everyone, "He never tried anything."* We looked at the minister with faces that pleaded with him to ignore her. He must have read our expressions, because he said, "No, dear, I think you'd better not." We sighed in relief, then bowed our heads again, returning to our tears.

My grandmother did not want to go to my grandfather's funeral; we brought her flowers from the grave and the two-page program that summed up his life. We told her that they read from Psalm 144 be-cause that was where the marker was in his Bible when he died; that a soloist sang "If I Can Help Somebody" and "Amazing Grace." This seemed to please her and a smile covered her face for as long as we talked. Then it disappeared—forever.

Grannie lived five more months. Life was a burden she wore awk-wardly the rest of her days, like an oversize coat, through a spring and one last miserable summer. She had a final, severe stroke and lingered in the hospital a few days before a heart attack cut off her last breath, giving her the freedom to follow the man she had been married to for forty-two years. She died September 3, 1985.

◆　◆　◆

At the end of my three-month trial at the *Post,* I was summoned to see Ben Bradlee, the editor of the paper and the person who would decide whether or not I was hired.

"Just answer his questions. He could ask you about anything.

Don't be nervous; be straightforward," advised several editors, leading me to Bradlee's office. This was a living legend, a man who had led the paper through one major story after another, the largest being Watergate. They spoke of him with such awe—or was it fear?—that I felt like Dorothy being led to the Wizard.

Again, my ignorance helped me. I had not grown up wanting to be a journalist, had not gone to college and read about Bradlee in newspapers and magazines, so I was not as much in awe as some of my white colleagues. But he is the kind of man whose reputation precedes him, so that even if you never read about him, you know something of him. In this case, what I knew was that he had led the *Post* through major stories like the Watergate scandal, which brought down a president, and that people pointed to him as the man who had molded the *Post* into a prestigious newspaper. Most important to me, though, he was simply the man at the head of the only daily newspaper in Washington, the man who could end the puzzle for me: how was I going to send my daughter to college?

He has two legs and sticks them in his pants just like I do, I told myself, repeating an adage my grandmother taught me. Then I prayed, *Lord, let me find something we both have in common, some mutual ground to stand on.*

The preparatory group disappeared and Bradlee and I were alone in his glass office. We shook hands and exchanged greetings. I noticed his tanned skin and the gruff voice that rattled each word in his throat before releasing it. He was relaxed, leaning back in his chair. So I relaxed, too.

"Tell me about yourself. Are you married?"

I choked for a second, then spit out the truth, that I was separated and would probably divorce. That I had regrets that the relationship had come to this, but believed it was best for my husband, my daughter, and myself.

"Isn't it something how we can be so smart at everything else in life and be so dumb about love?" he said.

I was surprised at the ease with which he said this to a stranger, the way he assumed he and I could fit into the same "we."

"Tell me about your parents, your family," he said.

I spoke at length about my sisters and brother, my father, the marine and golfer who was now a chauffeur, and my mother, a housewife who had gone back to school to become a beautician.

"What do your sisters and brother do for a living?" he asked.

"I come from a young family; I'm the oldest," I explained, noting that I didn't become a journalist until I was twenty-nine and that everyone else was still searching for their life's work while being employed in jobs such as salesclerks and office clerks.

"I come from a family of late bloomers, too," he said. "I was a late bloomer myself."

There was some talk about goals and what I wanted to do at the *Post*. I was honest, telling him what I admired about the newspaper but also admitting that I would have continued to freelance if I didn't need a regular check to pay for my daughter's college tuition. It was a short, friendly conversation, not at all like most job interviews I had had in the past; we shook hands, and I left his office to return to the office of the assistant managing editor for the Metro section, who peppered me with questions about the conversation.

Seeing that I wasn't offering any information, he said, "It normally takes Ben a few days to make up his mind. You go back to the bureau, and we'll call you."

I felt confident, and amused that the common ground Ben Bradlee and I shared was problems with love and being late bloomers. On my way through the newsroom I stopped to chat with a few reporters. By the time I reached the elevator, the assistant managing editor for Metro was behind me, huffing.

"You're on," he said.

"What?"

"I don't know what went on in there, but Ben said to hire you. He hired you on the spot." The editor shook his head as he walked away.

Actually, that first meeting with Bradlee set the tone for most of our relationship. Whenever I stepped into his office, it was generally to talk about life or after he had sent me a complimentary note on some article or commented on what he considered my ability to tell the stories of ordinary people overcoming challenges. He talked to me about his son's learning disabilities and the courage he had seen in children. One day, we would discuss my past.

◆   ◆   ◆

My life was the calmest it had been in years, though I was hurting, still mourning my grandparents and the end of my marriage. It was as if a large part of me was missing; the pieces of me that had been a wife and a grandchild—and then a caretaker to my grandparents—were all gone. It was hard to feel whole. If there was a salve for my pain, it was seeing how proud Andrea was of my new job and watching her flourish as we turned our apartment into a comfortable home.

At the *Post,* I settled into an easy friendship with a young gay man named Cooper, an editorial aide working his way up the ladder to become a reporter. He was in his late twenties when I met him, though he would become like an older brother to me. He was one of the most handsome people I would ever meet, slightly over six feet tall, with cinnamon brown skin and wavy pitch-black hair, a thick mustache, and piercing dark brown eyes. When I walked down the street with him, other women, not knowing he was gay, looked at me with envy. In fact, the attention he got from women was so annoying that he wore a wedding band to keep away the aggressive ones, like the woman who followed him home from the grocery store or the woman who walked into his yard while he was gardening and offered him a bottle of champagne—and herself.

Cooper had a sense of humor that would creep up on you and make you laugh hours later. He used it gently; he was never brutal or brash. He knew I admired the work of a *Post* reporter named Sue Ann Pressley. Basically, I used her writing as a measuring stick of excellence, by which I judged my own work. So Cooper would compliment me on a story by saying, "You wrote the hell out of that. Almost as good as Sue Ann Pressley." Or he'd say, "You're a damn good writer," then pause, squint his eyes, and add, "But that Sue Ann Pressley is damn good, too."

At work, I became close friends with a white woman named Cindy, who reminded me of my North Carolina roommate, Judy, with her infectious laugh and quick wit. Cindy had an absolute love for people and a curiosity about life that I thought God reserved for children. She was also Cooper's supervisor, but she became his good friend, too. We lunched together in the park, the three of us plopping down on the grass to eat hot dogs and discuss anything, from literature to the latest dirty joke we had heard. Once Cooper had us laughing about the difference between white people and black people making potato salad.

"White people put too much stuff in it. They want to throw in all these fresh herbs," he proclaimed, recounting how his next-door neighbor, a white woman, insisted she bring potato salad to some neighborhood event. Cooper had questioned her about her recipe. "You know what she put in it?" he asked me. "Fresh fennel. I asked her if she couldn't bring something else."

He and I hung out together after work, going to eat at trendy restaurants or dancing at Tracks, a large gay nightclub where we went to hear the beat-driven sounds of "club" music. We stood outside on the patio during the summers of 1985 and 1986, dressed in our Bermuda shorts, watching people play volleyball in the sandlot or dance on the outside deck. From the moment I walked into that club, I was more comfortable there than I had ever been in any other club. At Tracks, I didn't have to say "no" so many times that I wished I could say it in ten languages. I was tired of dressing up, weary of playing the mating game, strutting around bars and dance floors in high heels and short dresses like a peacock in heat.

The spring of 1986 Andrea graduated from high school while Ziggy and Ben and my entire family looked on. Then I took my daughter to Atlanta to Spelman College, and we said a tearful good-bye, both of us realizing our life together would never be the same. For the first time since I was nineteen, I was truly alone. I was excited, and afraid.

Back at home, I woke up in the morning without the sound of music blasting. I lay in bed, trying to decide if I could live with the strange sound of silence. But as the mornings rolled by that question vanished. I enjoyed the quiet, creating my own morning rituals: meditating, drinking tea, and doing yoga. I ate fast food or no food, or cooked exotic dishes my daughter would have wrinkled her nose at. If

I was dating, I occasionally invited the man to spend the night—and I did not have to feel guilty.

But I missed my daughter to the point of tears some days. We had grown up together; she was my sister, my best friend. Now I scraped up money, juggled bills, and got loans to pay for her tuition and send her money for living expenses. To my surprise, Ben paid nearly half of her tuition. He was excited about Andrea's attending college. I could only imagine that he had some regrets about his own life and that, like me, he was glad to see our daughter achieve something we never had.

Now that I didn't have to rush home each evening, Cindy and I were soon inseparable, hanging out at farmer's markets and cheap restaurants that served fish and grits. Her goodness and honesty prompted Cooper to call her an angel—and I wondered. One of my black girlfriends asked me, "What is it like to have a best friend who is white? How does it happen?" I probably did not answer either question sufficiently, but I knew that one of Cindy's best qualities was that she recognized our differences, acknowledged them, and considered them blessings. She didn't try to be black; I didn't try to be white.

When I think of my first days at the *Post,* I see a picture in my head of people, most of them white, standing with their backs toward me—except for Cindy, who was staring right into my eyes. Entering that newsroom was like walking into a place where everyone was too busy with their work to pay any attention to you. Just the size of the place was awesome. It looked like there were two hundred people in one room, much larger than the *Miami News* or the *Washington Star* newsroom, where I had worked. Also, for me being a reporter felt more like a job than a career. I had been hired at a salary of $33,300 a year, just a few thousand more than I had made at the *Washington Star,* but more than I had ever made in my life, more than my father had ever made any year of his, and more than anyone else in my family had made any year. I was working for money, not fame or prestige—or pleasure. Let the young white reporters go for the Pulitzer and the management positions, I figured; all I wanted was my check. A by-product was the opportunity to write and learn to write better. But I was convinced more than ever before that my future was in writing books, plays, essays, magazine articles—anything other than for newspapers.

My joy was outside of the *Post,* attending writing classes, hearing authors read their work, living the life I never had a chance to live while I was growing up, trying to be a mama when I was still a child myself. To me, Cooper was divine, entering my life when it was absent of any intimate relationships with men, teaching me simply by being a good man, a rarity in my life. He was like an older brother, though he was actually eight years younger than I was. With Cooper, I discovered that in the company of gay men I was more comfortable than I had ever been with any other men. Gone was the possibility of sex, which always complicated my relationships and kept me feeling ashamed, since I always thought I slept with someone too soon. Then one day a therapist offered this suggestion: that I went to bed with men not seeking sex, but searching for a touch, the intimacy of love. That one suggestion freed me from years of guilt, years of labeling myself "bad" because I thought I was just a loose woman with few morals. Needing love was not bad; it was understandable, and though my method of finding it still had to be changed, the task of changing was easier when I began from the point of accepting—and, therefore, loving—myself.

Gay men were perfect men for me at this period in life, when I was alone and had time to look inside myself. Knowing how discrimination and prejudice hurts, they try harder than most men to shed their male egos and empathize with the problems women face. This added a grace to them that many other men didn't have. I had the best of both worlds: they held open doors as I passed through, painted my house, repaired my electrical appliances, and did minor repairs to my car. It helped, too, that they spoiled me with attention just when I was beginning to believe I deserved it. They sensed that I had suffered, too. I, like them, found solace in the "camp" of gay culture, the ability that gay people have of making fun of themselves to mock the world, though we all knew deep inside that we were hurting. The laughter, the camp, and the satire were necessary to survive—and I admired it as a form of coping, because in the other worlds in which I had lived the general reaction to pain and misunderstanding was violence and hatred.

Cooper and I shared all of this between us and still it was difficult for him to let down his guard, totally, with me. When it came to my blundering love affairs, he always listened, yet he rarely shared the details of his intimate relationships with me. I had to accept that he felt he could not discuss his sexuality with me because I was straight. I wanted to free him, the way he freed me, by his listening and by gently offering just enough advice to make me ponder what I might not have considered otherwise.

◆   ◆   ◆

I decided to buy a house, a place in the city. I longed to live near restaurants, museums, and theaters. The house I found was passed off by realtors as part of the prestigious neighborhood of Capitol Hill. Actually, it was on the fringe of Capitol Hill, skirting the boundaries of that gentrified neighborhood and hanging onto it for mere survival. Cooper needed to move out of his own house and he proposed we become roommates—but first he wanted to see my new place. He was supposed to meet me at 1:00 P.M. on a Saturday. I waited for him on the porch for about an hour; then I dropped by his house. No one answered the door. A few hours later, he hadn't called, and I was worried. He still hadn't called late that night, and since I was leaving the next morning to drive Andrea back to school, I asked Cindy to find him.

After a furious ten-hour drive, I called her.

"Bad news," she said.

"What?"

"Our friend was sick yesterday and he went to the emergency room at Howard. They didn't know what was wrong with him, so they sent him back home. He got so sick a friend took him to another hospital. Patrice . . ."

"Yes?"

"Cooper has AIDS."

Neither of us said a word. Tears poured from my eyes and I gulped back emotion. "Is he dying?"

"No, they don't think so. But he's real sick. He's got pneumonia."

Cooper's only brother had died of AIDS a year earlier, coming to Washington from Puerto Rico to spend his last days with Cooper. It was only then that Cooper had learned that his brother was gay, too. Listening to Cooper as he went through his brother's illness and death was as close as I had come to the disease. When Cindy and I noticed Cooper was sick and absent from work more often than he had been in the past, the word *AIDS* had entered my thoughts, but I quickly erased it. Cooper was too good-looking, too perfect, and too kind to have AIDS, I reasoned, knowing deep inside that such attributes have nothing to do with keeping death away.

When I saw him in the hospital he was thin and sweating with fever, but each day that I returned he teased me, just as he usually did.

"Look at your hair. Something must be up. You got a new young boy?" he asked.

Every day for several weeks Cindy and I visited him, because a decision had been made by the *Post* management to excuse us so someone from work could be with Cooper daily. He was the first person in the newsroom to have AIDS, and even though no one formally announced his illness, the word spread. Some people asked Cindy and me about his health. We were elusive because we wanted to protect his privacy. Most coworkers had educated themselves about the disease, since it was intruding more and more into everyone's life. Generally people were kind and compassionate, though later on there were a few incidents: friends who avoided Cooper or did not want to touch the coffeepot after he had handled it.

It was the beginning of an arduous year, when Cooper would go in and out of the hospital and teeter on the brink of death several times. He celebrated his thirtieth birthday at an elegant dinner party given by Gerald, another gay man who was like an older brother to him. Cooper had lost pounds off his once perfectly toned body, and he stopped wearing clothes that revealed his arms or legs. Soon he was unable to work.

It was more obvious with each visit that I was watching him die. Our conversations evolved to topics we had never before discussed. It was a wonderful by-product of dying slowly, that Cooper had time to gain courage until he was so brave he did not let other people's hangups stop him from being honest with them or himself.

Before I fell asleep each night I wondered why God had spared me, why AIDS had not existed when I shot heroin and had sometimes shared a needle with Ben and a friend. Like Cooper, I had been promiscuous when I was younger. Eventually the fear of AIDS pushed me to be tested twice, because I considered it a miracle that I was healthy. So when I looked at Cooper lying in his hospital bed, it was easy to imagine myself there. Only the thinnest thread of fate separated us.

Once he said to me, "I love men and women equally. I can't see the difference, or why I should love one more than the other. That has caused me a lot of hell."

I looked at the pain on his face and tried to imagine his life. Even before he said anything about it, I had thought my friend might be bisexual, but I knew so little about bisexuality. I knew that for a brief while he had dated a woman, a model who was as beautiful as he was handsome. It was the only time I had known him to date a woman, or have a relationship we could discuss. His bisexuality didn't strike me as wrong or sinful, only a special burden to wear in a world that said, "Choose one." In fact, I wondered how could it be wrong to love, period, and I toyed with the idea that maybe Cooper was a more evolved soul than I was, because he *could* love both sexes equally.

◆　◆　◆

Once while Cooper was hospitalized a male nurse entered his room covered from head to toe in some type of protective suit that made him look like an astronaut. Most of the doctors and nurses wore only rubber gloves as a precaution when they worked with Cooper, but this man was clearly more frightened than the others.

"Do you know what you have?" he asked Cooper. But before Cooper answered, the nurse turned his attention to Cindy and me, sitting on the bed on either side of Cooper. "Did you know you could get it from soiled sheets?" he asked us. "You don't want to breathe in too much of this air."

I was ready to give the guy a piece of my mind, then ask his supervisors to keep him out of Cooper's room. Several years later, I would recall that this happened in 1987, and realize how much had changed, how much more people know about AIDS. But that evening, I was ready to raise hell. Yet when the nurse left, Cooper calmed me by saying, "Poor man, to have to come to work and do a job that frightens him that much."

◆   ◆   ◆

Death puts things in their proper perspective, not only for the person dying, but for those witnessing it. It was happening to me. I became smarter than I normally was just from the lessons I learned standing beside Cooper's bed. Having an intimate relationship with a man was becoming less important to me as I watched my friend die. Cooper became my measurement for a man; I wanted someone to treat me as he did, someone to love me unconditionally because he looks at me through grace and not judgment.

There came the day when Cooper's past began to parade before him, people he had not seen in years but who had heard he was sick and needed to come to forgive or ask for forgiveness, to say, "Thank you," or clear their minds and hearts while there was still time. Cooper and I had discussed the similarities in our relationships with our parents. Now death gave him grace that allowed him to leap ahead of me. This shift in understanding changed everything; his father, not known for doling out affection, sat beside Cooper's bed and massaged his feet for hours.

Cindy and I stayed at the hospital late one night with Cooper's mother and Gerald. Cooper had lived through another difficult day of chills and fever and aching. Once he had called dying of AIDS "a horrible relief. You get a chance to think about death, but you also have a chance to get your life in order." But on this night, he was afraid to die. So Cindy, Gerald, and Cooper's mother and I recited the Twenty-third Psalm.

"Feel our love around you," I said. "You know we love you so much. Just sink into that warm, safe feeling of love."

I had no idea if I was saying the right thing; death is one of those acts for which you get no rehearsal. Even though I had sat with my grandmother before she died, she and Cooper were so different that I couldn't possibly treat them the same. I learned then that people die pretty much the way they lived, though in the end they all want the same thing: to be comfortable and comforted and to feel loved. For all other clues about what to do I turned to Cindy, who was once a volunteer at a hospice.

I didn't want to leave Cooper, but I kissed him, leaving red lipstick on his damp, cool forehead, and followed the rest of the people out of the room. Cindy and I stayed together at her apartment, stopping at a bar for margaritas first. The phone rang at 4:00 A.M. and Cindy answered. I sat up in bed and watched sorrow take over her face.

"Cooper is dead," she said.

We cried while we dressed. Gerald had said we could go to the hospital to see Cooper one last time before they took his body away. The four of us tiptoed back into his hospital room and found Cooper as peaceful as a sleeping child. All I could think of was how lucky we were to have known him, how blessed to be chosen to be his friends. As I looked at his face, I felt grief, but it was mixed with the sweetest joy I had ever felt.

Cooper's funeral was in an ornate old stone Catholic church not far from downtown Washington. In the midday sun a congregation of people walked from the *Post* up the street to the church. The next day a caravan of friends joined Cooper's parents to escort his body and his brother's body to their hometown of Philadelphia. His parents had decided to have the brother's body exhumed from the Washington cemetery, since all he had wanted was to be close to Cooper. Now that Cooper was leaving, his parents decided to take his brother with him. So close friends in a line of cars followed two maroon hearses. As we meandered through city streets, people stopped in their tracks, their mouths gaping open at the sight of so much death.

Cooper's mother did not want us to leave after the burial, so Cindy and I and six male friends spent the night in the family's rambling house. We looked at family albums, laughing at the fading pictures of the two curly-haired brothers we had just buried. We lounged on Cooper's twin bed in the room that had been left the way it was when he went off to college, with fading photos sitting on a scuffed chest and tucked in the corner of the dresser mirror. We sat on the long front porch, recounting tales of our friend. Then we laid down blankets on the expansive front lawn and ate hamburgers until the gnats swarmed at our ankles and lightning bugs blinked around our heads. Cindy and I slept in nylon gowns Cooper's mother gave us for gifts, in the beds she had brought from her native Germany. We listened to Cooper's father tell the story of how he met his wife when he was a U.S. soldier sent to Europe after World War II and he found her a scared young woman who had lost most of her family in concentration camps. Cindy and I fell asleep marveling at life's ironies, that we were on our first visit to the house that Cooper had described to us so many times, that we could be sleeping in his house—and he wasn't there.

Before Cooper died, I made him promise to return to me after he was dead so he could tell me what death was like. But after he died, I thought, *Cooper, if I see you, I'll die*. I was scared. Then a few days after we left Philadelphia, I lay down to take a nap. It seemed I was about to doze off when I looked up and saw the words, "He rise," in big, black letters in the air. My first thought was: *Terrible English*. Then I saw Cooper, grinning, wearing a navy blue blazer and khaki pants, standing in a doorway with nothing but light all around him. I felt his happiness in my body. He was jumping up and down, clapping his hands in glee like a child. I fell into a deep, peaceful sleep, watching him. I woke up knowing that I would never feel sorry for Cooper again—that I would miss his laughter and advice, our dancing and philosophical discussions, but in all my selfishness, I could never feel sorry that he had died. Cooper was happier than he had ever been.

Meanwhile, I was left to contend with life. I discovered that a man I had been dating was dating another woman at the same time. This only made me miss Cooper more, because he had suspected the guy was a cheat, had warned me about him, and now wasn't here to comfort me. I was shattered because this guy had fooled me so easily. I was worn from bad relationships, weary from a life of terrible misjudgments. I needed someone to guide me through the bullshit I was feeding myself, someone to help me sift through my perceptions and tell me what was worth keeping, what to throw out. I decided to go to a therapist.

Choosing therapy was to become one of the single most important decisions of my life. The counseling took up where all of the positive thinking and philosophy books stopped. Truth can be painful, but it can bring you limitless joy if you remain with it, consistently. For two and a half years I propped up my feet on a hassock and sank into a comfortable leather chair while the therapist led me back through my childhood, the birth of my child, my rapes, my marriages, my relationships with other men, and my jobs.

I was never the same again. In my relationships with men I would continue to stumble; sometimes I was still too desperate, too quick to fall in love, too obliging. But I never fell as low as I had in the past. Quite simply, for the first time in life I began to understand my own worth, to give myself great credit for the strides I had made. But when the therapy was complete, I didn't walk out of the therapist's office totally changed; I left in the midst of peeling back my old skin and growing into a new self. Only living could finish the process, could help a new me grow. I had to be tested and challenged; there was no other way.

A significant amount of therapy dealt, directly and indirectly, with my relationship with my father. One day it struck me as profoundly sad that I had never gone anywhere alone with him, had never had a father-daughter talk. In fact, since I had grown up and left home, we had hardly spoken. Before therapy, I had blamed this on my father, on his aloofness and insensitivity, on him for not asking me. But now, with my new sense of power and worth, I was strong enough to shoulder some of the blame.

"Daddy, wanna go out to breakfast with me Saturday morning?" I asked him during a visit to my parents. I knew that like me, he was an early riser.

"I don't eat breakfast," he said.

Old feelings of rejection welled up in me, and for a moment I was silent. Then the new me took over. "You don't have to eat. You can just drink coffee, or watch me eat," I said.

He nodded his head "yes."

On Saturday morning, I arrived at my parents' house about ten minutes late. I had driven slowly, trying to think of what to say to my father.

"I sure am glad you're here. Your father has been pacing the floor, looking for you!" my mother yelled as soon as I walked in.

My father pacing for me? Mother had such an imagination. But as soon as Daddy heard my voice he came up from the basement and walked out the door. I followed. In the car, I was uncomfortable. For the first few minutes neither of us spoke. I sneaked glances at him, trying to read his expression. But he wore his usual face, the one that was blank except for the deep furrows in his forehead, above his bushy eyebrows. His hair was dark gray now and, as usual, just a bit too long to be neat. He was deathly frail and his limp was more profound, but he was as proud as ever, still the boy who had run off to join the Marine Corps. His children complained frequently about his dress because he always wore his work uniform, even at home, one of several blue short-sleeved shirts and gray pants. He was wearing them now, as we rode to breakfast. I told him about the work I was doing on my house and about Sherrill's, the old diner where we were going.

He loved the diner, though he never told me. It was in his face, the way the bones in his cheeks expanded and his mouth widened to a grin, how the deep wrinkles in his forehead disappeared. All of the waitresses at Sherrill's were over fifty and the price of a breakfast of pancakes, eggs, and bacon was just under four dollars, two facts that fascinated Daddy and endeared the place to him.

"I can't believe there's a place in D.C. where you can get breakfast this cheap," he said. Then every once in a while, as he ate his toast, eggs, and bacon, he looked around at the old soda fountain and advertisements and mumbled, "Jiminy Cricket," or "dang," his way of expressing amazement.

We relaxed and talked and laughed about the children in our family, about how Christopher, who was five, could read the *TV Guide* and how Erin, who was seven and an amazing dancer with long legs, was going to start running track. I watched Dad drink three cups of coffee. I noticed the way his eyes had aged, milky now, with pupils that floated more than they focused. But his skin was still rich, like perfect dark chocolate candy, and there were hardly any lines or wrinkles anywhere other than in his forehead, and those came more from attitude than age.

We went to my house, which wasn't very far away. He had never seen it because when I invited him over for the house blessing, he had shrugged and said, "Why would I want to come over there? If you've seen one house, you've seen them all." That comment had wounded me, and I never asked him over again. But on this day, he sat on my front porch and drank a beer from my refrigerator, while I pointed out the different flowers I had planted. I called my sister Shelia, who lived nearby, so she could run over and witness Daddy actually sitting on my front porch.

Over the next week, my five sisters called me, one after the other, to repeat some compliment Daddy had offered on his own about his breakfast with me. They thought I had taken him to some expensive, swank café. I was surprised that he even mentioned our outing, and my chest swelled the way a kindergartner's does when she brings home a paper with a gold star and her father says, "Very good. I'm proud of you."

◆   ◆   ◆

At the invitation of a friend, I started giving inspirational speeches to classes at a job training program, telling the men and women about the days when I shot heroin and shoplifted, and then laying out for them, as best I could, how I had turned my life around. Mostly, I encouraged them to take advantage of the fresh start they were being offered at the training program—and to believe in themselves. Eventually I was asked to speak to the members of Rap, a drug rehabilitation program that was well known in the Washington community and was occasionally the subject of articles in the *Post*. I accepted the invitation, but I considered the slight possibility that a reporter might be on hand and what I was going to say could appear in some publication. I was going to mention some details about myself that my employers did not know, so I felt I had to inform someone at the *Post*.

"I'm going to talk about the problems I used to have with drugs," I told Leonard Downie, the managing editor of the paper. I wasn't specific, failing to mention my brief stays in jail or the charges. It was not that I made a deliberate decision to withhold that information, but rather that I was still uncomfortable repeating it to some people. The members of my audience at the drug rehab program would have a reference point, their own lives, to use to understand my past; I didn't know enough about Len Downie to know if he would or could understand. I was still ashamed, still thinking of myself as a bad person. In that frame of mind, there was no way I could tell anyone at the *Post* about my past.

But Len surprised me at the end of our chat. "Congratulations," he said. "You're to be commended for sharing your life in that way."

◆   ◆   ◆

Meanwhile, I was involved in a complaint filed by the union against the *Post* because it did not pay overtime to people who had reached a certain salary. About a year before the complaint, I had been put on a fast track for raises, to receive large increases in my salary every six months until I reached a pay comparable to my peers'. I had no idea I was making less than my coworkers. Then, after I had received two raises, a local magazine published an article showing a salary scale at the *Post* that listed me as the lowest paid female reporter.

As part of the preparation for the court case, plaintiffs were interviewed by the union lawyers, a rehearsal in which we were asked questions they thought the *Post* lawyers might ask. During my interview, the lawyer showed me the application I had filled out for the job at the *Post* and asked me if everything on it was true. One line jumped out at me: "Have you ever been convicted of a felony?" I had answered: "No."

"This answer is not true," I said, pointing to that line.

The lawyer, who clearly had expected another routine interview, jumped. I explained, and after some discussion, she suggested I admit the truth to Len, since he knew at least a little about my past. "Better to have it come out now, rather than in court," she said.

I went home and lay awake most of the night, searching for the words to explain why I had lied. Of course, I didn't think I would be hired otherwise. But I had lied so much about my past and now it had been so long since I was in jail that I could almost believe none of it had ever happened. I definitely wanted my job as badly now as I had when I had filled out the application. My child was in college, and she had to stay there. I wanted Andrea to have a chance to be a college graduate more than I had ever wanted anything else in the world. If I was fired, I didn't know what else I could do, what kind of job I could get. It had been years since I had done anything else—at least full-time. I thought about teaching, working in public relations, or going back to some sort of executive secretarial job. But despite my discomfort and fear, I was glad it had come to this; it was time to clear up this business of having to lie about my past. I wanted to be free of this burden that I had carried for nearly twenty years now, to be able to tell the truth and be accepted in spite of who I once was.

Len was not in the office the next day, nor was Ben Bradlee; I went to Milton Coleman, a black man who was the new assistant managing editor for Metro, the department in which I worked. I laid out everything—my involvement in the suit, the job application, and why I had lied. I didn't know Milton well enough to know how he would react. He had been a good friend to Cooper and his family during Cooper's illness and had been lenient with Cindy and me, allowing us to take all the time we needed from work to help care for Cooper. But this was different and might carry political ramifications for him in the corporate world in which he operated. So I waited, anxiously, to see what would happen next.

Milton contacted Bradlee and Len, and when Bradlee returned from vacation, he called me into his office. I was scared. It was worse than standing in front of the judge years ago. I did not have as much to lose then, or at least I didn't understand what there was to lose. Now, it was clear. If I lost this job, I would probably never work as a newspaper journalist again—and the good life I wanted for my daughter might be put on hold. Yet always my mind returned to this: I was tired of living like a fugitive, of hiding who I was, of denying half of my life, a crucial part that had helped me be the person who now walked toward Bradlee's office.

"You know this is a very serious matter," he began. "There is no room for lying here. We're talking about your career being on the line, whether or not we should fire you. You do understand, don't you?"

"I do," I said softly. Then gathering up my strength, I added, "I want you to understand me, too. I am sorry I lied, but I am tired of having to lie. I think I've paid for a mistake long enough. If I had told you the truth, would I have gotten the job?"

"Probably not," he admitted.

We were both silent. Then he told me a decision would be made as soon as possible, that he didn't think it was fair to have me wait for a long time.

My legs were so weak from fear that I could barely walk out of that office. The next day, Cindy walked into Bradlee's office. She told me afterward that she had pleaded on my behalf, offering her personal testimony about me. But months passed and no decision was made. My life was in limbo; I tried to save money for unemployment while a part of me denied it was a possibility. From friends who worked in various jobs at the *Post* I heard that I had been discussed at executive meetings and that people were polled about how they stood on the question of whether or not to keep me as an employee. I was told that Milton Coleman was fighting on my behalf. What was at stake, it was said, was not just what the company thought of me as a person, but whether or not the *Post* could afford to allow someone who had lied on a job application to continue working at the company. The *Post* was particularly sensitive about the ramifications of this since it had been publicly embarrassed when a reporter had won a Pulitzer for a story that was later determined to be a fake. Some people had always been suspicious of the story, but what had prompted closer investigation was the discovery by someone in the media that information on the reporter's job application at the *Post* was incorrect, or in other words, that she had lied on the application. Now, in meetings, they compared me to her, as they tried to decide the appropriate action.

Finally, after about five months, Donald Graham, the publisher of the paper, instructed Bradlee to make the final decision, because I was a newsroom employee and the newsroom was Bradlee's domain. A few weeks later, a very happy friend walked past my desk and whispered, "They decided to keep you." I did not realize how much anxiety had built up inside me over the months until I felt a heaviness rush from my chest. My whole body sighed. At home that night, for the first time in months I fell asleep shortly after getting in bed.

I waited for the official word, but it didn't come. By the third week, I was worried that my friend had somehow gotten the wrong information. I went to Milton Coleman and asked him if a decision had been made. He was surprised that no one had given me the official answer. Within the hour, I got a call from Bradlee's secretary, asking me to come to his office.

"Well, we've decided to keep you," Bradlee said, almost as soon as I took a seat. He seemed relieved, too, happy to deliver good news.

"You made the right decision," I said. "I appreciate it."

"I have to tell you, we wavered. But in the end, it was your talent that pushed you. If you weren't so damned talented . . ."

He said something else, but I didn't hear him. As we shook hands, he said, "And don't ever bother with that stuff again."

"You don't have to worry about me. I'm just glad to be rid of my past." I tried to sound strong. I was giddy and my insides felt as if they were sparkling. I rushed past Cindy's desk, whispering the news to her. She met me in the bathroom, where I sobbed with relief while she held me and cried, too.

That weekend I went out to celebrate, dancing all night with my sister and brother-in-law, first at a gay club called Bachelor Mill, a neighborhood bar with a small dance floor, and then at another, the Delta, where the crowd never showed up until about 1:00 A.M. We walked out of that club with our clothes soaked from sweat and stepped out into the sun, blinking our eyes to adjust to the new day. It had been a long time since I had danced to celebrate.

chapter thirteen

Witnessing

For my fortieth birthday, on May 19, 1989, I wanted to be surrounded by friends and family, by children and dogs, by as much vivid life as possible. Death had touched too many people in my life, from Cooper to his best friend, Gerald, now also dying of AIDS. My new best friends, Michael Harrison, a gay black man who worked at the *Post,* and John, who called himself the longest living AIDS patient, insisted I have my party at John's family's beach house, in a small black community near Annapolis.

People spread blankets out across the huge lawn while others sat at picnic tables eating food from the grill or played volleyball at the edge of the yard. Andrea waited on me, running to fetch whatever I needed, and we both marveled that I could be forty and she could be almost twenty-one. Ziggy's band performed, their reggae and jazz floated with the salt in the ocean breeze. John, the perpetual host who loved to coordinate affairs, ushered people to the table where my presents were being kept. He was such a lover of pomp and circumstance; he had programs printed up for the tribute to me, which featured a tape of sentimental songs and testimonials from some of my sisters and friends. But John was also a healer, and in that role he had personally invited my father to the party—and my father came, spending the day in a lawn chair perched in front of the band, but where he could see everything: the games, the children playing, the dogs running, the people cooking and eating and dancing. He sent his children and grandchildren across the yard to fetch him beer and food and only rose once, entering the house I imagine to go to the bathroom.

We partied until it was too dark, even with the yard lights, to play volleyball and people slipped their cool arms into their sweaters. As my family was cleaning up, John asked us to come back the next day for a crab feast. I spent the night at the house with John, and he confided in me later that he had invited us all back because he had never seen my father smile as much as he had there. I had noticed, too. I guessed that the smell of water, the seclusion, the crickets chirping and frogs croaking at night must have reminded Daddy of his real home, of rural Badin, North Carolina, the town he was born in and the town he had fled. I fell asleep thinking about how frail my father had seemed as I held his arm and helped him to the car. He stumbled beside me and I couldn't figure out if he was sick or drunk.

◆　◆　◆

Over the next year, I moved, traveled across the country, and attended two different colleges. But no matter where I was, death reached me. In thirteen months, six people in my life died, most of them people who had touched me daily, or who had profoundly affected me. I sat beside their beds, watching them hurdle lifelong challenges, spurred on by the ticking clock and their slowing hearts.

Death made me judge less and love more. Death taught me that you have a say in the way you go, that you establish patterns and habits early in your life that probably determine when and, to some degree, how you die. Not obvious patterns like the kinds of people we have sex with or how much alcohol we drink, but patterns based on how much faith, love, and fear we have.

It was agonizing to watch people I loved suffer. Yet by the time the last one in this parade of death had marched into eternity, I understood what a remarkable gift all of them had given. With grace and love, each had used his last breath to teach me.

◆   ◆   ◆

My sister Sondra and I drove down to North Carolina to take my father home from a visit to his sister. It was an opportunity for me to discover another piece of the puzzle that made up the whole picture of my father's life, to talk to his sister about their parents and about what my father was like as a boy. I was in the middle of my therapy, where truths were unfolding rapidly, one of the most astounding being that although my father appeared invisible in my life, I could not relegate him to insignificance. He was like the silence in a song, the pause where you hear nothing until you realize that without that gap in music, the melody would be totally different.

Aunt Fannie fussed over us and fed us. Sondra and I blabbered news about Mama and our siblings. Then Daddy and Sondra went to bed and my aunt, whom I had seen many times but barely knew, sat with me on her front stoop. She didn't have to be prodded to talk about her family; she was a willing bearer of history, especially anecdotes about her brother, whom she spoke of in reverent tones.

"Did you know your father can identify every bird that flies by here?" she asked.

"No." I was dumbstruck. It hit me as bizarre that a daughter would not know something so profoundly wonderful about her own father.

"I guess he don't talk to y'all about things like that 'cause he don't think you care about them," she said.

"Why would he think we wouldn't care?"

She paused, cocked her head, and studied me, as if she was trying to decide what kind of answer to give. Then she said, "Y'all are different. We're country folks. I wear overalls and get dirty. Your mother kept y'all so neat and dainty."

"See, that's where you're wrong," I told her. I was upset. "We're not dainty. I mean maybe we are, but I can put on my dainty little jeans and still get just as dirty as anybody else."

"Toad was never comfortable up there," she insisted, referring to the North and using her childhood nickname for her brother. Her voice rose a little: "But your mother would never live down here."

She hit a nerve that had long severed the two sides of the family, a nerve that ran between the country and the city folks and seemed as permanent as the Mason-Dixon line. My relatives were victims of a presumption passed down to many blacks, that those who left Jim Crow for the North were smart and those who stayed behind were dumb, if not crazy. But I had lived long enough to know the trip north was not my salvation, so out in that yard that night, my aunt and I reached an easy truce.

She told me how my grandfather, her father, had spent years in a sanitarium suffering from tuberculosis. Aunt Fannie recalled only once seeing Grandpa Ollie doing something alone with my father, when he taught him to shoot a rifle. I tried to conjure up memories of my father alone with his son and couldn't. My father never pointed out birds to my brother, never tossed a ball to him or taught him anything about how to be a man. I was examining the meaning of that when my aunt rattled off more family history, adding nonchalantly, "Of course, I didn't know your *real* father."

I hid my shock. Then a memory flooded back, unbidden: when I was about six years old, I had gone with my mother to her hometown in North Carolina. A lady had looked at me and said, "Oh that's the child you had by . . ." Mama put her finger to her lips and the woman was quiet. For weeks afterward, I had fun filling in the blank with the names of different movie stars. But soon I was bored with that game. I hadn't thought about the incident in nearly thirty-five years.

"Did you ever meet my real father?" I asked my aunt calmly.

"Never met him. They tell me he was much older than your mother. Owned a funeral parlor. Still lives in Greensboro." She paused. "You know anything about him?"

"I heard he was older," I lied. I sat with my aunt another ten minutes, then announced, "Aunt Fannie, that long ride just hit me. I think I'll go to bed."

As soon as I reached Sondra I shook her awake and recounted my conversation with Aunt Fannie.

Sondra laughed. "Isn't it just like Eleanor and Bill to keep a secret like that," she said of our parents. I laughed, too, though I was actually numb from the revelation. But I was happy about Sondra's reaction, because it occurred to me that she could have been sad or angry, since this new information meant she and I were only half sisters. There were twelve years between us; she had been six years old when I left home. Now, in our older years, the distance between us had disappeared. I put on my pajamas and climbed into bed, feeling closer to her. My heart fluttered so that I thought I would never be able to fasten my eyes tight enough to fall asleep. We whispered in the dark for only a short while; then, exhausted more from the revelation than the long ride, I was asleep.

We didn't mention our secret to Daddy because I didn't want to send up warning flares to Mama. Two days later I was standing with Mama in her bedroom.

"Is Daddy my real father?" I asked, repeating what Aunt Fannie had said.

"She's just trying to start trouble. That's why I don't go down there." Mama stuttered and rambled.

I wanted to believe her. The alternative was horrible: that the man I considered my father was not my father, that my mother could look into my face and lie to me every day of my life. If she could do that, what could a person do to me who loved me less?

It was as if someone had pulled the earth from under my feet and I was falling. To save myself, I did not prod my mother anymore. But I knew this was something that would not go away, so I came up with a plan to discover the truth for myself. When Mother went out one evening, Sondra and I searched her old telephone bills, looking for a number in Greensboro. We found it on a bill only a couple of months old. We scanned through her personal telephone book until we found the phone number, across from the name "Mr. James." I was at once elated and terrified. I took the phone number and name to work with me and convinced my friend Michael to call Mr. James at his job number, posing as an interviewer from the Census Bureau. I cautioned my friend not to call him at his house because I didn't want to cause the man any problems.

A short while later, Michael ran over to me with the first real information I had about this man. His full name: Irwin Alexander James. He was eighty-three, married, with two girls and two boys—not counting me, of course. He owned a funeral parlor and a dry cleaner; his wife was a retired nurse.

His age astounded me most. He was nineteen years older than my mother. I figured, considering his age, I didn't have years to decide whether or not I wanted to meet him or to talk to him. So a few days later, Cindy sat beside me in an empty office as I dialed his number. My fingers shook.

The phone rang, and a gravelly old voice on the other end of the phone spoke.

I was terrified. "Mr. James?"

"Yes."

"My name is Pat," I blurted. I told him my mother's name. "I'm her oldest child."

There was silence.

"Does that name mean anything to you?" I asked, my heart pounding, my feet ready to run.

He spoke haltingly. "They tell me you're my daughter."

The hollow in my chest spread. I thought, *First I am rejected by the only father I've ever known; now I am rejected by my real father.*

"What do you mean, 'they tell you'?" I was afraid to hear his answer.

"Er, I mean, yes, I believe you are my daughter," he said. Then his voice softened, as he added, "I never thought the day would come when I would hear your voice."

Those were medicinal words for the child in me who longed for a father to love her. But I did not try to fashion them into something they weren't. This was an old man who had just suffered a powerful shock and was struggling to find the proper words. He was not a father celebrating a reunion with his long-lost daughter. We talked another five minutes, and yet somehow I knew when I hung up that this man was not my real father. I had thought about the question of fatherhood before our conversation. In fact, I had thought about it a lot longer, during the last couple of years in therapy. Maybe my definition of fatherhood had been changing, fermenting, until my call to Mr. James settled the question.

My real father was the man who had cared for me all of my life, who made sure I had food to eat and clothes to wear. In fact, after my phone conversation, I would come to refer to Mr. James as my "sperm father." He allowed me to enter this world, but he had not helped me live in it.

I agreed to meet him, after I had discussed our conversation with Mama and we had all agreed upon a date. Before we said good-bye, he told me he had a picture of me and Andrea and he had some of my articles. This was unbelievable to me, that he could know so much about me, that my mother could supply him with this information while I knew nothing about him.

Over the next few days I picked up the phone several times to call Mama, but I hung up, dreading the confrontation. I had begun to feel sorry for her. What a burden she had carried. What tangled web of thoughts had prevented her from telling me the truth?

When I finally called Mama and told her I had talked to Mr. James, there was silence, then she asked, "Who is Mr. James?"

"My father," I snapped.

"Your father?" She said this as if she had no idea what I was talking about. "What do you mean, your father?"

We went on like that a few minutes, with me repeating that I had talked to my real father and Mama denying that was possible. "Bill Gaines is your real father. What are you talking about?" she asked. I hurt for her, because her thin voice told me she had never thought this day would arrive.

We hung up, having accomplished nothing. But a couple of hours later, Mama called me and said curtly, "Let's go to brunch together Sunday at Andrew's."

She began talking that day as soon as she got into my car. Secrets bottled up for years gushed out of her mouth. "It's true; Mr. James is your real father," she began. I wondered what it meant that my mother never called this man by his first name.

She told me she was fifteen when Mr. James started flirting with her; he was thirty-four. She used to baby-sit for him and his wife. She refused his advances until she was eighteen. Then, the summer before Mama left for college, she slept with Mr. James to spite her ex-boyfriend, who was going out with an older woman.

Mama went off to Livingstone College in Salisbury, North Carolina, as planned, arriving with a scholarship from her church and my grandmother's dreams weighing heavy on her back. She missed her next two menstrual periods. A girlfriend took her to a doctor for an abortion. But the doctor did something called "packing," which Mama believes meant he put gauze and other things that she wasn't sure of inside her womb to make her abort. Her period never came on, so she returned to the doctor. This time she recognized his nurse as the town drunk and ran, figuring she was fleeing for her own life; I just happened to be with her.

She had to face the inevitable: my grandmother. What Mama remembered hearing all her life was her mother promising, "If an old man ever touches my daughter, I'll kill him." This was because my grandmother was fourteen when she gave birth to my mother by an older man who ended up marrying a woman his own age. So Mama told my grandmother that she was pregnant by the young man that Grannie knew Mama had dated throughout high school.

When I was an infant, Mama met my daddy, the marine, at a dance, and before I was old enough to talk, they got married.

"I never told you because I always wanted my children to be the same," Mama said, tears trickling down her cheeks. "I didn't want one to feel any different than the others. All my life, all I wanted was a husband and children, one big happy family."

"We *are* one big happy family," I said, crying because I felt relief for both of us and joy that my mother had one less burden. I cried, too, because my mother and I had wanted the same thing out of life and neither of us got it the way we had dreamed it.

We stayed at the restaurant a long time, eating too much food and drinking too many glasses of champagne. I told Mama that I was going to tell Andrea and the other children. She halfheartedly begged me not to. But she knew I would. Weeks later, when I told my daughter, she was furious. "You mean to tell me I don't have any sisters and brothers, I don't have a father—and now I don't have any aunts or an uncle either?" she snapped. I don't want to have anything to do with him! I have all the family I need!"

I made a date to meet all my sisters at one of our favorite restaurants, a sprawling, dimly lit place with reasonable prices and a menu the size of a special sales catalog from Spiegel. My brother couldn't come, so I spoke with him later. While we waited for our food, I broke the news to them. There was a short silence; then my sister Carol asked, "How are you doing? How are you feeling about this?" The others mumbled variations of the same questions.

I looked around at these women, sister-girlfriends who had loved me when I was difficult to like, when I was the older sister who made their mother cry every night because she didn't know where I was or when I would be home. I remembered when Carol was a toddler who tripped and cut her forehead on the brick wall of a flowerbed. As Mama took her off to the hospital, Shelia and I, the only other children who had been born then, cried hysterically at the sight of our sister bleeding. Mama's friends could not console us; we cried until we were sick to our stomachs and had fevers. We calmed down only hours later when Mama returned home and showed us that our sister had not "cracked her head open," as we had heard one adult say.

Time had bonded me with these women. They were my blood, my first girlfriends, the first women I had loved. What love I had for myself I owed to them as much as to anybody or anything.

"I am still shocked by all of this," I said. "But I know I have more than enough family here to last this lifetime."

We all laughed. Then one person kissed the other and the kiss was passed around the table, from one sister to the next.

I told them I had agreed to meet the "sperm father" one day. After all of us were sure everyone was feeling well, we began the joning and bantering we had subjected each other to all our lives.

"I always told those teachers at DuVal you weren't my real sister," said Carol, referring to the bad reputation I had left behind at high school.

"At least now when you do something stupid, we know we're only half to blame," said Debbie.

They went on like this until Carol suggested a toast. "To sister love," she said, and we all raised our glasses.

One day shortly after my dinner with my sisters, I dropped by my parents' house to give my worried mother the good news about how

my sisters had reacted. Instead of registering relief, Mama begged me
to go downstairs and tell my daddy to go to the doctor.

"He's so sick he didn't rise early. And you know that's not like your
daddy," she said.

This was true. Even though he drank too much, my father, the ex-
marine, prided himself on waking at sunrise every morning. I went
downstairs, expecting to see him in his usual lounge chair, but the
chair was empty. Daddy was stretched out on his back on the sofa.
It was midafternoon and he clearly was not leaving the house any
time soon.

I looked at him and felt something I had never felt for him before, a
warmth that came from the new respect I had for him. I was nervous,
but I blurted out what I was suddenly anxious to say.

"Daddy, I know about Mr. James. I want to thank you for all that
you have done for me—for accepting the responsibility of taking care
of me."

"I did what I had to do," he grumbled, waving me away.

Normally, such a cool reaction to my sincerity would have angered
me. But I walked away laughing, because it was so typical of my father. At that moment I was happy to recognize his quirks, to know
that he was not a stranger to me in the way that Mr. James was.
Daddy's answer comforted me; it made things normal again. Or so it
seemed.

◆　◆　◆

I was leaving for the University of Michigan soon, having been
awarded a journalism fellowship to study for one full school year. Andrea was returning to Spelman; we made plans for her to visit me later
during spring break. Michael rented my house along with a guy
named Ted, whom Michael knew only as a gay man who had the reputation of being responsible and reliable. I got new storm windows to
keep out the chilling gusts of wind that slipped through cracks around
the old windows. The new windows, I was sure, would prevent Michael from getting the pneumonia that seemed to kill so many people
with the AIDS virus.

Michael told me that like him, his new roommate was HIV positive, and I found myself considering the possibility that both or either of them could get too sick to work and be unable to pay the rent. *Is it fair to refuse to rent to someone who has the AIDS virus?* I asked myself, pondering the question for several days. In the end, I chose humanity over a smart business move, though I protected my investment by putting aside money in case they did get sick and I had to pay the mortgage.

Gerald, Cooper's friend, was getting sicker. He had been in and out of the hospital. Once he called all of his friends together to say good-bye and to talk to us about his memorial service. He was frail and weak, and most often I found him lying on his back in bed. When I was ready to leave for Michigan, I went to say good-bye to him, bending over his bed to plant a kiss on his forehead. "This is it," I said, and moments later I sat in my car trembling, shaking, and sobbing.

I did not want to be with strangers when Gerald died, so I began my daily prayer: *Gerald, please don't die while I'm in Michigan; I won't be able to handle it.*

Before Michigan, I was going to New York for a conference. The promise of a year without working excited me more than anything, but my father's bad health was like a fog surrounding me, so that I could not see anything clearly or enjoy anything nearly as much as I could have if he were well. My mother and I had agreed to go to North Carolina to meet Mr. James before the end of the summer, but now we postponed the trip. On the day that I left for New York, my father went to the doctor. By the time I called home long-distance the hospital had decided to keep him.

"They're running tests to see if it's cancer," one of my sisters said.

Before I left New York, it was confirmed: Daddy had cancer. I cursed God and His dramatic ironies. This was the father I had just gotten, the man I was beginning to understand and appreciate after years of not even trying. This was the man I discovered had chosen to take me into his life to care for as his own. God gave me a father I did not know, and now He was teasing me, dangling the life of my real father on a string.

◆ ◆ ◆

It was late August when I arrived in Ann Arbor, Michigan. The city already smelled like the damp yellow leaves of early fall. The air touched your skin, cool and moist in the mornings and crisp and chilly in the evenings. I lived in an efficiency apartment on the ninth floor of the city's tallest building, twenty-six stories high. If I looked straight out my huge picture window, not letting my eyes drop to the parking lot below, I could escape into brilliant purple-and-orange sunsets.

I had rented my house in Washington to Michael, the young gay black man who had become one of my best friends. Shortly after he started working at the *Post* as a copy aide I had run into him at Tracks nightclub, both of us disappointed to see someone from work at a place we each considered our hideout. But on our second run-in there, we danced together, and we became regular partners, cutting loose with each other, getting crazy. His body and face reminded me of African sculpture, tall and finely chiseled, with a strong, angular nose and well-defined lips on a face the color of rich molasses.

He spent the night at my house several times a week, cooking in the large kitchen, filling the house with the smell of exotic spices as he experimented. I enjoyed the food he cooked, though he wrecked the kitchen in the process, using every pot and pan. Sometimes before going to sleep, we read poetry or snippets of our favorite prose aloud to each other. He would introduce me to John, a gay black man in his late twenties, a perpetual volunteer, always involved in a community project, always giving. John reminded me of a child, diving into what-ever he was doing with unabandoned glee, madly in love with life and curious about everything. He had a little girl's face, too, with long, curly eyelashes and perfectly pink, full lips.

"I'm the oldest living AIDS patient and I want to keep that title," John loved to say. He had had AIDS nearly seven years when I met him. But he was never sick, always full of energy and hard to keep up with.

We had been an inseparable threesome for a couple of years, until I broke up the crew to go to Michigan. Now Michael, bubbling with excitement, called me to announce that he had gotten a job as a re-porter in Massachusetts. Then John called. He was concerned that Michael would not take good care of himself once he moved. It was true that John, with his mothering ways, made Michael more health-conscious, making sure he took his medicine, got his sleep, and watched his diet.

I called Gerald, who was very sick now, and for the first time he said, "I'm tired, Patrice." He said it with such exasperation that I was sure he was telling me he was ready to die. Too much was happening at once: Gerald was dying; my father had cancer; Michael was moving out of our protective circle. Whenever I talked to my sisters, they spoke in weary, whispering voices, and the news was never good. Daddy had bone cancer and it was in an advanced stage. My sisters Sondra and Vicki recounted how they had taken him home from the hospital for a family cookout. He was so weak that my brother and a friend had to pick him up and carry him into the house.

When he was in the hospital, I couldn't even talk to him, because the military hospital only had telephones in the hallway, which my father would never see again. Early one morning my sister Carol called me, sobbing. "The doctors said if you want to see Daddy, come home now," she said.

I left the next day.

◆ ◆ ◆

My father did not look like a marine. He was small and frail. His hands shook and his eyes were wild. You could smell his fear. I was so sorry for him, not because he was dying, but because he seemed to believe death would be horrible. I wanted him to know peace before he died, since he had always appeared tormented by something. I prayed to his mother and father and the other spirits I thought would greet him on the other side. I asked them to extend some peace to him now, before death, and, if possible, to help make his transition easy.

My daughter was coming to visit him as soon as she finished taking midterm exams. I had to go back to school, too. When I went to say good-bye to Daddy, my heart told me to fall across his bed and sob, because that was how I felt. But I couldn't push myself beyond the script we had played throughout our lives. Displays of emotion made him uncomfortable; I didn't want to cause him more pain. So I bent and kissed him on the forehead, thinking of how many times I had gone through this familiar gesture—with my grandmother, with Cooper, with Gerald. "I love you," I said.

"Why did you tell me that?" Daddy asked.

"Because I do," I said. Then I left, carrying tears in the corners of my eyes. Down the hall, I smiled at his last question, because it was so typical of him. He was not about to change now.

◆　◆　◆

Back at home, I stayed up all night talking on the phone to a friend, telling him about my relationship with my father. Just before the sun rose, I hung up and fell asleep. It was October 15, 1989; I had been in Michigan not quite two months.

The phone rang and my sister Debbie said between sobs, "Pat, Daddy is dead." I could not believe it, that I would have to live my life with only one parent. That it was even possible to do that. Already, I was thinking: If I could lose one, I could lose the other, and one day I would have no parents. This is how it all begins: one parent falls into the abyss, and then the other follows. I called my daughter. Within a few hours, we were both on planes headed to Maryland.

Once my father had gotten sick, I became dangerously forgetful, clumsy, and careless. One day in Michigan I walked into a bank, cashed my check, then dropped the envelope with all the money in it on the floor and kept walking. Fortunately, I went next door to the record store to buy records and, finding I had no money, returned to the bank. The tellers looked at me as if they were waiting to witness my self-destruction; then they pointed to a woman behind a desk, who handed me the envelope.

"My father is dying," I said to the woman.

I put a pair of shoes in the refrigerator, had to dig in the trash for a chapter of my novel, stood at corners waiting to cross the street even when the light was green. Now, when my sisters came to the airport to pick me up, I could not remember the names of their children. This struck all of us as hilarious, and we laughed, that too loud, half-hysterical burst of laughter that comes from being close to the edge.

The day after I arrived in Maryland, the phone rang at my parents' house. It was one of Gerald's good friends.

"I can't believe you're here," he said. "Gerald died yesterday. We were trying to call you in Michigan."

I sat at the dining room table crying and laughing at the same time, thanking Gerald and God. Gerald had died the same day as my father, which meant that now I got the news as I sat with people who knew him, too, who mourned his death with me.

While we made arrangements for my father's funeral, I found out that Ginny, my old neighborhood girlfriend and best friend from high school, was in the hospital recovering from a liver transplant. She had hepatitis, but her doctor had not diagnosed it until it destroyed her liver. She and I had kept in touch just enough to know the highlights of each other's life. Our mothers, who still visited each other regularly, shuttled messages and pictures back and forth for us. I went with Ginny's parents to visit her in the hospital. We wept at the sight of each other, all grown-up and older. We laughed recalling how we used to skip school, how we sometimes wore identical outfits and tricked people into thinking we were twins.

◆ ◆ ◆

My father's wake was at the same funeral home where we had held wakes for my grandparents. Some of Daddy's friends, gray-haired and balding ex-marines, stood guard over him, their aging bodies ramrod straight. Three of Mother's friends, beauticians from the salon where she used to work, sang a gospel song, fidgeting with a piece of paper when they couldn't remember the words. Their voices—all fine individually—trailed off in different directions. My siblings and I dubbed them "the Beauty Shop Trio," and though we knew they were sincere in their sorrow, we laughed because we figured Daddy was screaming, "Eleanor, what the hell are those women doing here!" He hated that beauty shop, because he had always resented that his wife had needed and wanted to work. As I listened to the Beauty Shop Trio sing, it was obvious to me that funerals are not for the dead.

Gerald's funeral was the same day as my father's. I thought I could attend both until that very day, when my father's funeral wrenched every ounce of energy from me. In perfect mechanical precision, Marine Corps guards in their dress blues lifted Daddy's casket from the hearse and carried it to the front of the small chapel at Arlington National Cemetery, their feet shuffling against the concrete in unison. I cried because my father loved the Marine Corps so much.

At the gravesite, I wept uncontrollably during the gun salute and then as the mournful sounds of "Taps" floated over the endless rows of white tombstones. I sobbed when the guards slapped the corners of the American flag, then folded it methodically, and a single soldier presented it to my mother. In the limousine, I cried again, surprising my own self at the depth of my grief. Sondra held me and calmed me. Lying in the cradle of her arms, I could not recall ever before letting my siblings comfort me. I was the oldest; I did the comforting.

"If I knew you could make me feel like this, I wouldn't have gotten married so many times," I told her.

Everyone laughed and our laughter made the somber air glow. The next minute we were telling "Daddy stories," about how his idea of a Sunday outing was to take us on drives and walks through Arlington Cemetery, to show us where famous people were buried. We couldn't appreciate it then, but our father, who was working at the cemetery at the time, was taking us to his office, showing us his work.

◆ ◆ ◆

The semester at Michigan ended and I headed home again for the Christmas break, thinking during the entire plane trip about the strangeness of being at home without my father. The house was so unnaturally quiet that although my father seldom made noise, I concluded that each person's breathing must affect the molecules within each room, sending invisible waves and ripples that touched the others. And so now each of us in the family felt different in that house; the rhythm of the air was not the same.

Ginny was in intensive care now and I couldn't see her, so I got my reports from her mother or from Ginny's best friend. The news got worse: Ginny was in very critical condition; Ginny was brain-dead and surviving on a respirator; death was inevitable. Her mother pleaded with Ginny's husband to give the doctor permission to unplug the respirator—and finally, two days before Christmas Day, the holiday she loved so much, he found the courage to do it. Ginny's mother called to tell me that my childhood friend was dead.

You cannot prepare for death. It socks you every time. You think you're prepared, but you can't know until that one moment that seems to last forever. I was stunned. I put on a gospel tape and sat in what was now my mother's kitchen, crying, not just because Ginny was dead, but because I had learned so much over the last months of her life about how different she had become. In high school, we were adventurous and daring, and though that sometimes worked against us, I considered our fearlessness to be our most redeeming and admirable feature. A friend told me Ginny had not come to my fortieth birthday party because it was near Annapolis and she was afraid to make the forty-five-minute drive alone. I wept over this, because this was not the adventurous Ginny I knew. What had killed her daring spirit?

From what I heard, Ginny had problems in her marriage, problems that some people believed should have pushed her to leave it, or to at least demand better. Hearing the stories, though, reminded me of high school, when our one great worry had been the fear of being alone. To two skinny, breastless black girls who felt inadequate in a society that worshiped flesh and whiteness, being alone meant being without a man, being found undesirable by a beau. Our devoted friendship was not enough. Though our lives had taken different routes—she had married after college and had remained married, and I had been married three times—I wondered now if we both had spent our lives just trying not to be alone.

I suffered over Ginny's life and death in a way I did not mourn my grandparents, Cooper, or my father. It was as if Ginny and I were almost one. When I considered her life, I felt her pain. It was a woman thing, I told myself. We women die in so many ways. Before a medical examiner proclaims us dead, we give our lives away.

◆   ◆   ◆

I flew back to my perfect life in Michigan. But I had been there only a week when someone called to tell me that Ted, Michael's former roommate and still a tenant in my house, had died of AIDS. I felt as if I were caught up in some bizarre black, black comedy. I put down the phone and laughed hysterically, talking to God aloud about His remarkable sense of humor.

But Ted's death was another rip in my heart, which I imagined already looked like Swiss cheese. I was comforted some by a call from his sister in Mississippi, who thanked me for letting him rent my house. He was happy there, she said. She had wanted to take him to live with her, but she thought the people in her small town would be cruel to someone with AIDS. I recalled how Ted had decorated the house so beautifully for Christmas and how immaculate he had kept it. I was thankful I was able to provide him his last home.

◆   ◆   ◆

My school year ended and I was back home. I sensed I had changed profoundly during my year away, but there was no way to know what changed me most: the deaths I had lived through or the months of contemplation. I moved in with Mama, taking the old bedroom downstairs, where my father used to sleep. The room still smelled like him, a mix of sweat and sweet cherry tobacco. Sometimes the scent was so alive that when I turned I half-expected to see him. Mama and I got along better now than we had when as a teenager I had fled that house. We were both in a compromising time of life, when our loneliness and will for peace matched the other's perfectly.

Andrea graduated from Spelman and a vanload of us went to Atlanta, including my friend John; Andrea's father, Ben; and his wife. My ex-husband Ziggy and his wife met us there. I spent my entire weekend in awe of the passage of time, recalling how my child had grown up with me, how often she had saved me with her small arms.

I had a month of vacation before returning to work, and John and I hung out, missing Michael everywhere we went. Michael had moved again, to Los Angeles this time. We called him often, sometimes at inappropriate hours after we were in a frenzy from dancing. Michael always ended with, "Come to L.A.!" and we sincerely wanted to, though neither of us had the time or money. We patiently listened as he gave us more details than we wanted about the most recent articles he had written. But we were truly happy for him, because we heard the pride he had in his job, and the pure, unadulterated glee delighted us.

Before I returned to work, I wanted to go to North Carolina to meet my birth father. I bought a cheap compact car, and Mama and I packed enough necessities for a week and hit the road. We stayed at a no-frills motor inn on the edge of Greensboro. Mama phoned Mr. James soon after we arrived, her voice uneasy, different than I had ever heard it. Then she called one of her girlfriends and made arrangements for her to pick us up in an hour.

I was angry. I hadn't driven five hours to see her old girlfriends.

"Mr. James said he'll call us at ten tonight," she said.

At 10:00 P.M., we were still at her girlfriend's house. Mama was eating a slice of pineapple upside-down cake while I stared at a grandfather clock, trying to hide my anger and disappointment.

"Mama, it's ten," I said.

"Okay, we'll leave in a minute," she replied.

We left at eleven. There was a message waiting for us that Mr. James had called. Mama went to bed, explaining that it was too late to call. I couldn't sleep because my head was full of too many questions, the major one being why was my mother behaving the way she was.

"Mama, when was the last time you saw Mr. James?" I asked as we ate breakfast the next morning.

"Oh, not since you were four or five," she said.

I was surprised, since they had kept in touch by phone and through letters.

Mr. James called to say he would come by our motel room that evening. My mother's nervousness matched my own. By the time he knocked at the door, Mama and I had each had two large drinks from a fifth of Rémy Martin.

"You get it," Mama said.

I opened the door slowly, and a white man walked in. He wasn't really a white man, but you could only tell that after you looked closely. His skin was pale pink; the jowls on his face hung low. Nothing on him looked like me. I looked at Mama for confirmation. He stuck out an unsteady hand and said, "Are you Pat?"

I nodded. He said something and walked toward Mama, leaving me frozen. He was white and old and round. That was what ran through my mind. He was just about five feet, six inches, not tall and stately like the father I knew. When I faced him, I saw gray eyes. When he spoke, a southern drawl slid out his mouth, but it bore neither black nor white inflections. I felt like I was five years old, as if I didn't have the adequate intelligence to deal with what was going on. Stepping back into propriety, I fixed all of us drinks and told him about Michigan, Andrea's graduation, and my job.

I sat in a chair across from him and rolled my eyes over every inch of his face, trying to find some hint of me. His nose was bridgeless like mine; his lips were thin, too.

My mama stayed seated on the bed, with her arms folded in front of her, just as stiff as a mannequin. She spoke in a syrupy, childish voice that I had never heard before. I felt sorry for her. A woman normally proud, she was now obviously ashamed of all the weight she had gained. But there was also something else happening that wasn't as easy to pinpoint. My mother had become the young baby-sitter again and Mr. James was the elder businessman who intimidated her. Mama was a child, giggly and shy.

I took photographs of Mr. James, knowing that this moment was too important to be left to memory. He did not have many wrinkles, but his skin looked tough, like leather. His clothes were neat, but dated and not coordinated. He wore a brown plaid blazer, a maroon sweater vest, and brown slacks. His shoes were scuffed brown wingtips.

He stayed about an hour, but I cannot recall most of what we said. I remember he laughed easily and had a wit that made me wonder if humor could be inherited, because it was the one part of him most like me. When I went in the bathroom after him, I saw that he had missed the toilet some and peed on the floor.

He did not disappoint me so much as wake me up. He was just as imperfect as the father I had known all my life. In a way, it was a relief that he wasn't someone who swept me off my feet and made me envious of his real children. By the time I got home and my sisters and brother asked what he was like, I had reduced him to one line: "He looks like an old white man, and he can't pee straight." It was clever and devoid of emotion. I had decided the man I met seemed kind enough to be a father, and could be one of the best fathers living. But he was not *my* father.

I told him I would write him sometime, or maybe send a card, but I was careful not to promise too much. Why open up a Pandora's box when his life was winding down? As for me, I was content with the family I had and I was still trying to understand the father God had given me.

In the end, I never wrote my birth father, or saw him again. I do not even know if he is dead or alive.

◆   ◆   ◆

By late July of 1990, Michael, now working in Los Angeles, had grown too sick to walk to his mailbox. I found out while talking to him by phone, after I questioned him about something I wrote in a letter. He admitted he had not gone to the mailbox in weeks. I called his mother in New York and encouraged her to visit him immediately, trying to hide the panic in my voice, telling her that he needed a mother's care and someone to force him to go to the hospital. She did not know her son was gay; she had no reason to suspect he might have AIDS.

She went to Los Angeles the next day. Later, she told me Michael burst into tears when he saw her. He must have been so exasperated from trying to be brave and strong. Mrs. Harrison found him alone, sleeping on a mattress that a friend had carried from upstairs and laid on the living room floor for him. When he had to go upstairs to the bathroom, he crawled.

At the hospital, they told him he had a collapsed lung. Shortly after his arrival, the other lung collapsed. The diagnosis was pneumocystis pneumonia, caused by AIDS. His mother called me in tears. She asked if I knew he had AIDS. I told her, "Yes," as gently as I could. For her, it was the beginning of a long struggle to try to answer the questions: Why? Why was her son gay? What had she done? Where had she or his father gone wrong? All I could do was tell her that I believed her questions were misformed, because no wrong had been done, that I sincerely believed people were born with some predetermination to become gay, bisexual, straight, or asexual.

I talked to her and Michael daily by phone. He had kept his illness a secret from his friends and coworkers, most of whom had no idea he was gay because Michael was still living in that small, cramped world called "the closet," which was too tight for friends to fit in. So no one knew Michael was in the hospital. This meant his only visitor was his mother. He was in a stark room without cards or flowers, except for the ones John and I sent.

"You are denying yourself love, which could help you heal," I told Michael by phone. "It's not fair to your mother. It would comfort her, to see that you are loved."

So he gave me permission to call his editor, a woman who happened to be an old friend of mine. I told her the truth, but I also told her he wanted to keep the exact nature of his illness a secret. Immediately friends began to visit and the bulletin board in his room filled with cards and letters, some from his old coworkers at the *Post,* whom I told of his illness with a note on the office bulletin board. There was one card from a police chief in a small town that Michael covered as a reporter. The card had a note inside that said: "Hurry and get well. People are starting to say you have that faggot disease."

◆　◆　◆

Mrs. Harrison had to return to New York briefly, so John and I flew to Los Angeles to be with Michael. When I saw him, I nearly cried. The fine, chiseled face that had reminded me of African sculpture was a skull with skin stretched taut across it. In his frail face, his eyes and mouth looked monstrously large.

Again, my life had come down to sitting beside the bed of someone facing death, helping him comb through his past. Michael and I talked about his difficult relationship with his father. I was convinced that part of the reason God had me sit at Michael's side was so that I could help lead him back to the love he had for his father when he was born. Every chance I got, I nudged him to try to forgive his father, telling him about the peace I had now since that Saturday morning I had taken my father to breakfast.

The doctors informed us that Michael had to have an operation if he was ever to get out of bed and live a normal life again. They needed to patch up his lungs so he could be detached from the machine and breathe on his own. We called Mrs. Harrison to come back. Michael had not wanted his father to visit him, I'm sure because he was afraid of his father's reaction if the elder man found out his son was gay. Mrs. Harrison had only told her ex-husband that their son had pneumonia. But now, facing an operation, Michael asked to see his father.

Mrs. Harrison told me, "There's going to be a problem when Mr. Harrison sees John."

I wasn't sure I understood, but she didn't hesitate to explain. "John is too effeminate. Michael Senior is going to know he's gay," she said.

I was offended. "Don't worry about it," I snapped.

"I hope he leaves before Mr. Harrison comes," she said.

I looked at her. Did she realize I loved her son and John equally? Did she understand that I was convinced that Michael would not have lived as long as he had if it had not been for John looking after him as if he were a child?

Of course, I could not tell John what she had said. I didn't want to hurt him. Yet as the day drew near for Mr. Harrison to arrive, I tried to form the words. As it turned out, John had to return to Washington before Mr. Harrison's arrival. I drove John to the airport in Michael's superplush Honda, a recent acquisition he had been able to afford with his new salary from his reporter's job. I sneaked a glance at John, trying to gauge his condition, emotionally and physically. He had developed a nagging cough in California but shrugged it off as he usually did with the explanation, "Chile, that's my bronchitis."

"John, you got to promise you'll never die on me," I said. "I don't think I could live without you."

I reached over and squeezed his hand. I saw him to his plane, would have boarded it with him and strapped him in his seat if I could have. Instead, I kissed his cheek; then we both hugged, then stared at each other one more time, with tears in our eyes.

"Michael isn't going to die, is he?" he asked.

"No," I said, hoping he could not hear my fear.

◆   ◆   ◆

When I saw Michael's father, it was like looking at a version of my friend with ebony skin. I could not believe Michael could dislike this man and yet have copied so many of his mannerisms, the way he held his tall body, the straight, wide smile. But Mr. Harrison was a man who could scare a boy, particularly a son. He talked too loud sometimes and too often.

Mr. Harrison came with color photos he had taken on a recent fishing trip with some buddies, and when he showed them to me he paused to carefully describe the sunsets and the moon, and he said, "Yeah, I got to take Michael fishing. There's a lot of things I have to do with that boy." He told me, too, that a friend had questioned his coming to check on someone who was twenty-six years old. "I told her I didn't care how old he was; if my son needs me, I'm coming," Mr. Harrison said.

Hearing him speak reminded me of my own father and how many men, particularly men of their generation, could not bring themselves to say, "I love you." I had always believed that Mr. Harrison loved Michael, even if he didn't know how to show it. Now I had heard the proof and I couldn't wait for Michael to hear it, too.

At the hospital, I recounted that story. Michael smiled. I told Mr. Harrison to show him the fishing photos. But the awkwardness between father and son returned and the elder man did not mention the beautiful images he had so easily described to me, until I begged him. As he laid out in words the streams where he fished and the land on which he had slept, Michael looked at him with eyes full of love.

"I have to take you fishing when you get out," the elder man said.

A tear ran down Michael's cheek. Mr. Harrison dropped his son's hand. But the moment had lasted long enough. Mr. Harrison left to return home that day, promising Michael he would return soon. I believe, though no one told him, he suspected, or even knew, that Michael had AIDS. Michael went into surgery the next day. Mrs. Harrison and I sat at the hospital, waiting. I tried to comfort her, but I felt lousy myself. I was focused on this thought: Michael, my wild dance partner, the frenetic cook, would rather die than be tied to a bed.

When we saw Michael after the operation, he was barely conscious, with tubes up his nose and in his mouth. The doctor talked to us by phone from another part of the hospital.

"It doesn't look good," he said. "He may not last through the night."

Mrs. Harrison and I sobbed, leaning against the counter so we could stand.

"Do you have to put AIDS on the death certificate?" Mrs. Harrison asked the doctor, her voice shaking with emotion, whimpering.

"I'll see what I can do, but I can't lie," the doctor said.

Once I would have considered any mother callous for thinking about the wording on a death certificate instead of grieving for her son. But I had learned to have more compassion. Within two months, this woman had learned that her son was gay, had AIDS, and was dying. Any one of these facts alone easily demanded years of contemplation from a parent.

Michael made it through the night. And the next day. Sometimes they took him off the respirator to let him breathe on his own for short periods. We prayed that the times would get longer and longer. But they didn't.

I had to get back to my job, even though I knew it meant leaving Michael one last time. Anyway, I wasn't sure I wanted to be a witness to his last breath. Mrs. Harrison's brother was coming to Los Angeles, so I didn't feel I was abandoning her. I stood over Michael's bed, taking my last look at him, trying to soak him through my pores, to inhale him with all my breath. I stared into his eyes—and he stared into mine. He was telling me he loved me; I could feel it.

"I love you," I said.

His lips moved. He was trying to talk, to tell me he loved me.

"I know. You love me, too," I said.

He gave me a thumbs-up signal. I kissed his forehead and backed out of the room, slowly, hearing the quiet shish of the machine as it breathed for him, backing up until I could not see him or hear his lungs filling with air.

Michael died two days later, on September 12, 1990. He was twenty-six years old.

◆   ◆   ◆

John celebrated his thirtieth birthday shortly before Christmas with a dinner party in the basement of the Quaker church in Washington where we had held the memorial service for Michael. John always used his birthday as a fund-raising event for some charity. On this birthday his friends donated money to the house for men with AIDS where John worked. A woman sang gospel music and people offered testimonies about John, which turned a festive event into something resembling a funeral. While this frightened me, the testimonies were healing for John because they showed him how much he was loved.

I spent all the time I could with him now, seldom going out to dance, since every time I was in the middle of a gay nightclub I only thought of the suffering in that community and all of the friends I had lost. Shortly after his birthday, John was sick. He went into the veterans' hospital, which he knew amused me because I always had difficulty imagining him, with his swishing hips, in the army.

After losing Michael and now seeing John sick, sometimes my insides would shake uncontrollably, and I considered going to the doctor for tranquilizers. At work, I wrote about AIDS, not as much as I wanted to, perhaps because my editors recognized that I was now obsessed by the subject. If I thought of any other story idea, it was about gay people. It took me hours to write short articles. I wasn't fully aware of this, though, not until much later, when it was almost too late to save my job. I thought because I rose in the morning, got dressed, and made it to work on time, I was doing fine. What I did not comprehend yet was that I was slipping into a depression, a deep funk that was going to get worse.

I visited John every day at the hospital, often two or three times a day. One morning I stopped by on my way to work and just as I was about to leave, John had a seizure. Doctors and nurses ran in, and machines replaced me. I stood in the hallway, paralyzed with fear. The virus had reached John's brain, the doctor said.

When I walked in, John didn't perk up as if he recognized me; he didn't look in my direction. After I said something to him, he said, "Oh, Patrice, it's you." I stepped outside to see the nurse.

"Can he see?" I asked.

"No. Not at all," she said.

"When did that happen?"

"This morning," she said. "And you know how I found out? I walked in to say good morning when I came on. He asked me which one I was. I said, 'You don't know me by now?' He said, 'I can't see you.' I was more anxious than he was about it. I called in the doctor and they checked him. He's blind.

"I couldn't believe it," she said. "If I woke up blind, I'd be screaming."

I asked him about his sight. He told me, as calmly as if he were talking about the weather, "I couldn't see when I woke up this morning."

"John, weren't you scared?"

"I knew it could happen. And my eyes have been getting bad. I expected it. Anyway, I'm not afraid."

I left it at that. "I'll be your eyes," I said.

He squeezed my hand.

I stayed until evening. When I left, a young woman he had dated was still sitting beside his bed. I explained to him that a writer friend of mine was in Washington on business and we were going to see Gil Scott Heron perform at Blues Alley. I considered canceling my plans and staying with John instead, but I knew that wouldn't please me either.

Nothing pleased me. What I wanted, no one could give. I wanted Michael back—and Gerald and my father and Ginny. I wanted John to walk out of the hospital right at that moment. There was no place on earth where I felt good, as peaceful and happy as I had been when John and Michael and I used to dance until dawn. I had so much nervous energy that I could not sit still for any length of time. Even at the hospital, I paced. So I kissed John, squeezed his hand, and said good-bye.

At the club, all I thought about was John. I seemed absurd to myself, saying inappropriate things, fidgeting, feeling totally on the edge. When Gil sang, I drifted away. I reminisced until sweet memories brought tears to my eyes; then I came back to the present and worried about how John was feeling right at that very moment. I whispered, "I love you," to him. Then the process started all over again: drifting, reminiscing, and worrying. It was tortuous, and it wore me out. When I got home, I went to bed and welcomed sleep. It was about 1:00 A.M.

About 4:00 A.M. I woke up to go to the bathroom. As soon as my feet touched the floor, I heard a voice inside my head say, *John is dead. He has gone to the other side.* I felt a sweet release, more peace than I had felt in months.

I went back to sleep, but only for another fifteen minutes before the phone rang. It was John's sister. "John died about a half hour ago," she said. I think I answered, "I know." Then I went back to bed and fell into an amazingly peaceful sleep. It was February 9, 1991.

I wanted to write his obituary for the *Washington Post.* It would be my last gift to John, I told myself. But John's mother said no, because the *Post* had a policy that the cause of death, in this case AIDS, has to be published. John's mother didn't want the word *AIDS* mentioned. This struck me as ironic at first, because no one had been more open and free than John. But he had also always respected the wishes of his mother. Her denial was only a reminder to me that John was dead, that it was his mother who was alive and would have to deal with such things as prejudices and fear. John was free from all of that now, the earthly burden of being gay. In the midst of my grief, my heart screamed, *Lucky you, John!*

As for myself, I cried often—and anywhere: on the subway, in stores, walking through a parking lot. I stayed away from popular movies that people described as sad, because I knew I would get hysterical. But the meaning of sad had changed for me, too, so that any hint of sorrow or pain to someone made me weep. Then there were the usual things that prompt tears from any grieving person: a sentimental song, an old photo, someone who reminds you of the dead person you love. At work, I received the worst performance evaluation I had ever gotten in my life. My editor basically told me that if I didn't straighten up, I was going to lose my job. This was my wake-up call. I had not realized how depressed I was and now I searched for a way to shake it off, because I could not afford to lose my job. If that happened, I feared I would go over the edge.

I went away to a monastery for a weekend, sitting alone in my room, staring at the distant mountains. When it was dark I went to the chapel and prayed for strength and understanding; for the will to live, to live the way John and Michael would want me to. I prayed for my grandparents and for Cooper, my father, Gerald, Ginny, my tenant Ted, for Michael and John. I prayed that I would not lose my mind.

I went to mass before the sun rose, when the earth was wonderfully quiet and still. The monks chanted in Latin, each syllable seeming to fill me with peace. I had a half-hour session with a priest who told me, "We are blessed to be alive now, at a time when the world is struggling with questions such as whether or not homosexuality is a sin." His words dissolved some of my grief, and I felt the joy I had felt when I was with Michael and John. I had begun to think that having gay friends had only caused me suffering. Now I thanked God for those friendships.

It came to me before I left the monastery that my life thus far could be broken into three parts: there was my childhood, when I learned that I was black and struggled to understand what that meant; there was my young adult life, when I searched for the definition of a woman and what my relationship should be to a man; and there was this time, the exciting time, when I had gone beyond sexuality, beyond woman and man, to humanness. Witnessing death and living through the holocaust of AIDS had somehow made me more alive.

But I was not totally healed. I did not dance the summer of 1991, though I missed dancing terribly. One night I even put on my soft flat leather dance shoes, my Lycra pants, and a big cotton shirt, perfect for soaking up sweat. I was ready to go to a club until I passed a mirror and saw my sad, empty eyes.

"Who will I dance with?" I cried.

chapter fourteen

Joy

winter and a spring passed, a danceless time when the world stood still and I did not see the leaves fall or the flowers bloom. I missed Michael and John more than I knew it was possible to miss anyone or anything, more than I missed all the mischosen lovers and husbands.

But when grief lifted long enough for me to feel the warmth of the sun, I saw clearly that my sorrow was a blessing. My father and friends had embellished my life with love and left me better than they had found me. Together we had learned things we could never have learned alone. I rose one morning, looked into the mirror, and saw a face with no tears. Instead of walking in a daze, I could see. Everywhere I turned, I saw stories: Who were these little boys who ran out at the stoplights to try to wash my windows? When did black teenagers start wearing the red, black, and green colors that black activists had worn in the seventies? When I went on an assignment, I saw several stories besides the one I had gone to cover. So at work, I was no longer consumed by stories about AIDS. The words came faster, so I wrote more articles, which pleased my editor and meant my job was no longer in jeopardy.

When I finally went to the gay clubs, coaxed by my sister Shelia and her husband, I stood on the dance floor and scanned the room, half-hoping to see people I knew were gone. I searched faces for signs of who would die next, but all I thought of was a line in a book of poetry by Lucille Clifton, which said, "We are all next." I was afraid to make new friends who were gay, so I didn't speak to anyone, content to just stand there and remember happier times, when my best friends laughed and danced and beckoned me to join them on the dance floor.

It was miraculous to me that life continued despite my grief. The world turned on its axis, the sun rose and set, as if the universe didn't take notice of my loss at all. My niece, Terrin, was christened and we all saw the empty space where John should have stood as one of the godfathers. I joked that now he could be her fairy godmother, and I laughed, knowing somewhere he was laughing, too.

To get over thinking of myself as alone, I proclaimed myself to be company enough for me. To prove this, I started going out with myself, though people who saw me probably thought I was "alone." On my first date I went to a late Saturday night movie. Afterward I bought a Sunday paper, went to a coffee shop, drank cappuccino, and ate a dessert heavy in calories. It was such an enjoyable date that I took myself out more often. I went to museums, music performances, and dance concerts. Occasionally, I went to a good restaurant, though I found it harder to enjoy myself on that kind of date.

On the rare occasion when I thought about a man, I mouthed an unrealistic prayer: I wanted a man without a history, one born the day before I met him, created by God to love only me. Knowing this was impossible, I had no need to look. I was too scared to love, too afraid to trust anyone. An inventory of my relationships with men offered little encouragement. I was so paranoid about death, too, that I assumed if I found someone who loved me passionately, he'd die. It wasn't in the stars for me to be coupled with someone, and I wasn't angry about this. In fact, I was relieved. For the first time in my life, I sincerely did not care about being in love.

I went to a cabaret with my siblings, a precious evening when everyone had baby-sitters and nothing else to do. We were giddy with excitement, posing for five-dollar family photos seven times, so each of us could have a copy. I met a guy named Chris, who asked me to dance several times, then politely asked if he could take me out to dinner sometime. I gave him my phone number, despite thinking, *Why do people bother with that line when they know they're not going to call?* By the second dance, I had seen enough of him to figure he was younger than I was, though I couldn't tell how much younger. He wore a suit and a white shirt, which made me a little uncomfortable, because I had never dated anyone who was either conservative or practical enough to wear white shirts. But I followed him onto the dance floor and admired his firm butt and the smooth motion of his hips. I liked the way he said "Thank you," softly after each dance and led me back to my family with his hand at the small of my back.

He called the next day, and we went to dinner the next evening. When he came to pick me up, I had barely said, "Hello," when I blurted out, "I have something to tell you: I'm old."

He laughed. "How old are you?"

"Forty-two," I said.

"That's not old," he answered.

I wasn't prepared for that response. He was supposed to run out the door. As it turned out, he was eleven and a half years younger than I was. Some months after we had been dating, my sister Carol, who worked with him, told me she had told him my age the night we met. When I asked Chris about this, he said, "Just wanted to see if you were going to tell me the truth." I found out he was as playful as I am, and this was just the first of many tricks we pulled on each other.

I fell in love with him slowly. Not after three months or during romantic trips together. Not after roses or the exchange of expensive gifts. It took at least a year of friendship, and even then my love for him didn't boil over; it simmered for months, then rose slowly, but steadily, like yeast bread.

He thought I was strange: a straight woman who was only familiar with gay clubs. A forty-two-year-old woman addicted to house music, who asked questions like, "Do you ever think about God?" or "Do you know what your purpose is here?"

To me, Chris seemed narrow-minded and conservative. He said

homosexuality was a sin. He preferred rap music to house music. I was a vegetarian and he loved meat. I would have thrown up my hands and walked out of his life, except he was kind and considerate and he kept his word.

He was not at all what I had prayed for. In fact, the history he brought with him was proof again that God had a heck of a sense of humor. Before me, Chris had dated two women at the same time, one whom he was once engaged to and another who became the mother of his child. When I met him, his daughter was about eight months old and he wasn't dating either woman; he was weary and taking inventory of his life. But first he had to tie up the frayed ends of these relationships; he had to work to turn sour love affairs into good friendships.

How can I trust such a man? I asked. But the question itself was arrogant. This man was no different than myself, no more perfect, no more sinful. Like me, he had struggled with life. For my life to change, I had to conquer my fear that every man would reject me, cause me pain, or leave me in some way. While I wished for an easy out, God knew the only way to overcome my fears was to go through them and not around them. Or in other words, God obviously believed that in my case there was no better way to learn to trust a man again than to meet the challenge of trusting one who had cheated on other women—recently.

For months I wished I had met Chris later in his life. Much later. When both of his relationships were faded photos he pointed to in a battered album. I was still afraid a man I dated would disappear without ever calling me again, or sleep with other women and flaunt it. Meanwhile, Chris still received desperate calls from both of his ex-lovers. At times he was a patient friend, nudging them to see he was not a part of their future. "I don't think that's going to happen," I would hear him say softly. Other times he was angry at their reluctance to move on and berated them, "Don't call here anymore if that's all you want to talk about." Both reactions made me uncomfortable. When he was friendly, I thought he needed to be tougher; I wondered if he was really over the relationship himself. If he was nasty, I imagined he would treat me that way, too.

It is tortuous, learning to trust. Yet I decided not to walk away, because deep inside I believed he was honest—and doing the best he could. He was trying hard and that was something I had not had before, a man in my life who was trying hard to make things right. I had never been so patient before. What sustained me was a powerful sense that I was learning something very crucial. In the past I had ignored the truth and had suffered greatly. Now I stared the truth in the eye—and I suffered. It was becoming obvious, though, that this time my pain was coming from carrying my past with me, carting around my fears from previous relationships and pinning them on Chris.

We had plans one evening for him to come over to my house and spend the night. He called to say he was too tired from working overtime. I figured even if he was tired he could come over just to sleep in my bed, so I suspected he was lying. About midnight, after tossing and turning, I got into my car with my heart racing faster than the engine and drove twenty minutes to his parents' house, where he was living. Cruising down their street, I slowed down to search for his car; it wasn't there. I was fuming. My faith had vanished. Making a U-turn to head home, I looked up at the street sign and saw that I was on the wrong street. *Damn neighborhoods where houses look alike,* I thought, smiling. A reprieve. He just might be home. Sure enough, when I turned down the right street, there was his car parked in front of his parents' house. I was happy until the thought flashed in my head: *Another woman picked him up in her car.* Then I knew I was getting ridiculous. I could always believe he was lying, I could think of one scheme after another, if I wanted. It was my choice. I decided to go home and sleep, praying before I did that the truth would make itself evident. And praying harder that I would recognize it when it came.

I nearly walked away once, when he used on me the overemployed line: "I need more space. You always seem to be holding onto me." I disappeared for a weekend, gave him enough space to build a new life, if he wanted it. I partied with friends, spent the night away from home, and didn't call. He left a barrage of messages on my machine, begging me to call and come by. After some discussion about space, each of us admitted we liked the closeness of our relationship, even though it sometimes frightened us.

Chris didn't want me to meet Janice, his daughter's mother; I was dependent on him for what I knew of her, a position I didn't like. I saw her through his perceptions, which I figured were warped at best, since they were no longer friends. This also gave him control, or power, over both of us—whether or not he knew it or used it. The longer he and I dated, the more this irked me, because if I was going to help him with their child, I needed a relationship of my own with this woman, even if the relationship was comprised only of saying hello and good-bye. I needed to have a sense of her myself. It was fear that placed him between us. He was afraid, I am sure, that neither of us women could handle a relationship with the other, and so he appointed himself the referee.

When I was finally in her presence, Janice treated me like an ugly chair chosen in desperation, one that Chris would surely remove when he came to his senses. My feelings for her went from jealousy to sorrow. When I was at my weakest, I felt jealousy. I felt sorry for her when I saw myself in her, loving too desperately. At those times, I wanted her to love herself at least as much as she did Chris.

What alarmed me more than anything was the discovery that I was jealous of Chris's daughter. For months I couldn't even admit that to myself. But then I began to see that I considered her visits intrusions, though once she was with us the feeling disappeared. Finally, it was changing diapers, reading books with three-word sentences, and rocking her to sleep that overwhelmed my misgivings. I loved her immediately, first because I naturally love babies for their innocence and honesty, then because there were a countless number of reasons to love this one: for her button nose, her endearing, quiet way, the love she returned so freely. I knew she had come to teach me something, too. I thought of her as a brave, loving spirit who had been born into what was chaos.

Once again, admitting an imperfection allowed me to work on changing it. Behind my jealousy was the feeling that after years of feeling neglected and abused by men, I wanted a man's undivided attention. On weekends, I wanted to be pampered, not to help pamper or watch someone else be pampered—even if that someone was a child. It was an admission that certainly made me feel less than noble, or less perfect than we all sometimes imagine we are. Yet when I dared to whisper my concerns to a friend, she surprised me by telling me she had the same feelings about her own children sometimes. "Sometimes I just want them to go away so my husband and I can be alone the way we used to be," she said nonchalantly, while I waited for lightning to strike her. Instead, she walked away as regal as always.

Then, there was the practical question of whether or not I even wanted to be a stepmother. I had raised one child and was enjoying the freedom of not searching for a baby-sitter or worrying about cooking a well-balanced meal for a kid. On some days, I decided being a stepmother wasn't for me. Then just as quickly, I decided it was. Months passed, until I saw more joy than intrusions in my new role. I learned to be more patient than I had been in years, to put down the novel I was reading so I could read nursery rhymes aloud. I rediscovered the beauty of sitting on the kitchen floor and rolling a ball. Then catching it. Then rolling it again. Repetition became the norm and in time, it, too, took on a new meaning. How many times could I read "Little Miss Muffett"? How many times could I play "ring-around-a-rosy"? I was forced to slow down and view the world differently. The clubs would survive without my dancing. I could rearrange my writing schedule and still get the work done. I relaxed.

My fears were getting knocked down, one at a time. But a major fear remained. For the first time in my life, I feared death would snatch someone who seemed totally healthy. It was ludicrous, I told myself. Yet I thought of an old movie I had seen, where everyone a woman met died, until she believed she was somehow killing them. Once Chris arrived at my house a half hour late and I burst into tears, releasing pent-up emotions, explaining that I had imagined he had gotten killed. If it rained, I saw him crashing his sports car on a slick highway. On a nice day, I saw the sun blind him as he sped around a corner. I created scenarios in which he was robbed and gunned down, beaten to death in a fight.

Then, a few days before Christmas, Chris and I were supposed to go shopping. Shortly before I left home to meet him, he called to say his throat hurt. I told him to gargle and promised I was on my way. But traffic was heavy and I was in no mood to rush. By the time I got to the apartment, he was doubled over the toilet, gagging and spitting.

"Call an ambulance," he said.

Chris had already called his father, and he arrived shortly before the ambulance. The medics couldn't find anything wrong with Chris, though he was clearly uncomfortable and by now was having difficulty breathing.

It is happening, a voice in my head said. But it wasn't the clear voice that spoke at times when I knew I heard the truth. This was my own fear talking to me.

The ambulance left and Chris's father and I rushed him to the hospital emergency room. We waited. Chris was examined and everyone seemed baffled until a doctor looked at him and said he might have a rare throat virus the doctor himself once had. Chris's throat was swelling, and if it continued, he could choke to death.

But the doctor needed a specialist to confirm the diagnosis. It was an extremely rare virus, usually appearing in small children, seldom in adults. The doctor sent us to another hospital to meet the specialist. We waited there a couple of hours. When he finally arrived, he told us they would have to operate quickly to insert a tube down Chris's throat so he would have a passage to breathe through. "There's a fifty-fifty chance it will work," he said.

I couldn't believe this was happening. I felt totally at God's mercy. In the past, I had believed I knew what was going to happen, even if I denied knowing. Yes, I knew Michael and John were going to die once they got sick. But this was different. I didn't know what to expect.

I sat with Chris's father in the waiting room, unable to feel. How long did we wait? I do not know. Finally, the doctor came out and announced that the operation had worked. But now Chris had to stay in intensive care, where they could watch him and make sure he did not develop an infection, which could kill him, too.

I stayed with Chris's family because it seemed the only place on earth where I had some peace. I spent time with my family, but I missed Chris more then, because my relatives, though concerned about Chris, were jovial and full of the holiday spirit. I was weary with sadness and worry. I spent every hour I could next to his hospital bed, praying and staring at him. *Love can save people,* I said to myself, so I surrounded him with signs of love: bright red hearts taped to the wall, a photo of us, a picture of his daughter. Janice came to the hospital to see him. I was at his bedside when a nurse, looking baffled, came to say, "There's a woman outside who says she's the mother of his child. She wants to come in?"

The nurse made the last statement as if it were a question. "She can come in," I said.

"She has a child with her and the child can't come in," the nurse said.

Chris was only half-alert and heavily sedated, but he shook his head no when his daughter was mentioned. I understood that he didn't want his child to see him with tubes up his nose. I told him I would go out and keep his daughter so Janice could come in. As I walked out, I imagined all of the nurses were staring at me. Because only family members were allowed to visit patients in intensive care, Chris's parents had once referred to me as his sister, while another time we told a nurse I was his fiancée. Some of the staff even referred to me as his wife.

I went to the reception area and greeted Janice, who looked worried and frightened. I talked to her about Chris's condition and offered to keep her daughter while she went in to see him. While I sat waiting, the elderly receptionist, who had become my friend after two full days spent together, said, "She was creating a ruckus, you know. She said she was his wife first. She insisted we let her back there. It's embarrassing, isn't it?"

"No, it's not. It's life," I snapped. I was immediately sorry, though. From our conversations I knew the woman was seventy-three years old and very traditional. To her, this episode must have seemed straight out of a soap opera. She offered her comment gently, as if to say she was sorry for my embarrassment.

"Believe me, I am not embarrassed," I said. "She is the mother of his child and she loves him dearly."

It wasn't as easy as I made it sound, but in my emotional state I was trying to do what I felt was right, what I hoped someone would do for me. I wasn't a martyr or some unusually kind and understanding person. I was a woman in love with a man I thought could die, and if he died, I didn't want it on my conscience that I had stopped him from seeing Janice one last time. I had seen enough people die to know that in the process there are sometimes things they must say to ex-lovers and ex-friends, words of forgiveness, words that help heal. How could I deny someone I love that opportunity?

But there was just fifteen minutes or so of visiting time left, and when Janice had taken up most of it I sent the receptionist in to get her.

"I told her, but she didn't move," the receptionist said timidly.

I sent a nurse in. Then finally Janice came out, when there was just a few minutes of visiting time left. I said good-bye, rushing past her to Chris's room. I was angry at Janice and my heart beat madly because I had not told her and because I was desperate to check on Chris.

For nearly a week he remained in intensive care. I bought his Christmas gift and wrapped it. I spent the day with his family, videotaping the celebration so he could watch it when he was well. I forced myself to eat—sometimes—but I never tasted the food. Chris began to come around; he was awake for longer periods. They removed the tube that ran down his throat and untied his hands, which had been secured so he wouldn't snatch the tube out. They allowed him to eat. Each step was a milestone, proof from God Chris would not die. When he slept, I sat at his bedside monitoring his breathing, listening to the beeps on machines I did not understand, watching his chest go up and down. When he couldn't talk, we wrote notes back and forth to each other. Usually he inquired about his daughter and other family members; or he asked me to do something for him, to get him water or wrap a gift he had already bought for someone.

I came to expect that each day I was at the hospital Janice would come, always just before visiting hours ended. But what I wasn't prepared for was Chris's reaction. Each time she arrived, he asked me and whoever else was in the room to leave. Because Chris could not speak well, he just waved good-bye to me and that was my cue to go. With that one gesture, all of my insecurities and fears returned. Why didn't he want us there at the same time? Why did I have to leave when she came?

The first time it happened I returned the next day to find their scribblings to each other. His note that said: "I love you and I'm glad you're here," his notes asking about their child. I felt rejected and re-called every man who had ever two-timed me. I had worried, cried, prayed, and hurt over his being sick and now he was going to leave me and return to her because she was the mother of his child. This was what my fear said to me. A brush with death could do this, I reasoned. There was nothing I could do about it. So I went through the motions of being a good friend, the same friend I had been to others whom I had nurtured and prayed over and tried to make well. I went to the hospital every day, but I was wounded and dispirited. The day before he was released, I walked into his room and went into a tirade, listing everything he had done wrong to me since he had gotten sick.

"I have been here every visiting hour. I stayed as long as they let me. I have been through hell these last few days. Then as soon as Ja-nice comes, you tell me to leave. You have never thanked me for any-thing. You take me for granted, and I'm tired of it."

He listened dispassionately, reading a magazine, not responding at all, which really pissed me off. Weeks later, when I replayed the scene in my head, I realized that to a man who had just battled death I must have seemed ridiculous.

He was being released the next day, and he asked his father to pick him up and take him home. But I couldn't stay away, so I accompa-nied his father. Chris ignored me. We went to his parents' house. I gave Chris his Christmas present, an expensive watch I knew he had admired. I expected him to go to his apartment, where I would nurse him, since he had been ordered to stay in the house for a week or so. But he told me he was staying at his parents' house. There was no burst of happiness. No huge thank-you. I wanted to hug and kiss him, to sleep with my arms wrapped around him while thanking God for helping me get over my greatest fear. But it wasn't going to happen that way.

I went home and waited. And waited. An eternity passed, though it was really just a couple of days. On the last day of the year of 1992, Chris called to ask if I would take him to the bank. I picked him up. Before I left him, I pleaded with him to tell me what was wrong. He said simply, "I need time to think." I silently completed the sentence: *about whether or not I want to stay with you or return to Janice.* I knew Chris well enough to realize that he was trying to figure out if God had made him sick to tell him it was his duty to be with Janice so they could raise their child together. So I left him alone, though I hurt, horribly. I could not eat or sleep. I was possessed, because I felt helpless. There was nothing I could do. I knew this was something Chris had to work out, and yet I wanted to scream, "That isn't what God is saying, Chris!" In my heart, though, I knew I could not say that I understood God well enough to be His interpreter.

I was trying to deal with God's latest irony in my life: that I had feared I would lose Chris to death, when now I could lose him to life. I was driving myself crazy with thoughts, with analyzing and trying to figure out where things went wrong, with trying to guess at what he would do, suffering over my own helplessness. He called and left a message on my machine, wishing me a happy New Year and saying he would probably be asleep around midnight because his medication made him tired. I went to a party with one of my sisters, aching through every dance and every laugh, hurting through the screams at the New Year, kissing my brother and two of my sisters. Aching. Aching.

But I had made up my mind earlier that day that if my heart continued to beat through the night I was going to New York to visit some friends on New Year's Day. Actually, a girlfriend suggested the getaway because she knew I loved to travel and that I used weekend excursions as a way of healing. Also, she had once feared she was dying after she was diagnosed with cancer; she understood what Chris was going through, that he probably needed the time alone. I went to visit some friends who lived on Long Island, near water and across from a park, a place where I could be surrounded by nature again and be cleansed of my pain.

On New Year's Day I arrived at their house, battered and feeling blue. But within hours I was transformed into their dear friend, a person loved, missed, and appreciated. Their eleven-month-old son licked my cheeks and hugged me. I was still anxious, but my racing heart slowed down to near normal as I watched him take tiny steps, chasing ducks in the park. I meditated in the quiet morning hours, sitting with my legs folded and my hands resting on my knees, palms facing the ceiling. God spoke to me, I am sure, and said: "You will never feel the power of love until you release all your fears. If you could let go of fear, love would rain down on you and joy will be yours forever."

After my meditation I knew that it was my ego that had felt rejected at the hospital, not me. My ego played games and thought one wave of a hand could dismiss love. My true self, the one that understood the real meaning of love, knew that I could not love Chris any less than I had loved Michael or John or my father. In fact, I could not love Chris any differently than I loved them. Love in its purest form treats everyone the same. Whatever Chris wanted was what I should wish for him, just as I would have for Michael or for John.

I remembered interviewing a thirty-something woman once about how she was able to muster up the will to run marathons. "I can do it because of my husband," she said. "Because he believes I can do anything; he inspires me."

As she spoke my body was engulfed in the most peaceful, joyous warmth I had ever experienced in my life, and I knew without anyone telling me that what I was feeling was pure love. Somehow I had tapped into the love she and her husband felt for each other. Even the palms of my hands and the bottoms of my feet were warm. But more memorable than the warmth was the joy in my heart. I felt a happiness I had never known. It lasted only seconds. I never told anyone, but after feeling it, I knew I wanted that feeling for my life.

I called my daughter, who was back at home. She said Chris had called and she had told him I was in New York, which had surprised him. *At least he's calling,* I thought. I phoned him and left a message telling him where I was, leaving the phone number. He called and I heard his daughter in the background, which was my first clue that he was feeling different; when I left, he had not wanted to see his daughter because he wanted solitude. Our chat was pleasant. He asked me to come see him when I returned.

Back in Washington, I stepped off the train a healed woman. I was by no means my normal self, but I was not the defeated person who had left for New York. I at least knew that if Chris told me he was going to spend his life with Janice, I could handle it. I would cry some days, but I would live—and one day, I would be absolutely fine. I even had a backup plan: to move to Los Angeles and study screenwriting and write articles for magazines.

The day after I returned I went to see Chris.

"I had to ask myself, 'Why me?' " he explained. "I needed to think. I wondered if I was doing something wrong. It crossed my mind that maybe I was supposed to marry Janice so I could be with my daughter every day."

I had guessed all of this, but for some reason I felt better now that he had said it. We went to dinner and talked for hours about life. We began to make love, but just touching made us cry, so we stopped and just held onto each other.

"I love you so much," I said, tears streaming down my face.

"I understand. I love you, too," he said.

Then we talked again—for hours. It marked a new beginning for both of us, solidifying our relationship the way only struggling and overcoming great difficulties together can. Finally, I felt I had lived through all of my fears in our relationship and I began to relax in a way I had never relaxed with a man, the way I got comfortable with girlfriends.

I noticed things I had missed before. One day I followed Chris in my car as he drove his daughter to the day-care center. I watched him lean over and talk to her and play with her and kiss her. He was always affectionate and patient with her, but this day it struck me that he was doing everything I had wished my father had done for me, what I had hoped my daughter's fathers would do for her. The "good father" had finally entered my life, but not in a way I had expected. *How ironic,* I thought, *that he is someone else's father.*

Yet to this day Chris reminds me of my own father: his work ethic, his sense of family and tradition, his love of evenings at home and time spent playing with children. But I always say God in His graciousness added to Chris those things I ached for from my father: hugs and kisses, words of encouragement and praise, "I love you," whispered softly in my ear. Through Chris, I am learning more about my father, more about trust.

I know that it is true that you don't have to search for love, that it is always here with us, within us, and around us. The problem is you can't see it until you first love yourself. After I loved me, Chris appeared. I felt as if Michael and John had chosen him and they were now opening their arms, releasing me to someone else. After all, they repeatedly had told me that they could not envision me with a man my own age, or an older man. "You have to get a younger man. You *need* a younger man," they said over and over. So I laughed when I found out that Chris was younger, and I looked around suspiciously, trying to find evidence that Michael and John were near.

I was puzzled, though, about Chris's view of gay men. "Maybe Michael and John didn't send him," I said. But my daughter answered, "Mama, what better person for them to send him to than you? With you, he'll change."

I had changed. I could look at my daughter, a college graduate who was a kind and giving woman, and see what I had done right. Chris and I found each other at the right time, when we both stood at the crux of major change, ready to move on to whatever was next. After months of struggling, of breaking each other in like comfortable shoes, stretching and tugging until we were a perfect fit, we started planning our wedding and our life together.

◆　◆　◆

I finally wrote an article that I had held inside me for years, a piece laying out in black and white some of my pseudo-secret background—hinting at my bout with heroin. I wanted to show my struggle to learn to love all of me: my crooked buck teeth; my ugly right thumb I caught in a mimeograph machine when I was high on marijuana; my self who loved so easy and so hard; the me whom I kicked and scolded and never loved half as much as I loved men barely worth a hello.

It was an article I had suggested writing at least five years earlier, but then an editor had told me it would be career suicide. He was probably right. But the *Post* had since hired another reporter with a background similar to mine. Nathan McCall, I discovered, had been to jail and initially had not been hired by the *Post* because he had told them about his background. In talking to Nathan, I realized that between the year when the *Post* refused to hire him and the time he came to work there, the *Post* had found out about my police record and dealt with what to do with me. Could management's experience with me have helped Nathan get hired? Would our experiences help others in the future? The thought pleased me, because I can never forget how difficult it is getting a job when you have a police record.

Then Nathan opened a door for me. He wrote an article about his life of crime—and I saw that he wasn't hated and dismissed because of it, as the editor had predicted I would be. At first I considered that Nathan's story was more acceptable than mine because it was somehow more acceptable, macho even, for a man to write about his past crimes than for a woman to discuss hers. But then I realized the truth was that the world was different back when the editor advised me not to write such an article. Back then, we lived in a world that slayed the political aspirations of presidential candidates who were unfaithful to their wives. Then, the world never would have tolerated a president who put marijuana to his lips, even if he didn't inhale it. It was surely not a world willing to accept the truth: that we are not perfect in the way that we think, that we have never been since we entered this world and will never be until we leave again.

The message of the article was so important to me that I worked intensely on every word, delicately crafting a lead that would draw people into it, spending hours forming the last sentence so people would ponder it for days after they put down the paper. I wrote and rewrote, mixed in slivers of interviews with the young girls who reminded me of myself, and I was careful not to break the mood when I switched from my story to theirs and back again. I had concentrated so much on the process of writing that I forgot how intimate the article was.

That Sunday when it was published, I rushed to the store to buy a newspaper, to make sure the sentences were just as I remembered. I turned to the page, read the first line: "At the D.C. jail every Saturday, young black women line up for visits, many of them toting babies on their hips." It was a scene that reminded me of my life, the next line said. But before I reached that line, I burst into tears and could not stop crying. I screamed, "This is my life! This is my fucking life!"

I was so surprised at my reaction that I frightened myself. I was overwhelmed by sadness. I shook and sobbed. I picked up the phone to call one of my sisters, or my best friend from work, Cindy, or someone. But I couldn't stop crying, so I put it down. I put down the article, too, and I did not read it until weeks later.

Waiting for me at work were messages from book agents who saw ways in which my article could become a book. I called a friend who was an agent, someone who had already been encouraging me to write a book. Five months later I had a book contract, the first major indication that my new angels were working overtime. I had only hoped to use my words to encourage people to acknowledge their imperfections and, in doing so, look less harshly at others. That included others who still made mistakes, like the people I wrote about and interviewed daily. The addicts. Juvenile delinquents. Young single mothers with five children. And teenage girls who dated hoodlums, following them down a treacherous winding road of mistakes. Whenever I interviewed one of these girls, I saw myself in her face. But now I wanted people to know when they looked at those girls, they were looking at me. When they failed to have compassion for them, they spat in my face. It wasn't a book I wanted; it was redemption from the burden of carrying this story inside me. I wanted to open my chest, rip out the past, and free myself to fly.

There were still secrets about my life that I had not told Chris. I knew I would have to tell him before we got married, but since that was months away, I kept putting it off, until I got the book contract. Then I knew I had to tell him before I told the rest of the world. Ashamed of having married and divorced three times, I had only spoken of my last marriage. Three failed marriages would surely scare him into leaving me, because any sane person knew a person divorced three times was a failure. I was petrified. For weeks I lay awake at night going over in my head what I might say to him and all the possible ways in which he might react. I waited for the perfect moment, until I only made myself more miserable with my worry.

One evening after we had made love, showered, and snuggled up in bed to watch television, I knew it was time to make my move. Chris asked for a sandwich and I went to the kitchen to make it for him. But I couldn't concentrate, so I walked back into the bedroom to make my confession. "There's something you should know," I said, weakly. "I've had one abortion, been raped twice, and been married three times."

He looked relieved. "Hell, I thought you were getting ready to tell me something about the food," he said. "Where's the sandwich?"

"Did you hear me? Is that all you're gonna to say?" I must have looked like an inflatable question mark, ready to float away.

"You've had a very busy life, haven't you?" he said.

I walked out of the room, smiling. He didn't bat an eye when I mentioned the three marriages. I forgave him for not offering his sympathy about my rapes because I had alluded to them before and he had consoled me. Besides, on this evening I had blurted out the news as if the rapes were incidents with no more weight in my life than the others.

◆ ◆ ◆

I returned to Beaufort, South Carolina, to do some research for my book, to visit my childhood friends and walk across the land that had been my family's home when my father was a young, fearless marine and I was a little girl learning what it meant to be black. When I returned to Washington, I dreamed my father was standing beside me. His straight gray hair was rumpled and he wore a brown tweed suit I didn't recognize. He leaned over my bed. His breath was warm on my face. We looked into each other's eyes. His eyes spoke to me. He kissed me and I jumped, waking up, still feeling his breath and his presence.

I fell back asleep happy, because my father's eyes had said so perfectly: "I . . . am . . . very . . . proud . . . of . . . you."

◆ ◆ ◆

In addition to the book contract, the article from the *Post* opened up new opportunities for me to give inspirational speeches to groups I had hoped to reach: women in prison, teenage girls from troubled families, young men in a rites of passage program, which the court had ordered them to attend.

The article was nominated to receive an award for "Best Commentary" from the National Association of Black Journalists, a professional organization with thousands of members working in radio and television and on newspapers. Winning an award from this group was comparable to winning a Pulitzer to me. I considered both impossible, so I buried the nomination in the back of my mind. Then a girlfriend at the *Post* passed my desk and whispered, "You're a finalist."

The conference was in Detroit. I spent my first couple of days screaming at people I hadn't seen in years. By the afternoon of the awards program, I began to entertain the possibility of winning. I was ironing a pair of my pants in a friend's room when she asked what I was going to say if I won. I rattled off something. But after I had closed my mouth, I gave the question serious thought. The way I looked at it was: "If I had the attention of more than a thousand people for three minutes, what would I say?" I decided it was important for me to tell my purpose in writing the article and to thank people who had helped me through the difficult months in which I overcame paralyzing grief. Then I wanted to make some sort of statement about AIDS, but more specifically also about homosexuality. I could feel the presence of Michael and Cooper. I was sure they were walking beside me. I knew how much they would love to be in my place, how much they had loved being journalists, how hard they had worked to be good at what they did. But I knew, too, they were smiling now, happy for me. Yet my heart ached.

Within our professional group, I had heard crude, mean jokes about gays. I had also heard an uncountable number of homophobic remarks by people otherwise caring and compassionate. I knew gay journalists who were still in the closet among their journalist peers because they wanted to be politically involved in the organization and feared being open would limit or destroy that possibility. I thought maybe if I won, in my few minutes onstage I could gently nudge people to look at their prejudices toward gay people. But by the time I had finished ironing, I had put the possibility of winning out of my mind again.

The program was at the Fox Theatre, a huge old movie theater that had been refurnished to historical accuracy, with gold gilding and crystal tier chandeliers. I watched the fashion show as women walked around the lobby, their beaded dresses sparkling, and men strolled in perfectly tailored suits. When the lights went down, I sat back and enjoyed the program, which had always awed me with its sophisticated production. I didn't look at the printed program because I didn't want to know when my category was coming up. I laughed, applauded for winners, and generally enjoyed myself until the emcee called out the nominees for the commentary category.

My heart raced. I was thrilled to see my article on a huge screen. At that moment I regretted deeply that neither Chris, my daughter, nor my mother had been able to come with me. But I hadn't pressed anyone to come because until that very moment, while I stared at my article projected on a movie screen, I had not realized how exciting this event was. I was savoring the moment when I thought I heard the emcee call my name.

I looked at my girlfriends next to me. They were staring in my face. Then it hit me. He had called my name. I had won! I bounced and skipped down the aisle to the stage. "I like it up here," I said, looking down at the crowd. People laughed. I put my hand over my heart to hold it inside my chest. The thoughts came faster than I could speak. I was breathless.

"I thought if I told people that I used to shoot heroin in my arms, and I went to jail, and people used to look at me and see nothing, that it would help them look at some of the young people in our community who are smoking crack and shooting drugs and carrying guns and see they could be future journalists. I felt it was worth it to me. To open my heart. For them. What has happened has been a lot of wonderful things, including I got a book contract."

People applauded. I was amazed and at the same time heartened that they even cared.

"A couple of years ago I was so depressed I couldn't think of story ideas. Within a thirteen-month span, I lost six people in my life. . . .

"I'd like to accept this in memory of one young black journalist who died of AIDS. I would love to be able to say his name, but although it became public that he died of AIDS, he died in fear people would know he was gay." I stopped to breathe. I was thinking of Michael, yet in the brief pause I realized I had to say something for Cooper, so I added for him: "We as a group and people need to look inside our hearts and open our hearts to all people so they will no longer live half-lives, but live fully—in front of us." Again people clapped, and I felt encouraged. "We are losing brilliant young sisters and brothers who die in fear and alone, because they do not want us to know—and that should not happen."

I thanked two friends who had encouraged me during my depression and recovery from grief, and Milton Coleman, who had stood by me when the *Post* nearly fired me for hiding the same truth whose avowal was now being celebrated. "I'd like to thank all of you for seeing fit to honor me like this. Thank you so very much."

As I said the last "thank you," I was struck by the inadequacy of the words. How could I convey to anyone how much that award, that moment of being honored, meant to me? As I turned to leave the stage, the entire audience stood and cheered. They were not honoring a wounded child who had put a syringe full of heroin in her arm, or a scared young woman who had shoplifted and cheated every chance she got, not the woman who was raped and abused and who got married three times by the time she was twenty-six, not the woman who had never loved herself. It was as if I stood on top of a mountain, and to my back was my past and to my front were the spotlights shining on the path I was to walk next.

I had pondered, particularly during my time of grief, why we have to go through what we do in life to learn. Why do some of us take a more difficult path than others? I know people who believe that because I was not born poor or handicapped, I should not have struggled, or that somehow my story, and therefore my life, is a fraud or not legitimate. But I am convinced that you can stand in one place and struggle; you can live on an island alone and never meet another person, and still fight one demon after another. The only struggle that matters is the one that occurs inside.

"We are born perfect," I tell young students when I speak at schools. "We know this in the crib, but as we grow, we forget. Then life becomes our journey back to perfection, or at least back to the time of remembering."

Onstage, I felt as if God had reached down His hands and raised me up. It was a moment of grace. A voice in my head said, *Now you see? This is why you shot dope. This is why you went to jail. This is why you were lost. So that you could one day go out and spread the word, that there is no greater love than love of self.*

The award was not the culmination of anything. It was a beginning. As I walked, my legs wobbled so badly I was afraid I would faint. One of Cooper's friends met me in the aisle on the way to my seat. I collapsed in his arms, sobbing, as he whispered, "Oh, Patrice, Cooper is smiling now."

An hour later, my legs were strong. I danced like a maniac, for Cooper and Michael and John; for my father, who was so proud of me, though I did not know it until he was dead. I danced for my life, in celebration of it and not in spite of it. Sashaying. Twirling. Laughing.